"This valuable volume provides solutions to poverty that really work, in contrast to many well-intentioned but harmful solutions that are popular in much of society today. It cont̶a̶i̶n̶ practical and biblical insights from the ̶ ̶ ̶rts who have spent a large portion of ̶ ̶ in how economies actually function in ̶ ̶ y useful theological insights on the prob. ̶ ̶ poverty."

Wayne Grudem, Ph.D.
Research Professor of Theology and Biblical Studies
at Phoenix Seminary

"This book engagingly addresses poverty from a biblical point of view, convincingly demonstrating the case for free enterprise as the best means for the transformational development of the poor."

Luis Bush, Ph.D.
International Facilitator of Transform World Connections

"This book soundly tackles the most important social task of Christians over the next twenty years: the urgent need to break the chains of poverty for the world's billion-plus poor. *For the Least of These: A Biblical Answer to Poverty* critically balances the discussion between the poor in biblical times and who they are today, as well as examining the economic principles behind poverty and prosperity. The book's empirical analysis reveals that great progress has been made—and sound methods discovered—for breaking the chains of poverty. The editors are to be praised for their unique concentration on both biblical principles and sound empirical research to determine what works and what doesn't to free the poor from poverty."

Michael Novak
Author of *The Spirit of Democratic Capitalism*

"The Institute for Faith, Work & Economics has done an excellent job of recruiting a number of outstanding theologians and scholars to put together this primer on how Christians should address the issue of poverty. The writers have even-handedly dealt with the biblical mandate to show compassion for the poor in an effective and moral way. The various essays are sound both theologically and economically. Any Christian interested in his duty to the poor will gain significant insights by reading this book."

Paul A. Cleveland, Ph.D.
Professor of Finance and Economics at
Birmingham-Southern College

"You're probably familiar with the following justification for redistribution: we in the west are rich because we stole our wealth from everyone else, the rest of the world remains poor because we won't share, and it is the church's responsibility to alleviate these historic injustices through income redistribution. The essays in *For the Least of These* suggest that this emotionally appealing story is wrong. In this volume, you will find a combination of careful biblical exegesis and economic analysis that will cause you to rethink some of your assumptions about the sources of poverty and prosperity."

Art Carden, Ph.D.
Assistant Professor of Economics at Samford University

"This book is a timely update on historical truth. The appeal to natural and revealed law is superb, confirming the timeless principles of basic economic development and their relation to the compassionate command to serve the poor and help them to achieve self-dependency, dignity, and the ability to become givers to the community themselves."

Hal Jones
President and CEO of Global Hope International

"We are confused about the causes of and solutions to poverty. *For the Least of These* provides one of the most adept considerations of this very human problem, asking readers to consider both the Scriptures and the market as complementary moral guides to helping the poor. One leaves this volume with a greater understanding of the complexity of poverty, a wiser zeal for helping *the least of these*, and a greater hope that finally some are paying attention to how the Scriptures are central to human flourishing."

Gerson Moreno-Riano, Ph.D.
Dean of the College of Arts and Sciences at Regent University

"Christians are called to "do good to all people." But how to help? History demonstrates that good intentions are not enough. *For the Least of These* ably explores our moral obligations to others—and the even tougher issue of how to effectively help those in need."

Doug Bandow, Ph.D.
Senior Fellow at the Cato Institute

The Least of These is what Christians have needed for quite some time—a book tackling the issue of poverty that is both theologically and economically sound. Top biblical scholars, theologians, and economists all contribute to clearly and charitably explain what both the special revelation of Scripture and the general revelation of economics reveal about the nature of poverty and how we can alleviate it. Anyone interested in how Christians can best minister to the poor should consult this volume.

Shawn Ritenour, Ph.D.
Professor of Economics at Grove City College

"As Christians, we must re-imagine our call to Good Samaritanism to include a right view of economics if we are to fully love our neighbors with our hearts and our minds. This book is a robust tool to help you in your journey toward a fuller theology of Good Samaritanism, one that takes into account the driving forces fueling human flourishing across the world."

Chris Horst
Director of Development at HOPE International
and author of *Mission Drift*

"I typically turn and run from books with entries by a dozen authors. But not this one: the chapters of *For the Least of These* are tied together by a rich, shared commitment to Holy Scripture and a heart for genuinely helping the poor in ways that affirm, rather than undermine, personal dignity. On the eve of the Great Society's fiftieth anniversary, theologians, practitioners, and reformers here sound a clarion call to a better, more biblical way of loving our neighbors—one that challenges many tenets of today's welfare state.

"Today in exciting new ways, the church is waking up to a more faithful approach to integrating faith and work. As many Christian college students look head-on at modern poverty, this book offers a practical, first-rate response to the question of how to follow our Lord's command to love and effectively serve the poor. I recommend it highly."

Josh Good
Values & Capitalism Program Manager at
the American Enterprise Institute

FOR THE
LEAST
OF THESE

A BIBLICAL ANSWER TO POVERTY

Anne Bradley and Art Lindsley, editors

WESTBOW·
PRESS
A DIVISION OF THOMAS NELSON
& ZONDERVAN

Contents

Part 2: Markets and the Poor

Part 3: Poverty Alleviation in Practice

About the Institute for Faith, Work & Economics

The Institute for Faith, Work & Economics™ (IFWE) is a nonprofit, 501(c)(3) Christian research organization committed to promoting biblical and economic principles that help individuals find fulfillment in their work and contribute to a free and flourishing society. IFWE's research starts with the belief that the Bible, as the inerrant word of God, provides the authoritative and intellectual foundation for a proper understanding of work and economic truths that, when properly followed, can help individuals, companies, communities, and nations flourish. For more information, please visit www.tifwe.org.

About the Editors

Anne Bradley, Ph.D. is the Vice President of Economic Initiatives at the Institute for Faith, Work & Economics, where she develops and commissions research toward a systematic biblical theology of economic freedom. She is a visiting professor at Georgetown University and has previously taught at George Mason University and at Charles University, Prague. She is currently a visiting scholar at the Bernard Center for Women, Politics, and Public Policy. She served as the Associate Director for the Program in Economics, Politics, and the Law at the James M. Buchanan Center at George Mason University. She received her Ph.D. in economics from George Mason University in 2006 during which time she was a James M. Buchanan Scholar.

Art Lindsley, M.Div., Ph.D. is the Vice President of Theological Initiatives at the Institute for Faith, Work & Economics, where he oversees the development of a theology that integrates faith, work, and economics. Most recently, he has served as President and Senior Fellow at the C.S. Lewis Institute since 1987. Prior to that, he was Director of Educational Ministries at the Ligonier Valley Study Center and Staff Specialist with the Coalition for Christian Outreach in Pittsburgh, Pennsylvania.

He is the author of *C.S. Lewis's Case for Christ*, *True Truth*, *Love: The Ultimate Apologetic*, and co-author with R.C. Sproul and John Gerstner of *Classical Apologetics*. He has written numerous articles on theology, apologetics, C.S. Lewis, and the lives and works of many other authors and teachers.

Dr. Lindsley received his B.S. in chemistry from Seattle Pacific University, an M.Div. from Pittsburgh Theological Seminary, and a Ph.D. in religious studies from the University of Pittsburgh.

About the Authors

Anne Bradley, Ph.D. is the Vice President of Economic Initiatives at the Institute for Faith, Work & Economics, where she develops and commissions research toward a systematic biblical theology of economic freedom. For more information about Dr. Bradley, see the "About the Editors" section.

Arthur C. Brooks, Ph.D. is the president of the American Enterprise Institute. Previously, he was the Louis A. Bantle Professor of Business and Government Policy at Syracuse University. He is the author of ten books and hundreds of articles on topics ranging from the economics of the arts to military operations research. His most recent book is the *New York Times* bestseller *The Road to Freedom: How to Win the Fight for Free Enterprise*. Other books include *The Battle*, *Gross National Happiness*, *Social Entrepreneurship*, and *Who Really Cares*. Before pursuing his work in public policy, Dr. Brooks spent twelve years as a professional French hornist with the City Orchestra of Barcelona and other ensembles.

Peter Greer, M.P.P. is president and CEO of HOPE International, a global nonprofit organization focused on alleviating both physical and spiritual poverty through Christ-centered microfinance in some of the most challenging places around the world, including Afghanistan, Democratic Republic of Congo, and Haiti. Under his leadership,

HOPE has expanded its network from three to fifteen countries and now serves over 300,000 active clients.

He received his undergraduate education in international business from Messiah College and completed a master's degree in public policy from Harvard's Kennedy School, with a concentration in political and economic development and executive education from Harvard Business School. He lectures nationwide on microenterprise development, social entrepreneurship, and poverty eradication. His books include *The Poor Will Be Glad*, co-authored with Phil Smith, *The Spiritual Danger of Doing Good*, and *Mission Drift*, co-authored with Chris Horst.

Lord Brian Griffiths of Fforestfach, Ph.D. is vice chairman of Goldman Sachs International and chairman of the European Middle East and Africa Business Practice and Compliance Committee. He was appointed professor of banking and international finance at the City University in 1976 and was dean of the City University Business School from 1982 to 1985. He became director of the Bank of England in 1983 for two years and from 1985 to 1990 served as head of the Prime Minister's Policy Unit and special advisor to Margaret Thatcher. He is currently a member of the Select Committee on Economic Affairs and until recently was chairman of the Archbishop of Canterbury's Lambeth Fund. He is also chairman of Christian Responsibility in Public Affairs.

R. Mark Isaac, Ph.D. is the John and Hallie Quinn Eminent Scholar and department chair of economics at Florida State University. He received his Ph.D. in social science from Caltech in 1981 and taught for many years at the University of Arizona before moving to Tallahassee in 2001. He is the author of numerous journal articles and book chapters and is also an ordained ruling elder in the Presbyterian Church.

Walter C. Kaiser, Jr., Ph.D. is the Colman M. Mockler distinguished professor emeritus of Old Testament and president emeritus of Gordon-Conwell. He also served as the seminary's president from 1997-2006. Prior to coming to Gordon-Conwell, he taught Bible and archaeology at Wheaton College, Wheaton Illinois, and taught at Trinity Evangelical Divinity School in several capacities. In addition to teaching in the Old Testament Department, he was Senior Vice President of Education, Academic Dean, and Senior Vice President of Distance Learning and Ministries.

He has contributed to such publications as *Journal for the Study of Old Testament, Journal of the Evangelical Theological Society, Christianity Today, Westminster Theological Journal,* and *Evangelical Quarterly.* He has also written numerous books, some of which are: *Toward an Old Testament Theology; Ecclesiastes: Total Life; Toward an Exegetical Theology: Biblical Exegesis for Preaching and Teaching; Hard Sayings of the Old Testament; The Messiah in the Old Testament;* and *A History of Israel.*

David Kotter, M.Div., M.B.A. serves as visiting scholar and senior research fellow at the Institute for Faith, Work & Economics. He teaches graduate economics, finance, and global business for Indiana Wesleyan University at the campus in Louisville, Kentucky. Professionally he worked for Ford Motor Company as the finance director of a manufacturing plant in Europe, as a financial analyst at the world headquarters in Michigan, and as a financial advocate for the minority supply base. After attending seminary later in life, he was invited to be one of the founding pastors of CrossWay Community Church and by God's grace saw the church grow from under eighty people to over eight hundred.

He graduated summa cum laude with an M.B.A. and a B.S. in engineering from the University of Illinois and an M.Div. and M.A. from Trinity Evangelical Divinity School. He is currently working on his Ph.D. in New Testament studies at the Southern Baptist Theological Seminary.

Art Lindsley, M.Div., Ph.D. is the Vice President of Theological Initiatives at the Institute for Faith, Work & Economics, where he oversees the development of a theology that integrates faith, work, and economics. For more information about Dr. Lindsley, see the "About the Editors" section.

Marvin Olasky, Ph.D. is editor-in-chief of *World* magazine and holder of the distinguished chair in journalism and public policy at Patrick Henry College. He is the author of eighteen books, including *Compassionate Conservatism*, *The Religions Next Door*, *Abortion Rites*, *Fighting for Liberty and Virtue*, and *Prodigal Press*. He has co-authored ten more and has written 2,800 articles for publications ranging from *World* to the *New York Times*, the *Wall Street Journal*, and the *Washington Post*. He earned an A.B. from Yale University in 1971 and a Ph.D. in American culture from the University of Michigan in 1976. He served as a professor at the University of Texas for two decades and provost of The King's College from 2007 to 2011. He is also a senior fellow of the Acton Institute and has chaired the boards of City School of Austin and the Austin Crisis Pregnancy Center.

Lawrence W. ("Larry") Reed, M.A. became president of the Foundation for Economic Education (FEE) in 2008. Prior to that, he was a founder and president for twenty years of the Mackinac Center for Public Policy in Midland, Michigan. He also taught economics full-time and chaired the Department of Economics at Northwood University in Michigan from 1977 to 1984. He holds a B.A. in economics from Grove City College (1975) and an M.A. degree in history from Slippery Rock State University (1978). He holds two honorary doctorates, one from Central Michigan University (Public Administration—1993) and Northwood University (Laws—2008). His writings have appeared in *The Wall Street Journal, Christian Science Monitor, USA Today, Baltimore Sun, Detroit News, and Detroit Free Press,* among many others. He has authored or co-authored five books, the most recent ones being *A Republic—If We Can Keep It* and *Striking the Root: Essays on Liberty.*

Jay W. Richards, Th.M., M.Div., Ph.D. is the author of *Money, Greed, and God: Why Capitalism Is the Solution and Not the Problem* and *New York Times* best-selling book, *Infiltrated: How to Stop the Insiders and Activists Who Are Exploiting the Financial Crisis to Control Our Lives and Our Fortunes.* Dr. Richards is also executive producer of several documentaries, including *The Call of the Entrepreneur, The Birth of Freedom,* and *Effective Stewardship.* He has a B.A. with majors in political science and religion, an M.Div., a Th.M., and a Ph.D. in philosophy and theology from Princeton Theological Seminary.

Robert A. Sirico, M.Div. is the president of the Acton Institute. He received his Master of Divinity degree from the Catholic University of America, following undergraduate study at the University of Southern California and the University of London. He co-founded the Acton Institute with Kris Alan Mauren in 1990 to educate religious leaders in fundamental economic principles. His writings on religious, political, economic, and social matters are published in a variety of journals, including the *New York Times,* the *Wall Street Journal, Forbes,* the *London Financial Times,* the *Washington Times,* the *Detroit News,* and *National Review.*

Rev. Sirico has provided commentary for CNN, ABC, the BBC, NPR, and CBS' *60 Minutes*, among others.

In 1999, Rev. Sirico was awarded an honorary doctorate in Christian ethics from the Franciscan University of Steubenville, and in 2001, Universidad Francisco Marroquin awarded him an honorary doctorate in social sciences. He is also currently serving on the pastoral staff of Sacred Heart of Jesus parish in Grand Rapids, Michigan.

Glenn Sunshine, Ph.D. is currently chair of the history department at Central Connecticut State University, a research fellow at the Acton Institute, and a faculty member for the Centurions Program. He received a B.A. from Michigan State University in linguistics, an M.A. from Trinity Evangelical Divinity School in church history, and a Ph.D. from the University of Wisconsin-Madison in renaissance and reformation history. He is the author of *Reforming French Protestantism*, *The Reformation for Armchair Theologian*, and *Why You Think the Way You Do*, along with scholarly articles on history and historical theology. He also writes popular level articles regularly for the Colson Center.

Dato Kim Tan, Ph.D. is the founder Chairman of SpringHill Management Ltd (UK), a fund management company in biotech and social venture capital investments. Dato Kim is the Chairman of the NCI Cancer Hospital (Malaysia) and a board director of a number of companies in Malaysia, India, the UK, South Africa, and the USA. He is an advisor to a number of government agencies in Asia on biotechnology and is a board member of the Asia Pacific Economic Cooperation (APEC) Life Science Forum. He is the Chairman of the West Surrey & North Hants Innovation and Growth Team (UK). He has a Ph.D. in biochemistry and is the inventor of sheep monoclonal antibodies and a Fellow of the Royal Society of Medicine. He is the co-founder of Transformational Business Network, the UK charity with social transformational businesses in developing countries, including the Kuzuko Game Reserve in South Africa and the Hagar Social Enterprise Group in Cambodia.

Richard Turnbull, M.A., Ph.D. is the director of the Centre for Enterprise, Markets, and Ethics, a new UK-based research institute and think tank aiming to articulate the vision of an enterprise economy from a Christian perspective. He spent nine years working in the City of London as a Chartered Accountant before ordination in the Church of England. He served as a rector of a church in southern England before being appointed principal of Wycliffe Hall, Oxford, in 2005 where he served until his new appointment in 2012. He has served at the highest levels of the Church of England's General Synod and authored four books: *Anglican and Evangelical?*, *Shaftesbury, the Great Reformer*, *Reviving the Heart—The Story of the Eighteenth Century Revival*, and *A Passionate Faith—What Makes an Evangelical*.

Foreword

By Arthur C. Brooks, Ph.D.

The Christian gospels make it abundantly clear that Jesus calls on us to care for the poor. What is not at all clear, however, is the best means by which Christians living in a modern, industrial society—particularly one in which the state has built a large, technocratic edifice ostensibly devoted to solving the problems of poverty—can and should carry out the Lord's directive. This volume takes on the challenge of beginning to answer that question.

It is important to note that this is not a new discussion, but rather a very old one that began to fade from the public consciousness during the twentieth century. Throughout much of American history, poverty and the relief thereof were discussed in an explicitly moral or religious context. The care of the indigent was largely the function of the church and of mutual aid societies, many of which were founded and guided by explicitly religious precepts. Discussing poverty relief without also discussing religious institutions, faith, and Scripture would have been largely unfathomable to America's founders.

The Progressive era changed all of this. Over the course of the twentieth century, the relief of poverty went from being the function of private religious and philanthropic charities to a function of the state—increasingly on the federal level—administered not by people giving their time, treasure, and talent to their fellow men out of compassion, religious duty, and moral obligation, but by the administrative state distributing the funds of others collected through taxation. For better or worse, this represents a massive change from what America's founders—much less the ancient Israelites and early Christians – would have seen as philanthropy.

The spiritual implications of this change are profound. As Richard Turnbull discusses in chapter five, it has removed the principle of voluntarism from the equation; and without voluntary action, virtue is hollow.

This leaves Christians in a difficult position. While they are called to help the poor, it is unclear how they can best fulfill this injunction, particularly when the state claims to be doing this on their behalf. In an environment in which far too many aspects of life are politicized and in which people of faith are increasingly under attack, how can Christians fulfill their biblical responsibilities? What insights can they gain from economics and from faith that could help them be better stewards of the poor?

Beyond a proper orientation toward the government safety net and personal charity decisions, there are questions about our capitalist system as well. Should we oppose it as a force that harms the weak, support it as a vehicle for prosperity, or something else? The answer is actually quite simple: There has never been an economic system that does more for what Jesus called "the least of these" than capitalism and free enterprise.

Consider your life chances if you were born in London in the mid-eighteenth century. If you were one of the lucky few to make it to working age, you would work six or seven days a week, earning an income that paid for only the barest necessities of life. You would probably be illiterate and never stray more than a few miles from the place where you were born. You would work until your death, which was not unlikely to come at the hands of another Londoner or by one of the plagues that regularly swept the city. And if you had children, their lives would likely be no better than yours.

Capitalism, through the Industrial Revolution, changed all of this for the poor. Markets, trade, and capital accumulation lifted people by the millions out of grinding poverty. Scientific and engineering advances came on the back of this system. Childhood mortality plummeted. Class mobility increased. And enough wealth was created so that people could, through voluntary means, share with those who were left behind. Even the definition of poverty changed; today's poor have access to medicines, technologies, and creature comforts that were unavailable to even the wealthiest titans of industry a century ago.

As Lord Griffiths and Dato Kim Tan discuss in chapter seven, we see a similar cycle playing out today in developing countries. In the past forty years, eighty percent of the world's worst poverty—defined as people living on less than a dollar a day—has been eliminated. This is not because of the IMF, the World Bank, foreign aid, or global socialism. It is because wealthy countries have lowered trade barriers, and because countries like China and India, which were once committed to socialism, have embraced—albeit tentatively and imperfectly—markets and trade. Simply put, more capitalism has meant less poverty across the globe.

As an economist, the case for free enterprise as the best means for helping the poor could not be clearer. But as a Christian, it is not always evident how what one knows empirically about economics and what one believes about Christ's teachings intersect and interact. I do believe—and I think readers of this book will as well—that it is insufficient to understand only the economics or only the theology of poverty alleviation. If we believe that we are called to help the poor, we must understand both. Properly understood, economics and faith have a great deal to teach one another.

This book, then, is an important resource for understanding what the Hebrew Bible and New Testament say (and do not say) about the poor. By putting in context and in conversation the ideas of both the ancient Israelites and the early Christians, we can better understand what it means to be commanded to care for the poor, the distinction between "riches" and "wealth," biblical attitudes towards property rights and wealth redistribution, and the ways in which work is a holy act.

The later chapters of this book are devoted to discussing what practical solutions for poverty reduction, as informed by a Christian worldview, might look like. How does economic liberty reduce poverty? How do markets promote morality? How does a welfare state strip people of their agency? And what is the difference between charities that offer a handout versus a hand up? In other words, these chapters pull together what previous chapters have discussed concerning Christian faith and economic evidence that teach us about helping the poor and advance the discussion of what this means for us in practical terms and in our personal lives.

Jesus teaches that "The poor you will always have with you." That is, poverty is not something that we can cure. But Christians can have compassion for the poor, and by applying faith through reason, can ameliorate suffering and help improve the chances of future generations.

Introduction

By Anne Bradley, Ph.D. & Art Lindsley, M.Div., Ph.D.

Over two hundred years ago, Adam Smith, a moral philosopher and the father of modern economics, wrote his most famous work, *An Inquiry into the Nature and Causes of the Wealth of Nations,* in which he set out to understand why and how nations accumulate wealth. Smith's book was written in 1776, on the eve of the most explosive growth and capital accumulation human history has ever known. Prior to this time, most of the human experience was a struggle to survive and was characterized by early death, disease, corruption, and oppression.

The question raised by Adam Smith is one that still plagues us today. Why do sub-Saharan Africa, parts of Latin America, and countries in South Asia remain poor while the developed world thrives? We believe Adam Smith's question has an answer, but that some societies have failed to implement the necessary biblical and economic principles that must undergird a flourishing society. Thus, to answer the question, we must start with Scripture.

Christians understand that wealth is not an end in and of itself, but a necessary means of giving people choice, access to vital goods and services (like clean water and medical care), and an opportunity to serve and care for others. It is simply no accident that if you are reading this book, you live in the richest time in human history and are likely one of the richest people in human history. The World Bank has never been as optimistic about global poverty elimination as it is today. In China alone, since 1978 over 600 million have been lifted out of extreme poverty. Global poverty rates have been halved since 1990 and are on pace to be halved again. The only way this has been possible is by embracing the biblical principles of private property, the rule of law, ingenuity, productive work, and well-functioning global markets that encourage and reward our God-given creativity and talents.

For the Least of These: A Biblical Answer to Poverty was written to provide an alternative perspective for addressing the problem of poverty from both a biblical and economic point of view, presenting a framework that will allow us to become better stewards of the earth's scarce resources and simultaneously to bring about a flourishing society.

The Bible calls on us to care for the poor, demonstrating Christ's love as well as our own. All too often, however, Christians turn to the secular state as the answer for poverty rather than grasping their own responsibility and realizing that the best long-term solution is to enable people to use their gifts to serve others and to exchange goods and services through market trade. Government is impersonal and bureaucratic in the way it addresses poverty, and, as such, often destroys rather than elevates the God-breathed dignity of the poor. By contrast, the local church and nonprofit organizations are better positioned to adapt aid to the unique needs of specific individuals because they are closer to those they are trying to help, and are thus more knowledgeable and nimble in how they act.

The Bible not only calls on believers to care for the poor, it provides many reasons to do so. There are many specific biblical commands in regard to this, and they are often mentioned. Believers must obey.

What is not often mentioned, however, is that a central reason for helping the poor is that they are made in the image of God. As such, we should desire that each person not only survives but thrives and flourishes in every area. This does not only mean that we should provide food for the starving; it also extends to creating opportunities for education, the development of gifts, and the resources to start small businesses, all of which will enable the poor to provide for their families and, eventually, to create jobs for others. Thus, the best way of alleviating long-term poverty is not giving people money (and welfare, etc.), but providing opportunities through markets for them to provide for themselves. In the last twenty years, twenty-five countries have virtually eliminated poverty within their borders in this fashion. However, in the United States—a country with one of the world's highest per capita incomes—the trend is toward an increasing dependence on federal and state aid. Because a biblical and economic framework was ignored or unknown when adopting these programs, we have created dependencies that are enslaving the poorest to a life of food stamps and welfare checks with no hope of personal fulfillment. These programs—managed by a secular, bureaucratic state, and in spite of the best of intentions—are unable to address individuals as unique and special, created in the image of God with intrinsic dignity. As such, they trap the poorest among us in a life-long cycle of despair because we are not embracing the biblical narrative of work and its value for personal fulfillment, honoring Christ, and creating value through service to others.

In situations of desperate need, aid must necessarily be provided, and there may be a place for government to provide a safety net so that people do not starve and health needs do not go unaddressed. But this is not a sufficient condition for poverty alleviation. We must make sure that people do not starve, but we must also make sure that they live in an opportunity society, where they can be contributors to the common good. The biblical role of the state is one that guards human rights, upholds a rule of law, and protects private property. The government does this in its call to punish the "evildoer" (Romans 13:4). In other words, government's role is more negative (to prevent evil) than positive (to provide goods and services). Some relevant biblical and economic questions here are: How much should and can the church do? How much is the government able to do? What can markets do? There is certainly a role for government, the church (and nonprofit organizations), and markets in bringing about a flourishing society. The question is, in what proportion?

The first section of this book will carefully examine the biblical passages on poverty, looking occasionally at wrong deductions or false understandings held by some. It will also shed some light on the questions mentioned in the previous paragraphs about the role of the church, government, and markets. In the next section, we get a historical perspective on how the church has addressed poverty, how markets can be a significant part of the solution, and whether markets are moral. In the final section, we will look at practical applications of the previous sections and how these extensions can be utilized to alleviate poverty.

We hope that each section can contribute to your understanding. This book could be a text for a course, or individual chapters could be used for assigned reading on different topics. Certainly, it is acceptable to read chapters that particularly interest you. However, it is important to read the earlier chapters as a foundation for the later ones. Above all, we want this to be a biblical perspective on poverty.

Our desire is that you might be stimulated to think deeply about the problem of poverty through biblical glasses. But it ought not to stop there. Reading this book is meant to lead to prayer about what you should do to respond to this concern. Each person has a different calling. Some may be called to work full-time addressing these issues. Others may be motivated to contribute money and resources. Still others may be moved to set up businesses that employ people in need. Search for what your response should be to the challenge of Scripture.

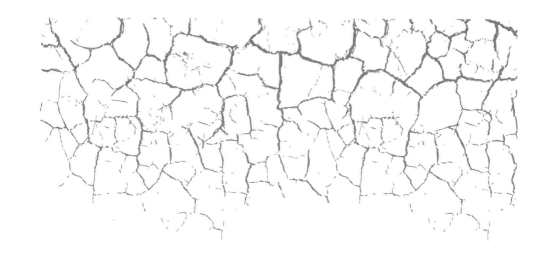

PART 1

A BIBLICAL
PERSPECTIVE
ON THE POOR

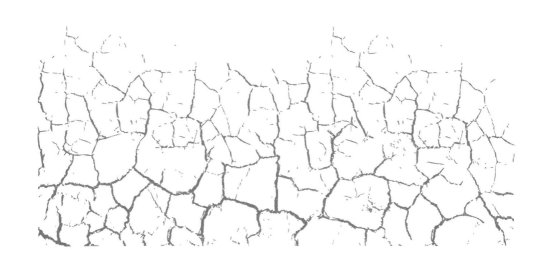

This chapter will examine poverty from a biblical perspective in an effort for us to better understand our call to care for those who fall into different conditions of poverty, both material and spiritual. It will also consider a biblical perspective on the rich and their responsibilities to the poor as well as the historical role of the state and the church in caring for the poor. Based on these discussions, it will then provide biblical principles for caring for the poor that must take into consideration the importance of work, moral proximity and subsidiarity, and a heart for giving.

Understanding the Poor

To determine whether God is on the side of the poor and opposed to the rich, we must first understand whom the Scriptures mean when they talk about these groups. Starting with the poor (although some passages talk about poverty metaphorically), in the vast majority of cases, the word refers to material poverty—people who are hungry, naked, homeless, etc. Economic poverty is also typically accompanied by a broader lack of resources and connections that makes the poor particularly vulnerable to oppression and abuse. They are frequently identified as widows, orphans, and foreigners who also lack social connections. Throughout the Old Testament, God warns against mistreating the poor, the widow, the orphan, and the foreigner, and promises to judge those who abuse them. Clearly, treatment of the poor and disadvantaged is a very important part of biblical ethics.

At the same time, this does not mean that the poor are *de facto* virtuous. To be sure, poverty is not necessarily a sign of God's displeasure. The poor can be blameless (Proverbs 28:6) and wise (Ecclesiastes. 9:15). But other Scriptures warn us that drunkenness, gluttony, and laziness can cause poverty (Proverbs 23:21), as can chasing fantasies (Proverbs

28:19). The Bible also warns about the danger of some temptations that are particularly enticing for the poor. The most obvious temptation is theft to get food. This can be easily extended to other types of criminal behavior motivated by the need or desire for money, including gang-related activities, drug dealing, etc. This in turn points to the reality of 1 Timothy 6:9-10: "But those who desire to be rich fall into temptation, into a snare, into many senseless and harmful desires that plunge people into ruin and destruction. For the love of money is a root of all kinds of evils. It is through this craving that some have wandered from the faith and pierced themselves with many pangs."

This passage is frequently associated with those who are already rich, but the rich are not the group being addressed; it is those who desire wealth, and specifically those who are not yet rich, who are being cautioned here. This is an important reminder that greed and worship of money are not vices peculiar to the rich. In fact, the people I know who are most obsessed with money are not the wealthy but those who have to struggle to get by. Envy of the rich is another sin that Scripture warns against (e.g. Psalm 73). This ties in directly to the Tenth Commandment, which forbids coveting a neighbor's possessions. The classical definition of envy is the desire to tear down anyone who is ahead of oneself, to take away what is that person's because he or she has more than oneself. Whether one cloaks this in the language of "fairness" or "income redistribution," envy and covetousness remain sins.

In other words, the Bible is realistic about the causes of poverty: people can become poor through no fault of their own, but poverty can also be the result of foolish decisions and actions; further, there are some sins to which the poor are particularly susceptible. Poverty is thus not a guarantee of virtue or righteousness.

So why are the poor described as blessed? The issue is not poverty per se, but rather the attitude of humility and reliance on God that it can produce in us. This is why Matthew's version of the beatitude isn't just "Blessed are the poor," but "Blessed are the poor *in spirit*" (Matthew 5:3). Reliance on personal wealth or government help (Psalm 146, especially verses 3-4, 7-10) for security is foolish, because they do not last. Rather, we need to place our hope in God alone.

Understanding the Rich

What about the rich? Although as we have seen, Scripture has some very harsh things to say about the wealthy, this does not mean that all of them are evil or under divine judgment. Abraham, Isaac, Jacob, and Job were rich and yet were also approved by God. Just as poverty doesn't guarantee virtue, wealth does not guarantee vice. Scripture tells us that God gives us the power to make wealth, and that he delights in the prosperity of his servants (Psalm 35:27), which includes material prosperity (Deuteronomy 28:11-13). So it is clear that the wealthy are not necessarily corrupt.

Why, then, the condemnations of the rich in Scripture?[2] Once again, the issue is not wealth or poverty per se. Leviticus 19:15 tells us, "You shall do no injustice in court. You shall not be partial to the poor or defer to the great, but in righteousness shall you judge your neighbor." God's concern is for righteousness and justice, but this verse tells us that justice does not mean being partial to the poor, contrary to what many social justice advocates argue. Justice means judging fairly according to the law and on the basis of truth without regard to social class.

And this is precisely why the rich are so often condemned in Scripture. In our fallen world, the rich and powerful have historically taken advantage of their power to increase their privileges at the expense of the poor and weak—the widows, orphans, and foreigners who are under special protection in the Mosaic Law because of their vulnerability. A careful reading of the texts attacking the rich demonstrates that the condemnations are almost inevitably connected to one of two things. The first of these is how they made their wealth. The Bible does not see money-making as a zero-sum game, as if the only road to wealth is through exploitation; but it does recognize that the rich do sometimes further enrich themselves at the expense of the poor.

For example, the rich are condemned in Scripture for failing to pay workers promptly and completely (Deuteronomy 24:15; James 5:4). Workers should be paid a just wage for their labor and should not be exploited in any way by their employers. Taking advantage of another's misfortune is also forbidden in Scripture, for example, in the prohibition of taking a cloak in pledge for a loan (Deuteronomy 24:12-13, 17) and of charging interest on loans (Leviticus 25:63).[3] The rich are also condemned for using the courts to defraud the poor (e.g. James 2:6). In today's terms, there are multitudes of ways people with money can use the legal system to take advantage of the poor. Perhaps the most obvious way is to drag out litigation to force your opponent either to give up or to go bankrupt, though there are other ways to game the system with high-end lawyers. Another modern approach would be for the well-connected to use zoning regulations to block anything that would interfere with their own quality of life—thereby pushing highways and toxic, hazardous, or undesirable industries into poor neighborhoods.

To put it differently, the rich are not always oppressors, but oppressors are almost always rich. And that is why they incur condemnation in Scripture. Chapter three gives specific examples of wealthy men who are not condemned.

The rich can also fall into other traps, particularly by relying on wealth for their security (e.g. Psalm 52:7), which in turn leads very easily to presumption, as if they rather than God were in control of their destinies (Luke 12:16-21). This is exactly the opposite attitude of the poor in spirit. And, of course, the rich can be just as greedy and enslaved to money as anyone else. Having money does not create any of these problems; rather, money reveals what is inside us and magnifies our character for good or for ill. And for too many in our fallen world, it is for ill.

Responsibilities of the Rich to the Poor

Along with how the rich make their wealth, the Bible is also concerned with how they use their wealth. It condemns, for example, the wealthy giving themselves over to luxurious living and ignoring the needs of the poor (e.g. Amos 6:1-7; Luke 16:19-31; James 5:5).[4] Instead, the Bible teaches that those who are better off have positive responsibilities to those who are poor. Simply put, we are to see to it that their needs are met, and we are to do it in such a way that we preserve their dignity (e.g. Deuteronomy 24:10). In the Old Testament period, almsgiving was not a major part of the culture. Rather, there were other mechanisms in place to take care of poverty in ancient Israel, notably through providing the poor with opportunities to work. Since work is part of what it means to bear the image of God, this sort of workfare affirms the dignity of the poor while meeting their needs.[5] The most important example of this was the law of gleaning (Deuteronomy 24:19-21). Landowners were prohibited from harvesting every last bit of their crops, but were to leave some for the poor who could come to collect it. The poor were thus required to do some work for their food, which in turn kept them from being reduced to complete dependence on charity and thus preserved their dignity.

The second key point about government is that Jesus is Lord and Caesar is not. This may seem obvious, but we rarely realize today how important and radical that statement is. In the ancient world, religion and government were inseparable. Kings ruled by divine authority or were seen as gods themselves. As such, nothing was beyond their control.[8] The early Christian proclamation that Jesus is Lord challenged this concept of governmental power at its very core. As Jesus taught, Christians were prepared to "render unto Caesar the things that are Caesar's"—they were not rebels in that sense—but they refused to render to Caesar the things that were God's. This amounts to a *de facto* insistence on limited government. And as a result, the Romans considered Christians seditious and subjected the church to nearly three hundred years of sporadic persecution before Constantine finally decriminalized Christianity. Christianity is, therefore, unique among the world's major religions in that it established itself in society without the support of the state. And since the church had been independent of the state for centuries, after Christianity was legalized, religion and government were, for the first time, seen as separable, with each having authority in its own sphere without interference from the other, though cooperating in areas of mutual interest.

The distinction of church and state had enormous implications for society. As George Weigel has argued, the church's independence from government created the possibility of other areas developing their own authority separate from the state. Schools, business, labor, family, and other institutions emerged as largely autonomous spheres operating with minimal state regulation. And it is precisely this that created Western civil society.

What has this got to do with poverty? During the Middle Ages, social welfare programs were handled through a variety of intermediate agencies, including guilds, lay religious groups, monasteries, and churches rather than through governments. With few exceptions, states relied on these independent charities to handle social welfare.[9] When the Reformation came, governments in some areas took social welfare functions away from the churches; but for the most part, charity continued to be handled by families, private individuals, benevolent organizations, and churches all the way into the late nineteenth century and even the twentieth century.[10] This emphasis on local solutions is the flip side of Schneider's idea of moral proximity discussed earlier: just as individuals have greater responsibility to those closest to them, so the solution to problems should come from those closest to them.

This principle, which Catholic thinkers call "subsidiarity," argues that governmental institutions are subsidiary, or secondary, to more immediate groups in finding solutions to problems. Thus social welfare is better handled by families first and then by local charitable institutions rather than by governments. Only if a situation is sufficiently widespread or intractable should government get involved, and even then it should be handled on as local a level as possible. The principle of subsidiarity thus does not reject governmental involvement in poor-relief out of hand, but argues that it should be a last resort after other institutions prove unable to provide solutions. If it is necessary for the government to get involved in certain circumstances, the results will be better if the government is closer (more local) to those in need.

From a biblical perspective, an approach to poverty based on subsidiarity has several advantages:

- It reinforces the responsibility of families to take care of their own.
- It helps develop compassion and love of one's neighbor.
- Encouraging voluntary charitable institutions helps promote civic mindedness, care for the needy, and thus virtue in the

populace (one responsibility of government, according to Romans 13).

- It fosters liberty by encouraging citizens to take responsibility for their communities rather than relying on government to do so.

Subsidiarity was the underlying principle of social welfare in the United States up until the New Deal, which began to shift responsibility for the needy away from private and local organizations toward the federal government. This process was accelerated in the 1960s by the Great Society and the War on Poverty.[11] These marked progressive steps away from subsidiarity. In essence, social welfare became a top-down system. Primary responsibility was vested in the federal government; many of the programs were administered through the states, but there was little local involvement—exactly the opposite of an approach guided by the principle of subsidiarity.

While this approach did have some positive results, it also had a number of serious negative side effects. First, this approach requires regulations for welfare to be written in such a way that they apply to everyone across the board. Unfortunately, since local conditions vary so much, nationalizing welfare creates one-size-fits-none policies that cannot adequately address the specific needs in particular communities. Even beyond that problem, however, federally mandated policies can produce unintended consequences that cause more harm than good.

When I was growing up in the 1960s, my mother taught in inner-city Newark, New Jersey. Most of her students were on welfare and therefore did not live with their fathers; in an effort to prevent cheating, the welfare laws stipulated that families would receive reduced benefits if the father lived at home, because he presumably would be working and thus be ineligible for the program. But there were no jobs, so to make ends meet, the fathers had to leave. The net result was that the Great Society drove fathers out of their homes, destroying the fabric of the African-American family. In the 1950s, the illegitimacy rate among blacks was lower than among whites, largely because of the influence of black churches. In the 1960s, an alarmed Daniel Patrick Moynihan warned of the impending destruction of the black family when the illegitimacy rate hit twenty-two percent; by 1994, it had risen to over seventy percent. Single-parent households are the most important predictor of poverty, yet that is precisely what the "War on Poverty" created. The result has been a permanent underclass, locked in a cycle of dependency on government—exactly the opposite of the kind of true aid to the poor advocated in Scripture.[12]

Another problem that flows from the increased dependency that the welfare state has produced is increased corruption in government. In a fallen world, governments are inevitably corrupt; in fact, St. Augustine described government as institutionalized injustice. Augustine tells us that government always acts for its own power and glory, and therefore that abuse of power is a natural part of the system. In democratic societies, the most obvious example of this abuse is vote-buying through legislation: politicians win by promising their constituents more and more benefits (paid for by the government and someone else's taxes). A quotation generally attributed (incorrectly) to Alexander Tytler, a late-eighteenth to early nineteenth century jurist and history professor in Scotland, tells us: "A democracy cannot exist as a permanent form of government. It can only exist until the voters discover that they can vote themselves largesse from the public treasury. From that moment on, the majority always votes for the candidates promising the most benefits from the public treasury with the result that a democracy always collapses over loose fiscal policy"[13] Or, as Alexis de Tocqueville said, "The American Republic will endure until the day Congress discovers that it can bribe the public with the public's money."

Federalizing social welfare leads to two other consequences as well. First, because the federal government is ill-suited to handling welfare, it requires an ever-expanding bureaucracy to write regulations and administer the programs, making it inefficient and generally ineffective, while, at the same time, increasing the reach and power of the government. This results in skyrocketing costs that drive governments to bankruptcy; and when that happens, the truly poor and needy end up worse off than they started. Second, dependency on government decreases liberty—defined by John Locke, for example, as the ability to dispose of one's self and one's possessions according to the dictates of reason.[14] Those dependent on the government have disincentives to try to find a way out of their situation. I have personally had numerous people decline to work with me in a business I own because they were afraid of losing government benefits. Since Scripture teaches that work is good and tells us to work so that we have the ability to give to others, this kind of dependency saps virtue and limits freedom to act even in your own interests, because it leads you to rely instead on the government to pay your bills and take care of you.

Government-run welfare is also a disincentive for churches and citizens to get involved in taking care of the poor; we pay taxes for other people to do that for us. Although there is no shortage of soup kitchens, homeless shelters, halfway houses, and other places of need where we could volunteer, few actually get involved, at least in part because we figure we have subcontracted those jobs to the government. We no longer feel responsible to care for the poor since we pay taxes, and without direct responsibility we do not develop virtue and, instead, step away from liberty and toward another form of dependence on the government: we rely on it to take care of our neighbors so we do not have to.

None of this implies that government, even at the federal level, should not be involved in welfare. Scripture may assign other roles to the government as its primary function, but it does not forbid government involvement in caring for the poor. What subsidiarity does mean is that government, especially the federal government, should not have the central responsibility to care for the needy. That responsibility properly belongs to more local agencies, and especially to the church. Even here, however, there are many misconceptions about New Testament models on how this is to be done.

The Church and the Poor

There can be no question that the early church was involved in caring for the poor. The church in Jerusalem in Acts 4 is perhaps the most obvious (and most misunderstood) example of this, but we can look as well to the aid delivered to the church in Jerusalem from churches in Asia Minor and Greece as an additional example of caring for those in need within the Christian community. But these early Christians did not only take care of their own poor. They ministered to the sick and dying, purchased slaves to set them free, clothed the naked, and fed the hungry whether they were Christians or not. This was recognized by Julian the Apostate, the Roman Emperor who attempted to repaganize Rome after Christianity was legalized. Julian complained, "These impious Galileans [i.e. Christians] feed not only their own poor, but ours as well." Julian's reaction was based on the fact that the pagan world was not much given to charity, and so the church's role in feeding the poor created a space in Roman society that was not under imperial authority and, therefore, undermined his rule. As the church has moved away from its ancient practice, it has surrendered this area once again to Caesar.

Historically, evangelism had always been linked to social welfare programs, ranging from feeding the poor to establishing hospitals and schools. In the early twentieth century, American church leaders, inspired by German liberal theology, essentially abandoned evangelism in favor of the "Social Gospel" and a nearly exclusive emphasis on this world. Conservative theologians rejected this change as a betrayal of true Christianity, but unfortunately they reacted by focusing exclusively on evangelism and the afterlife, while ignoring the relevance of the gospel of the kingdom for this world. American evangelicalism is still suffering from the aftermath of this division, which has discredited Christianity in the eyes of many young people in the country.[15]

The fact is, the emphasis on an exclusively other-worldly gospel does not do justice to the teachings of Jesus or Paul, as Ron Sider, Jim Wallis, and more recently Ched Myers and Shane Claiborne have argued. Unfortunately, many of these "progressive evangelicals" have largely baptized the programs of the secular left and confused them with a biblical vision for caring for the needy. Wallis, for example, has tied himself to government solutions for poverty through his close association with secular progressives and funding from the atheist George Soros. Claiborne and Myers see economic redistribution as an essential component to the gospel: Claiborne's *The Irresistible Revolution* tells us that "rebirth and redistribution are inextricably bound up in one another," and Myers's *Sabbath Economics* presents a vision of Christianity that is one hundred percent economic, with no mention of the spiritual dimensions of salvation. *Sabbath Economics* illustrates a number of important themes in this movement, along with its problems. The book's premise revolves around three points: God provides enough for his people if they restrain their appetites and live within limits;

differences in wealth and power are not natural and the community of faith must correct them through redistribution; the prophetic message of Scripture calls us to redistribution, which is what makes it good news for the poor.[16]

The first point comes from Myers's interpretation of the story of the manna, which teaches us that God provides for us but that accumulation is forbidden. In fact, Myers sees the entire manna episode as a parable about the superiority of hunter/gatherer society and local horticulture over intensive agriculture, cities, and the resultant slave-based imperial economies.[17] Moses did not see it this way (Deuteronomy 8:3), but Myers evidently thinks he understands the point of the manna better than Moses did. The prohibition of accumulation is further reinforced by the story of the rich young ruler, about which Myers concludes, "Whatever else the kingdom of God may be, it is where the rich are *not!*"[18] Evidently, Myers confuses it being *difficult* for the rich to enter the kingdom of heaven with it being *impossible*, an error he might have avoided had he not made the climax of the discussion Mark 10:26 rather than Jesus's own conclusion in 10:27.

The idea of redistribution comes from the Old Testament Sabbath Year and Jubilee—where property was returned and slaves set free—the Jerusalem church in Acts 4, and Jesus's description of his ministry as preaching good news to the poor (Luke 4:18). According to Myers, the only thing that would qualify as good news to the poor was the cancelation of their debts, and so Jesus's ministry was fundamentally about economics. He even argues that, although in the New Testament the Greek words for *debt* and *sin* are different, in Aramaic they are the same; and so when Jesus talks about forgiveness of sins he really means releasing people from monetary debt.[19] In other words, in rejecting modern evangelism's emphasis on the next life, he has made the gospel all about this world.

These assumptions guide Myers's approach to Scripture and lead to what can only be described as tortured exegesis of some of Jesus's parables. For example, in the parable of the vineyard, the absentee landowner is the one who faces judgment, not the tenants. Similarly, in the parable of the talents, it is not the ones who use their talents who are the heroes because, according to Myers, everyone would have recognized that the only way they could have doubled their investment was by exploitation. Here, Myers ignores the example of Isaac, who got a one hundred-fold return in his harvest (Genesis 26:12). He also misses the fact that the master was away for a long time (Matthew 25:19); even at the low rates of return he claims would have been acceptable, the servants could potentially have doubled the money without exploitation. The only reason to see these servants as exploitative is that if they are not, Myers's economic argument falls apart. Instead, Myers sees the servant who hides the talent as the real hero, because he refused to participate in an exploitive economic system. Myers's justification for this reading is that the third servant called the master a "hard man"—a term used for Pharaoh elsewhere in Scripture—and the master quotes it back to him without refutation (though in parallel passages the master makes it clear he is judging the servant using his own words). Both the tenants in the earlier parable and the third servant in this parable come to an unfortunate end, though Myers argues that this is not the result of divine judgment but the action of the unjust, oppressive system of the world, which always persecutes the righteous. The descriptions of their fate—being executed or cast into outermost darkness—are references to divine judgment in other parables, but to fit his assumptions Myers has to argue that they mean something different here. The examples can be multiplied.[20]

This forced exegesis (or to be more accurate, eisegesis—reading into the text rather than drawing the meaning out of it) is a sure sign that the assumptions Myers brings to Scripture are wrong. While his recognition of the relevance of the gospel to this world is laudable, his approach is wrong-headed, owing more to Marxist economic determinism than to a biblically faithful vision of economics within the community of faith.

But what of Myers's central idea, shared by other progressives such as Shane Claiborne, that the church is to be an anti-capitalist community based on voluntary redistribution of goods? First, the Bible is absolutely clear that those who have must share with those who have not. John the Baptist, Jesus, Paul, John, and James all tell us that the rich are obligated to help the poor. So, yes, in that sense, redistribution is a part of living faithfully before God. On the other hand, simplistic, communal redistribution schemes are neither biblically-mandated nor effective in truly helping the poor. Ched Myers cites the manna story as a prohibition on accumulation, but ignores the fact that the Israelites carried out great wealth from Egypt, some of which they contributed to the building of the Tabernacle. Evidently, despite the manna, God was not concerned with them holding on to property, even gold and jewels. This should not be surprising, considering that the right to property is grounded in the image of God and God's mandate to Adam in the Garden of Eden.[21] In fact, the inalienable right to property is critical to the Jubilee (one of Myers' inspirations for *Sabbath Economics*), as well as the laws prohibiting theft and covetousness.

But what about the "community of goods" described in the Jerusalem church, in which the believers "held all things in common" (Acts 4:32)?[22] This is a favorite verse for those who believe that redistribution is a central responsibility of the church. Yet a careful reading of the text and of the next few chapters shows that the Jerusalem church did not operate as a commune, whatever a superficial reading of this verse suggests. Read in context, "they held all things in common" is an example of hyperbole, the rhetorical device of using exaggeration for emphasis. The following verses tell us that, when there was a need, people sold their property to meet it. In other words, they recognized that their responsibility to their neighbors was more important than their ownership of their property, so they were quite willing to sell what they had to help others—but that means that they retained ownership of their property until a need arose that led them to sell it.

This observation is reinforced in the following chapter, where Peter affirms Ananias and Sapphira's right to their property and to the proceeds of its sale (Acts 5:4). In other words, private property was maintained in the Jerusalem church, and thus they did not literally "hold all things in common," although generosity was encouraged and practiced. Myers never explicitly rejects private property, and he does argue that redistribution should be voluntary; but since he also argues that accumulation is forbidden, it would seem that property ownership would involve the Christian in the kind of unjust economic system that Myers claims all believers are called upon to dismantle. How these two ideas fit together is not entirely clear.

The trajectory of poor-relief in Jerusalem does not stop in Acts chapter four or even five. Chapter six shows that the informal sharing of resources that had developed in the church did not work effectively; ethnic divisions led to a breakdown of the system that had to be corrected through a more organized approach to helping the poor (specifically, the widows) to be sure that all were adequately cared for. Because of this experience, the church in Jerusalem drew up rolls of widows who were dependent on the church, and appointed seven people to oversee the distribution of aid: the first deacons. At this point, the Jerusalem church numbered several thousand people, yet only seven were needed to deal with the needs of the church's dependents. This is a remarkably small number for such a large church. How did they make it work?

The answer is found in 1 Timothy. Evidently, the widows' roll in Jerusalem became the model for other churches, including the church in Ephesus. Paul tells Timothy that only certain widows were to put on the church's rolls; the rest were to remarry or be cared for by their families (1 Timothy 5:3-16). It is even possible that these widows were given specific responsibilities in the church. Early church documents indicate that the church had an "order of widows" whose job was to minister to women in ways that would have been inappropriate for men.[23] If true, this would be consistent with Paul's warnings against idleness and his insistence that those who can work should do so (2 Thessalonians 3:6-12). To put it differently, the church's regular distribution of food was limited to those who had no other options or resources and who devoted themselves to prayer and service to the saints (1 Timothy 5:5, 10). As a result, there were relatively few who were on the rolls, and the church in Jerusalem could therefore get by with only seven deacons. While Christians also engaged in extensive ad hoc charity to the needy, only a very limited number of people were allowed to become dependents of the church.

Of course, in addition to its regular charitable giving, the church also gave to help in emergencies, such as the famine in Jerusalem, for which Paul took up collections in Asia Minor and Greece (1 Corinthians 16:1-4). This is the context for 2 Corinthians 8:13-14, which Myers uses to argue that redistribution must be a regular activity of the church. But the situation described in this passage did not deal with "regular" giving within the church, but rather with a response to an emergency in a far distant church, one that gave an opportunity for a concrete demonstration of one of Paul's central ideas: the unity of Jews and Gentiles in Christ (cf. Romans 15:27).

None of this means that Christians are not called upon to share with those in need. We absolutely are, and on this point the progressive movement among evangelicals is beyond doubt correct. The apostolic church considered "remembering the poor" to be among its most basic moral imperatives (Galatians 2:10). The key question is how best to do this.

This analysis suggests that a balanced, Scripture-based approach to helping the poor is considerably more complex than the "community of goods" model, and takes into account such core biblical ideas as the significance of work and private property, along with the importance of loving our neighbor with actions, not just words. The issue of accumulation is particularly important here, because without it, economic and technological growth, medical advancement, the arts, and a wide range of other activities would come to a grinding halt. History provides numerous examples where a more biblically-balanced understanding of economics and responsibility to the poor had a massive (though under-appreciated) impact on society.

After the apostolic era, Christians continued to take care of human needs. Even prior to the legalization of Christianity, Christians took the lead in caring for the sick, even at great personal risk (as the Roman physician Galen attested). After Christianity was legalized, they more than anyone else fed the hungry (as the pagan emperor Julian the Apostate recognized). Throughout history, the church has also been heavily involved in education (as evidenced by the number of schools and universities that have been started by missionaries and churches). In the Middle Ages, nearly all organized charity was administered through the church or through parachurch organizations known as confraternities. These lay-religious institutions provided for the poor, either generally or through targeted giving to specific causes, for example by providing dowries for poor girls.Perhaps the most interesting example of Christian efforts to aid the poor is found in the medieval monasteries. St. Benedict of Nursia, whose rules for monastic life were the foundation for nearly all Western monasticism, mandated that his monks take a vow of poverty and at the same time be engaged in work—understood primarily in agricultural terms as production of goods. There were two reasons for this: first, in the ancient world, work was seen as demeaning, and thus having the monks work promoted humility; second, Benedict recognized that God gave Adam work to do in the Garden before the Fall, and so work was good no matter what society thought of it.[24] As we have seen, the Apostle Paul also taught this. But a curious thing happened:

Although many of the monasteries became corrupt—little more than country clubs for the nobility, who lived in luxury, whatever their vows said—other monasteries were vitally concerned with following a pure version of Benedict's Rule. The Cistercian order is a good example of this. The Cistercians made sure that the monks were all engaged in productive labor, and at the same time banned conspicuous consumption and luxurious living, insisting instead on a strict understanding of the vow of poverty. Productive labor resulted in increasing profits. While some profits were given away, the limitations on transportation and the relatively sparse population still left a surplus after giving to the poor. Since it was wrong to let the produce spoil, it was sold and the proceeds were used to purchase more land, since the monks' vow of poverty meant that the cash could not be kept or spent on conspicuous consumption. In turn, the new land increased the productive potential of the monastery. The thought was: if production is good, more production is better. The monks themselves could not work all of the land, and so they brought in tenant farmers who grew crops and gave a fixed amount back to the monastery. The monks thus provided employment for the lay people outside of the monastery, giving them meaningful work and a chance to benefit from their own labor. The net result was that a strict understanding of the monastic vow of poverty led the Cistercians to become very rich while also benefiting those who lived around the monasteries.

But the story does not stop there. The monks understood that, although work is good, drudgery is a negative result of the Fall. Christ came to redeem us from the results of sin, and thus as his followers we need to work to restore meaning to work by eliminating drudgery. As a result, the monks also used their excess profits to find ways to harness technology to do repetitive, mindless work rather than tasking people with it. Monks were the first to use waterwheels—a technology known to but never deployed by the Romans—to grind grain. The waterwheel was then adapted for a wide range of other uses outside of the monasteries, including operating bellows and trip hammers for forges, sawing lumber, fulling cloth, and making paper. These technologies further increased productivity while eliminating some of the drudgework associated with production. The monasteries were thus the beginning of many of the essential elements of capitalism, particularly the reinvestment of profits to increase production, motivated by a biblical understanding of work and man's creation in the image of God. The unintended effect of all this was to raise the amount of goods available to people and, therefore, raise the standard of living in Europe across the board through the central Middle Ages. This also produced important social changes, including most notably the conversion of the vast majority of European serfs to free peasants.

In the sixteenth century, cities began to regard care for their own poor as a civic responsibility. The Reformation heightened this trend, since without the Catholic confraternities that had been handling social welfare, someone had to pick up the slack in caring for the poor. At the same time, many reformers continued to insist (with varying degrees of success) that this should be an ecclesiastical function. At their best, town governments developed innovative and comprehensive approaches for dealing with the poor in a way the hodgepodge of confraternities and religious orders had been unable to do.

For example, when the city of Geneva converted to Protestantism in 1536, it replaced all of the Catholic relief organizations with a single "General Hospital." The hospital was a comprehensive social welfare institution that took care of all needs except communicable diseases. It used a vertically integrated, interlocking approach to provide for the needs of native deserving poor, orphans, the elderly, and those unable to work.[25] Orphaned, illegitimate, or abandoned boys would work on farms under the direction of the hospital, thereby learning the skills needed to be farmers. The grain they produced was then brought to mills, where other boys were taught to grind it into flour. The flour then went to bakeries, where other boys were taught to bake bread. The bread was then distributed to the elderly and infirm who could not work for themselves. Girls were similarly given opportunities to learn skills that they would need later in life. All of this was supervised directly by *hôpitaliers* (essentially, ecclesiastical social workers) and funded through the work of *procureurs* (fundraisers for the hospital). When Calvin wrote the church order for Geneva, he identified these offices as deacons in the church, thereby baptizing existing Genevan practice and creating a kind of mixed church-state institution. Even with the separation of church and state in America, the model of the Genevan hospital suggests that church-state cooperation in social welfare can be very effective. In fact, this kind of cooperation is actually practiced in many places in the United States today.

The examples of medieval monasteries and of Reformation Geneva show that dealing with poverty involves more than just feeding the poor; it requires economic structures that promote human flourishing holistically. Significantly, this does not mean reorganizing society to shift wealth from those who produce it to those who do not; rather, it means providing opportunities to all to earn their own way and providing a safety net for those who cannot.

Clearly, biblical ideas about work, the image of God, property rights, and generosity lead to sound economic thought and social welfare approaches that benefit society as a whole. The free market system built on biblical ideas about property rights, the dignity of work, and practices such as reinvesting profits to increase production, has done more to relieve poverty than any other economic system in history. Unfortunately, very few people in the church and in society today recognize the importance of these biblical ideas, the role of the church in economic thought, and the profound impact for good these things have had in practice.

Principles for Helping the Poor

To draw this chapter to a close, I would suggest the following principles drawn from the previous discussion as a starting point for dealing with issues of poverty:

The Importance of Work

In an era of ongoing unemployment, it is important to recognize the true value and importance of work. One of the areas that progressives often ignore is where wealth comes from in the first place, which is the essential starting point if we are going to find biblical principles for dealing with poverty. Work is simultaneously an aspect of man's creation in the image of God and the normal means God gives us to provide for our needs and for the needs of others. Sometimes people are genuinely unable to provide for themselves, but Scripture tells us we should all be seeking to work rather than to live off the generosity of others. Those of us who are employed or who own businesses need to value our work and do our best at it. We also should advocate for policies that will encourage meaningful work. And where possible, we should endeavor to provide training and opportunity for others as an expression of our love for our neighbor.

Churches can also be involved in these areas, but at the very least they should recognize the importance of business, investment, and employment as fundamental tools for promoting human dignity and the health and well-being of the community. The church must not demonize the wealthy, the financially successful, the business owner, or the entrepreneur. In too many cases, these groups are valued only when it is time for a capital campaign. The church also needs to rediscover and teach the cultural mandate, that is, that all callings—including business and finance—come from God and are part of what it means to be created in the image of God. Rather than condemning business, the church needs to devote resources to supporting it and bringing the gospel of the kingdom to bear in the marketplace. This doesn't mean ignoring ethical abuses, but it does mean promoting kingdom values in business in order to prevent such abuses.

The Importance of Moral Proximity

The principle of moral proximity states that we have responsibilities to others in proportion to our relationship with them: those who are closer to us have more of a claim on us than those who are distant, with proximity determined by relationships rather than geography. For example, our church has a relationship with a church in Peru through the marvelous organization Compassion International. Through that relationship, our church is brought into close moral proximity with that church and its members, and we thus have a greater responsibility to support them than we have to support other equally needy and deserving churches elsewhere.

Following the principle of moral proximity, our primary responsibility is to our own family. Jesus understood the commandment, "Honor your father and mother," to mean that we need to provide for our parents even ahead of giving to the temple (Mark 7:9-13); and Paul tells us that we are responsible to take care of our grandparents rather than passing them off to the church (or the state) to take care of them (1 Timothy 5:4). We also have responsibilities to our descendants. Proverbs 13:22 tells us that we are to leave a legacy to our grandchildren, so we are to give them something to build upon rather than to leave them in debt. We thus have an ethical responsibility before God to provide for our own families ourselves. How this works out in our modern world is more complicated than it was in the first century, given Social Security, Medicare, insurance, unemployment, food stamps, and other public and private provisions to care for the elderly, unemployed, or disabled. Nonetheless, it remains our responsibility to see to it that our families are cared for regardless of what assistance is or is not available. After our families, we need to look at the other circles around us, including our churches, our communities, and connections to the wider world through institutions we are part of, as the next set of responsibilities we have.

The Importance of Subsidiarity

The principle of subsidiarity is very closely related to the principle of moral proximity. The difference is focus: moral proximity looks at problems and asks where I am personally responsible to act given my finite time and resources; subsidiarity looks at problems and asks who is best equipped to deal with them. Subsidiarity argues that solutions are best found on as local a level as possible, with higher level institutions becoming involved only when the problems are too big for lower levels to handle. In cases of human need, the process begins with the family; if the family cannot solve it, friends, community groups, and churches should step in. Only after these private agencies are exhausted should the problem move to government, and then once again on as local a level as possible. This is where a biblical approach to poor-relief flies in the face of what is done in most of the Western world. Rather than looking for solutions at the highest levels of government, subsidiarity is based on the premise that those closest to the problem have both the best understanding of the situation and of the individuals involved, and the most direct responsibility to solve those problems. This allows for solutions tailored to the individual situation rather than the one-size-fits-all approach necessarily taken by the state, and promotes virtue by encouraging the community to take greater responsibility for the welfare of its members.

The Importance of Giving

All of these principles mean nothing unless we follow biblical teaching about the importance of giving generously and even sacrificially to those in need. John Wesley's advice about money is worth quoting here: "Make all you can, save all you can, give all you can." James tells us that true faith leads us to give to those in need: "If a brother or sister is poorly clothed and lacking in daily food, and one of you says to them, 'Go in peace, be warmed and filled,' without giving them the things needed for the body, what good is that?" (James 2:15-16). And John tells us that if we do not give to those in need, we do not know the love of God: "... if anyone has this world's goods and sees his brother in need, yet closes his heart against him, how does God's love abide in him?" (1 John 3:17). Giving involves more than money; it includes our time. If we are too busy to help others, we are too busy. This includes direct involvement in people's lives, but also involvement in community organizations, particularly churches that have an active ministry to those in need.

History shows us that when the church carries out its calling to help the poor, it can have a profound effect on society as a whole. But it is important to do this correctly. It begins with encouraging businesses and economic development. These provide resources to help the poor as well as giving people the opportunity to work their way out of poverty. In terms of direct action, churches should recognize that helping the poor is not simply serving in a soup kitchen once a month; rather, the church needs to consider how it can help minister to the whole person and the full range of needs they may have, such as food, medical care, education, transportation, job training, etc. Few churches have the resources to deal with all of these areas. Instead, churches need to work together across denominational lines to coordinate their work in the community; even beyond that, they should work with secular social service agencies to see that the needs are met. Following the principle of subsidiarity, the church's first concern must be for the needy within its own community. But this does not preclude the church from taking on other charitable work further afield, whether in poor areas in our own nation or overseas. This is important work as well, but it must not replace meeting local needs.

Far from moving in an anti-capitalist, quasi-socialist direction, both the Bible and church history show that a two-pronged approach of supporting business and economic development and direct work meeting needs in the community is the best approach to promoting human flourishing in this world, and it does so in a way that also promotes godly living in this world in preparation for the next.

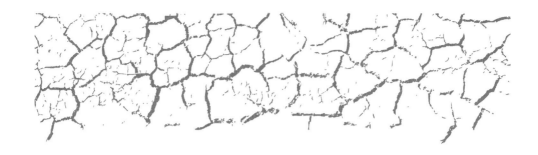

Poverty and the Poor in the Old Testament

By Walter C. Kaiser, Jr., Ph.D.

P overty is the state or condition of having few or no material possessions or evidences of wealth, but it must always be assessed as a relative condition to some spoken or unstated standard or criteria of the culture in which it is assessed. The word "poor" is often used in a relative sense. To take just one example, a poor person in America would appear rich in comparison to others in less developed countries, given that the poverty level in the United States is an income of $28,000 a year, whereas, in most other parts of the world, it is $800 per year or $2.00 per day.

This chapter will examine the biblical nature and causes of poverty from the perspective of the Old Testament. Chapter three will continue the discussion from the New Testament perspective. Poverty is frequently referenced in the Old Testament, demonstrating that God cares about the poor and so must we. This chapter begins with an Old Testament definition of poverty and then traces the plight of the Israelites, who began as slaves in Egypt. Generally, it was very difficult to escape the conditions of poverty in Old Testament times, where markets were small and sporadic and income mobility was largely unlikely, unlike modern conditions. This chapter will then discuss the Torah law regarding poverty and riches and the conditions that it created for caring for the poor, followed by an examination of how the conditions of the poor worsened under the monarchy, as some became wealthy at the expense of the poor through expropriation; their plight was taken up by the latter prophets as income inequality worsened. We then examine the poor in light of the wisdom literature. This chapter will end with a critical look at the role of the church in the poverty crisis and the state and public welfare issues related to caring for the poor—all in light of examined Old Testament teachings.

But let it be noted from the very beginning that poverty is not the greatest of all evils on planet earth any more than wealth is to be granted the honor of being the greatest of all goods and possible achievements that a person could attain. Even though some have suggested that a life of poverty is such a wretched state of existence that life is not worth living (Job 24:4-12), Proverbs 28:6 and Ecclesiastes 4:13 argue correctly that, at times, poverty is much to be preferred over the possession of great riches, especially if those riches are achieved by perverse or wicked means. The argument of both Proverbs and Ecclesiastes follows like this:

> Better is a poor man whose walk is blameless
> Than a rich man whose ways are perverse – Proverbs 28:6.

> Better is a poor but wise youth
> Than an old but foolish king
> Who no longer knows how to take warning – Ecclesiastes 4:13.

Scripture examines many causes or reasons for poverty, but these causes are, more often than not, attributed to human faults instead of to some action on God's part. For example, poverty may come because of laziness or sloth (Proverbs 6:10; 19:15; 24:30); or it may even result from living high on the hog (Proverbs 21:17); or perhaps it is due to just plain foolishness and stubbornness (Proverbs 13:18; 28:19). Poverty may come as a result of oppression and the greed of others (Exodus 1:13; Jeremiah 22:13), or it may come from events over which the individual has no control, such as a disaster, war, disease, fraud, earthquake, tsunami, or political oppression. These causes are just as real, and they need to be considered before one quickly tries to pass off all poverty as the heavy hand of God raised against the poor.

Nor has the plight of the poor been left as the least or last of the concerns of Scripture and the believing community. In fact, according the count of Rick Warren, a well-known pastor and author of *The Purpose Driven Life* (which has sold well over thirty-two million copies), 2000 verses deal with the issue of the poor in Scripture, even though the actual use of the term "poor" appears just over 200 times in the King James Version.[26] Warren was surprised when he first discovered these references. Up to that time, no one had brought this huge number of verses to his attention, despite the fact that he was seminary trained and holds a Doctor of Ministry (D. Min.) degree.

Prior to the release of Warren's book, in the 1970s, Jim Wallis of the Sojourners Community had already gone through the Bible with his colleagues and cut every one of the 2000 verses out of the Bible to demonstrate how significant this topic was for those who treasured the full message of the Scriptures. Many were shocked when Wallis held up his hole-y Bible, for it must have reminded them of Thomas Jefferson, who also cut up his Bible. It should be noted, however, that

Jefferson's goal was to remove those doctrines in Scripture that he found offensive; this was not Wallis's intent.

A point is to be taken from those who emphasize the Bible's 2000 references to the poor: it is time that the believing community reconsiders what Scripture has to say about the poor, the widow, the orphan, the oppressed, and about poverty itself. All too often, people show that they like to talk about the poor, but if and when they are challenged by their personal response to the needs and the presence of the poor, they immediately feel threatened. Not many will admit that they usually want to avoid facing the issue or dealing with the poor, but the truth of the matter still remains: there is a lot of room for growth in Christian graces in this area of accepting and caring for the poor, as well as in the more readily accepted areas of those holy living. Scripture states this fact bluntly:

> The poor are shunned even by their neighbors,
> but the rich have many friends. – Proverbs 14:20.

Believers are not only called to face the plight of the poor, but also to work together to address their needs in a way that honors the teaching of the word of God.

Definition of the Poor in the Old Testament

Traditionally, the poor are generally referred to as those who are destitute, lacking even the most basic necessities to keep body and soul together. At best, a poor person is one who has little or nothing in the way of goods, possessions, wealth, or even the means to maintain a subsistence level of living.

Since this is so serious a matter, it is not strange that we find a number of key Hebrew terms used for the "poor" in the Old Testament. The most frequent Hebrew term rendered as "poor" is the term *'evyon* and its cognates, which occur more than sixty times in the Old Testament. These reference persons who are poor in a material sense and are the truly needy and destitute of the basic necessities of life (Deuteronomy 15:7; 24:14; Psalm 109:16). *'Evyon* is often partnered with another Hebrew term, *'ani* (Psalm 109:16; 35:10; 72:12; 109:22) to refer to those who are 'afflicted' and 'bowed low' because of the oppression of the wicked—often the rich (Isaiah 3:14; Ezekiel 18:16-18)—even though they may truly have been trying to serve the Lord (Psalm 10:2; Isaiah 14:32)."[27]

Another Hebrew word for the "poor," *dal* or *dalah*—derived from the root *dalal*, meaning "to be low," "to languish"—was especially common in the poetry of the wisdom literature, appearing some twenty-two times, with seven instances in Proverbs. The poor mentioned under this term are usually those whose condition is exacerbated due to the oppression of the wicked (Job 20:19; Proverbs 22:16; Amos 4:1).

Another Hebrew term, *cheser*, carries the meaning of a "lack," a "need," expressed by those in want or in dire poverty (Proverbs 6:11; 11:24), those without the basic necessities of life (2 Samuel 3:29; Job 30:3; Proverbs 12:9). In this extensive vocabulary for the poor, however, there are other Hebrew words used less frequently, such as *dak*, the "downtrodden," and *miskan*, a "beggar," used only in Ecclesiastes (4:13; 9:15-16).

A Nation Begins in Slavery in Egypt

It must be remembered in all of this discussion that the nation of Israel began its existence as a nation of slaves in Egypt, and, after being delivered, spent forty years in the wilderness before arriving in the land of Canaan. Under those originating conditions, it was next to impossible for economic or class distinctions between the poor and the wealthy to develop; there just were no sharp divisions in those days between the poor and the rich, for the same heritage was shared by all. No one person or family seemed to have more than the next person or family. Moreover, when they came to the Promised Land, every Israelite was given a portion of land on which to settle. But even then the land did not belong solely to the individuals themselves, as they had been assigned portions within their tribes. These assignments were theirs to steward with no prospect of losing them, for in reality, the land belonged to Yahweh (Leviticus 25:23).

The Israelites knew what it meant to be marginalized and to experience slavery in another country. It was for this reason that they were to show mercy to others who found themselves in similar situations living in their land as aliens. Even Abraham, Isaac, and Jacob were described as resident aliens in their original dwelling in the Promised Land (Genesis 17:8; 23:4; 28:4; 35:27). That same designation was used for the Israelites' status while they were in Egypt (Genesis 12:10; 15:13; 47:4; Exodus 22:21).

Apportioning land to each family ensured that families always had a means of producing the essentials for a livelihood through the land that had been gifted. This meant that all in Israel would have a home as well as land that they could farm and use to produce additional products for sale beyond their family's needs.

The Teaching of the Torah Law about Poverty and Riches

What is most distinctive about the biblical understanding of wealth and poverty is the fact that Yahweh had a deep love for the poor. It was his desire that there should be no poor people in his covenant community (Deuteronomy 15:4). In order to maintain such a high standard, the book of the covenant (Exodus 20:22-23:19) set up what was known as the Sabbatical Year for debt service (Exodus 21:2). Since no one owned the land—it belonged to Yahweh—it could not be used as collateral on a fixed or permanent sale of the property when a person faced economic trouble. Thus, the only readily available bargaining power a debtor owned was his labor. Acting as a "bonded laborer," he could use his labor as leverage against his agreed-upon loan granted in expectation of his service. But even this was limited to a maximum indenture period of six years (Exodus 21:2; Leviticus 25:39). The loan was then to be totally cancelled and forgiven, and this indentured man or woman was to go absolutely free. A father could also sell his children for a limited period of time to provide food if the family had sunk to the bare edge of a subsistence level of living (Exodus 21:7; Nehemiah 5:5). Creditors often forcefully seized the children of debtors to satisfy unpaid judgments against their parents (2 Kings 4:1; Amos 2:6), but they also were to be released after a maximum of six years. This thought also affected the feeling of the children, for they too were obligated to care for their poverty-stricken parents.

The law also granted the poor the right to harvest whatever the land produced on its own during the Sabbatical Year in which Israel was to let the fields remain fallow (Exodus 23:10-11). There was also the provision that the corners of the fields were not to be picked clean, but they were to be left for the poor, the widow, and the orphan to harvest as part of their own upkeep (Leviticus 19:9-10; Deuteronomy 24:19-21). In short, all exploitation of the poor was strictly forbidden (Leviticus 25:22-27), as was all perversion of justice against their interest (Leviticus 25:43-53). Instead, the community was commanded to treat the poor with open hands, rather than manifesting tight fists (Deuteronomy

15:7, 11). This meant that special care should be rendered to such landless members as widows and orphans (Deuteronomy 24:17-18), all resident aliens (Deuteronomy 10:19), and the Levites, who had no property assigned to them (Deuteronomy 14:27). The basic thought was that Yahweh was the protector and defender of the poor (Exodus 22:25; 23:3; Leviticus 19:10; 23:22).

Permission was also granted for poor persons to help themselves to fruit or grain as they journeyed along the road through the property of others, a provision David Baker called "scrumping." For example:

> If you enter your neighbor's vineyard, you may eat all the grapes you want, but do not put any in your basket. If you enter your neighbor's grain field, you may pick kernels with your hands, but you must not put a sickle to his standing grain – Deuteronomy 23:24-25.

Permission was granted to satisfy one's hunger, but not to use this as an occasion to load up on produce from another person's property and then to cart it back home; no damage was to be done as a result of entering the property or sampling of its fruit or grains. This law was unique, for there are no other instances of such legislation in the ancient Near East. The point once again was this: concern for the needs of the poor took a significant position in defining the property rights held by the "owners" (really holders of the God-given land tenancy) of land. This also meant that theft was nuanced by this exception, for the right to satisfy a human need was a qualifier within the definition of what was considered theft and what was not.

These regulations, therefore, were not intended to produce a welfare state, but, instead, were intended to protect what were otherwise known as an enterprising people during exceptional times of difficult circumstances. The law was most interested in providing needed protection from unscrupulous persons who sought to take advantage of another person's misfortune.

Do not mistreat an alien or oppress him, for you were aliens in Egypt. Do not take advantage of a widow or an orphan – Exodus 22:21-22.

Do not deprive the alien or the fatherless of justice,
or take the cloak of a widow as a pledge.
Remember that you were slaves in Egypt,
and the LORD
your God redeemed you from there.
That is why I command you to do this – Deuteronomy 24:17.

The same law applies to the native-born and to the alien living among you
– Exodus 12:49.

When you reap the harvest of your land,
Do not reap to the very edges of your field
or gather the gleanings of your harvest.
Leave them for the poor and the alien.
I am the LORD your God – Leviticus 23:22.

These verses provide, therefore, one of the earliest references to the widow, the orphan and the immigrant. If these concepts were established as law, as they indeed were, then how did any in Israel become wealthy or rich while others became poor? As part of the covenant that God made with Israel, riches would come from obedience and faithfulness to the Lord, just as poverty and losses would result from persistent disobedience, laziness, or lackadaisical behavior (Leviticus 26:3-5, 9-10; Deuteronomy 30:11-20).

The ideal point of view was that "there should be no poor among you (cf. chapter 3 of this work), for in the land the LORD your God is giving you to possess as your inheritance, he will richly bless you" (Deuteronomy 15:4). God's perspective was to be the norm and the desired state of affairs; however, the text continued, with its usual sense of realism, "If there is a poor man among your brothers in any of your towns of the land that the LORD your God is giving you, do not be hardhearted or tightfisted toward your poor brother. Rather be openhanded and freely lend him whatever he needs" (Deuteronomy 15:7-8). Some might conclude that this is a contradiction of texts, but it was merely the difference between stating what God had made possible for all and the fact that, because of sin and other factors, less than the ideal would also occur. In fact, this very passage ends with this statement: "There will always be poor people in the land. Therefore, I command you to be openhanded toward your brothers and toward the poor and needy in the land" (Deuteronomy 15:11; cf. Matthew 26:11; Mark 14:7). Both teachings were true: "There should be no poor among you," and "There will always be poor in the land;" the difference was mainly in the obedience factor to the Lord!

Of course, some chose to be poor voluntarily, such as the Levites, some of the prophets, and Jesus himself. Such also seemed to be the state of all those who entered into the sectarian community of Qumran, the Dead Sea Scrolls community. In many lands of that day, some quite openly preferred slavery to what would otherwise be a state of poverty, as slavery under a benevolent master approximated something closer to what we would consider employment than either harsh bondage or servitude.

The Poor under the Monarchy and the Latter Prophets

The condition of the poor worsened during the days of the monarchy—especially under kings David and Solomon—as some became fabulously rich and others fell behind. The infusion of silver and gold to the monarchy, along with a number of other luxury products from afar in the royal court, spurred the growing disparity between rich and poor as the standards of living grew apart. As a result of this condition, the prophets began to take up the cause of the poor, particularly in those areas where the disparity brought forced labor for some (Amos 5:11, 12), the illegitimate enslavement of their fellow citizens (Jeremiah 34:8-11), and the loss of certain freedoms and rights that should have been offered to widows, orphans, and the poor (Isaiah 10:1, 2). Those who achieved wealth and riches and became socially strong could use that position of strength to oppress those of another class, namely the poor (Amos 2:7; 4:1; 5:11). The rich did not oppress the poor simply because they were rich but because they were sinners. Part of this oppression could be seen in an insatiable hunger for more land (Amos 8:4; Isaiah 3:15). This, in turn, led to driving the poor off their inheritance (Micah 2:2; Isaiah 5:8-10). As the prophets warned, Yahweh was sure to see such that outright disobedience of his law was punished (Amos 2:13-15):

> Hear this, you who trample the needy
> and do away with the poor of the land....
> skimping the measure,
> boosting the price
> and cheating with dishonest scales,
> buying the poor with silver
> and the needy for a pair of sandals,
> selling even the sweepings with the wheat – Amos 8:4-6.

> Learn to do right!
> Seek justice,
> encourage the oppressed.
> Defend the cause of the fatherless,
> plead the case of the widow – Isaiah 1:17.

An even more direct rebuke was given to the wives of many of those considered rich, those whom the prophet Amos dared to address as "cows of Bashan!" This must have caught their attention if nothing else did!

> Hear this word, you cows of Bashan on Mount Samaria,
> you women who oppress the poor and crush the needy
> and say to your husbands, 'Bring us some drinks!'
> The Sovereign LORD has sworn by his holiness:
> 'The time will surely come
> when you will be taken away with hooks,
> the last of you with fishhooks' – Amos 4:1-2.

Despite the forthrightness of many of these commands and accusations, they should not be seen as evidence of a "class struggle" in Israel. These injunctions were addressed to every Israelite, and, as such, laid on the conscience of everyone—from the king to the youngest child—the responsibility of making sure that the rights of every person were fully respected. Typically in the Old Testament, the issue of the poor was expressed as the plight of widows, orphans, and immigrants. Not all those who belonged to these classes were indigent, but some in these groups fell into precarious economic or oppressive situations at times; in their weakness they became vulnerable and subject to the predatory instincts of those who were stronger and possessed certain powers. The problem was, therefore, that some were tempted to rob the needy of their rights and the justice they deserved from their officials and the courts (e.g. Isaiah 10:2; Jeremiah 5:28) because those in political power allowed such state-sanctioned theft or indulged in it themselves.

Repeatedly, the prophets of the Old Testament called for special attention to the oppressed, the poor, the widow, the orphan, and the alien. One such typical charge to the people can be seen in Zechariah 7:9-10:

> Administer true justice;
> show mercy and compassion to one another.
> Do not oppress the widow or the fatherless, the alien or the poor;
> in your hearts do not think evil of each other.

This text is joined by another, Isaiah 58:1-12, which may be one of the strongest texts in defense of the poor. In it, the prophet Isaiah warned those who wanted to substitute deeds of mercy toward the poor and needy with times of fasting. The prophet was most clear as he challenged Israel to replace an improper emphasis on religious formalism and liturgy with real social concern for those who were hurting.

> Is not this the kind of fasting I have chosen:
> to loose the chains of injustice
> and untie the cords of the yoke,
> to set the oppressed free
> and break every yoke?
> Is it not to share your food with the hungry

and to provide the poor wanderer with shelter—

when you see the naked, to clothe him,

and not to turn away from your own flesh and blood? – Isaiah

58: 5-7.

True godliness and faithful walking with God have some very real economic and practical consequences, which Isaiah sets out in as plain a fashion as possible. One could not hide behind an orthodox theology while leaving his brother, relative, or neighbor out in the cold. This teaching rises to the same level found in the New Testament book of James:

Religion that God our Father accepts as pure and faultless

is this:

to look after orphans and widows in their distress

and to keep oneself from being polluted by the world –

James 1:27.

The Poor in the Wisdom Writings

Not all poverty in this world is the same—as we have already argued—for a normal standard of living in one country would not reach subsistence level in another. And Scripture does not always, or even mainly, deal with the causes of most forms of poverty as much as it deals with what one should do when someone falls into such hard times. Thus, it urges diligence and hard work as part of the cure for poverty, rather than an attitude that sits back and waits for wealth redistribution from the rich so that all can benefit at the same time and at the same level. For example, consider these examples from the wisdom books:

Lazy hands make a person poor,
but diligent hands bring wealth – Proverbs 10:4.

Laziness brings on deep sleep,
and a shiftless/idle man goes hungry – Proverbs 19:15.

He who ignores discipline comes to poverty and shame,
but whoever heeds correction is honored – Proverbs 13:18.

Oftentimes the poor are embedded in poverty not because of what they have done, or even failed to do, but because of what has been done to them. For example:

'Because of the oppression of the weak
and the groaning of the needy,
I will arise,' says the LORD.
'I will protect them from those who malign them' – Psalm 12:5.

In his arrogance the wicked man hunts down the weak,
who are caught in the schemes he devises – Psalm 10:2.

Despite the worse efforts of wicked men, the wisdom books emphasize that God is directly involved in acting on behalf of those who present such special needs. Few texts say that better than Psalm 146:9: "The LORD watches over the alien and sustains the fatherless and the widow, but he frustrates the ways of the wicked." This is not to claim that God was unfairly partial to the poor against the rich, for once again Proverbs 22:2 affirms that "The rich and the poor have this in common: The LORD is the Maker of them all." What is more, God has made it the king's responsibility, as his representative, to look after and care for the poor (Psalm 72:2-4).

A poor or hungry person must therefore do all that he can to care for his needs, but the believing body (along with the administrative establishment) is not given a pass and excused from sharing the hurts and needs of these wounded souls. Both truths are fully operative at the same time.

The Proper Means of Helping the Poor

Scripture clearly challenges Christians to have compassion for the poor, starting especially with the care of those in their own families, then for those in the household of faith, and then for their neighbors outside the household of faith; but it is often possible to confuse the end of helping the poor with the appropriate means of helping them. Not all economic and political programs are equally helpful in aiding the poor, despite pressures to think differently.

First of all, not all forms of poverty result from, or are even caused by, economic factors. Some causes may be traced back to personal predispositions, such as one's habit of not planning for the future. For example, wealthy people typically are future-oriented in that they may be willing to make sacrifices in the present in order to gain something in the future. However, those *outside* this class all too often demonstrate their inability to think beyond the present, and thus live moment-by-moment, suggesting that poverty involves more than merely possessing material goods.[28] After all, students, retired persons, and some laborers live on low incomes—at least for a period of time—but they have planned or are planning for their future goals and are willing to make sacrifices. This distinction is an important one, and one that needs to be taught. Saving and sacrificing for the future are very important.

Jim Wallis, editor of *Sojourners* magazine, is one who has spoken often of the great disparities between the wealthy and the poor. In his view, expressed some time ago, he claimed:

> The bottom fifth of American families get 6 percent of the national income while the top fifth get 40 percent of the national income, owns 77 percent of the wealth and 97 percent of the corporate stock.[29]

Apparently, Wallis views this as an immoral situation. And he, as an evangelical, is not alone in his view. Another evangelical, Ron Sider, also agrees with him on the need for a fundamental redistribution of wealth.[30] But does Scripture argue for this type of egalitarianism? The thought is that perhaps Leviticus 25, the law of the year of Jubilee, could serve as the basis for contending that Christians should pool all of their stocks and income-producing properties and businesses, and redistribute them equally to elevate the poor to a level similar to that of the rich. But this idea raises some questions. Is the Jubilee law normative for believers today? And is this a proper understanding of what that law intended to do, i.e., to redistribute wealth?

First, it is extremely important to note that Leviticus 25 was not at all concerned with "income equalization." Instead, it was primarily interested in keeping properties within family lines and restoring those lands that were leased for a stated amount of time back to the families who originally owned them. The maximum period a piece of land could be leased was forty-nine years; but since Yahweh alone ultimately owned the land, family lands could not be sold to another party in perpetuity; that property had to remain in the family line. Each family was to remain the only long-term holder of that land. If during that forty-nine year period, a kinsman-redeemer—a wealthier relative from the family—did not come forth to pay off the lease and repurchase the family's plot, the land reverted automatically to the original owner in the fiftieth year without any further economic obligations. The main point of the arrangement mandated in Leviticus 25 was to maintain an equal opportunity for all Israelites to maintain a base from which they could continue to earn an income and provide for themselves, as removing a family's land would also remove the incentives that family had to work and to invest in its own real estate holdings.

The Year of Jubilee law cannot be equated, as some have tried to argue, with certain Latin American "land reform" programs, for in the biblical instance exhibited in Leviticus 25, the original owner, or his kinsman-redeemer, was obligated to repurchase the land, exchanging compensation for the land and restoring dignity to the original family. This could hardly be seen as robbing one party to make another party happy. The prohibition against stealing (the eighth commandment) applied just as vigorously to governments and land agencies as it did to individuals.

These provisions in Leviticus 25 deliberately exempted houses in walled cities (Leviticus 25:29-30) and the release of foreign slaves (Leviticus 25:44, 45), but release was provided for those Hebrews who were in debt-bondage for the maximum six-year period from the sale of their labor power. Houses in walled cities and land were both forms of wealth. Only land that was farmed reverted back to its original owners, whereas the land with permanent structures in the city was not reversible.

The Government's Role in Alleviating Poverty

Professor John Davis related an interesting scenario from Roman history, as told in H. J. Haskell's book, *The New Deal in Ancient Rome.*[31]

Ancient Rome's welfare system began without an income test; only those who were willing to stand in lines for bread could take advantage of subsidized prices. When Publius Clodius (c. 92-52 B.C.) ran for the office of tribune, he offered free wheat to all, which was enough to get him elected (Lex Clodia, 58 B.C.). There were about 320,000 persons on the government dole when Julius Caesar came to power ten years later. By the time of Emperor Aurelian (A.D. 270-275), it had already become a hereditary right to receive government help. Daily, two pounds of bread were distributed freely to all citizens who applied. Pork, olive oil, and salt were periodically added to this dole without charge. But as might be expected, such reliance on the government had a deleterious effect on the people's incentives and character, for now they came to expect something for nothing. This handout from the government had to be financed with increasingly heavy taxes, which eventually strangled the Roman government.

Some would want to make a biblical case for such governmental largesse by appealing to the gleaning law of Deuteronomy 23:24-25, which permitted a person to glean the edges or corners of a neighbor's field when poor or in need. This privilege, however, was not to be abused. The poor were not to come into a neighbor's field with a "basket" or a "sickle," indicating that they were going to take more than what they needed to satisfy their immediate needs (Deuteronomy 23:24b, 25b). Yes, these folks could glean in the fields even at harvest time to collect what those cutting the grain had missed (Leviticus 19:9-10; 23:22; Deuteronomy 24:19-21), but they were also to respect those who sowed the fields and brought forth the harvest.

These biblical provisions are clear signs of concern and care for the poor and the needy, but modern solutions diverge sharply in how they address the same problems. First of all, the Mosaic laws did provide a "safety net" to catch any of the poor and needy facing hard times, but government was very limited in this role. The emphasis was more on the local level and on the need for individuals to respond, rather than leaving the work for the government to pick up.

In the second place, the Scriptures never advocated a wholesale redistribution of all income in an attempt to restructure society. The gift of help and aid came in a direct line, from the one who farmed the land with privileges given for gleaning, all the way down to the needy person. There was nothing impersonal about it, as occurs so frequently in our modern system of taxation and governmental help.

A third difference can be seen in the fact that these gifts of grain or fruit did not remove the incentives of the poor to work or even belittle the dignity of the person receiving help, for that needy person was expected to expend his or her own efforts at collecting grain by gathering up what was left in the field.

One could also add a fourth difference: generosity was commanded by God, but those who received aid needed to willingly respond. While the provider of grains and fruits was morally obligated to give, the one who received was similarly obligated to bury his or her pride and to work honestly for what was received. One need only consult the book of Ruth to illustrate this principle.

Public Welfare and the Biblical Evidence

How much does "public welfare" carry out the teachings of the Old Testament? How broadly should this concept be construed? Should it be a government program run by the state or the church?

Since the 1960s, "welfare" in the United States has been associated with three programs: (1) AFDC, i.e., "Aid to Families with Dependent Children," (2) Food Stamps, and (3) Medicaid. These programs were designed mainly to help non-elderly families. Social Security and Medicare were mainly for elderly citizens.

Welfare legislation was reformed in 1996 because the support system was spotty and differed from state to state. It often encouraged two-parent families to split up, leaving most welfare families without fathers. The reforms originally contained requirements to work as a condition for eligibility, which some decried as moving from "welfare" to "workfare." But what was so wrong about that?

The God of the Bible clearly desires justice and righteousness in human dealings with one another.[32] The Scriptures make it plain that it is sinful to "deny justice to your poor people" (Exodus 23:6). The trickier question, however, is this: How should concern for the poorer and weaker members of society be expressed? Should it be limited to members of one's own family, or just to those in the household of faith, or to all the poor and needy? Should this response come through private charity as a moral admonition for the non-poor, or through some state or federal action as a legal obligation?

Scripture does mention that the poor have "rights" (Exodus 23:6; Deuteronomy 24:17; 27:19; Jeremiah 5:28), but what if private charity is not sufficient to meet those needs? Do those same needs require the government to meet them? The answer to that question is: Yes, they can, for Psalm 72:1-4, 12-14 clearly put such a burden on the king. Thus, the Bible does commend a special concern by the king and his officials for those who are poor through no fault of their own.

But when believers are called upon to assist the poor and needy, both the rich and the poor are called to show mutual responsibilities. The rich should include a willingness to give a compassionate loan, access to one's fields in a fallow year, or the right to glean the edges or corners of the field. And the poor should show a willingness to put the labor needed to harvest the grain as Ruth the Moabitess demonstrated.

Assistance to the poor was to be as decentralized as possible. The Bible exhibits an aversion to hierarchy and centralization as the answer to the problem of poverty. Of course, there were those in government who enforced the law of God in Old Testament times; but in general, oversight of these helps was left to the elders or members of the family. The preference, as much as possible, was for a decentralized administration.

The hardest issue in the poverty discussion is what to do about "ghetto poverty." Most of our major cities are overburdened with a concentration of people who often exhibit a high percentage of fatherless families, welfare dependency, high teenage pregnancy rates, high unemployment levels, excessive high school dropout rates, and sky-rocketing rates of criminal and drug-related activity.

How does one deal with those who live in this technological age, but who have few employable skills, are unwilling to commit to a permanent marriage relationship, have little accountability from family, and are prone to criminal and drug activity? Where does one begin to crack a problem of such dimensions? From a scriptural point of view, the first place to start is with the gospel of Jesus Christ. The outcome of this will show up in a restoration of a strong concept of the family. From God's perspective, the family was always the first line of defense in all societies. Parents cannot absolve themselves of their responsibilities for their own children. Strong family leadership will bring health to both children and parents. Without support from one or both parents in the home, society is in an unhealthy situation and is likely to fail. State and federal governments cannot act as surrogate parents as successfully as real parents can and were meant to act.

"Public housing units" have not proven very effective in many poverty areas, for they entrap and isolate the poor from the rest of society, giving the poor few opportunities for employment, good schools, churches, libraries, and the like. Such "projects" have been a temporary means for many major cities to remove the problem from constant notice of the rest of society. The poor need housing that is not isolated and concentrated, but, instead, is scattered throughout the community where jobs and better social structures are available for support and learning.

A need also exists that the church is uniquely positioned to meet, i.e., making available church people to act as mentors by spending an evening or more a week providing tutoring and remedial education for those who come from poor schools and are struggling to keep up. Often, this can be extended to create surrogate families to serve as models where one-parent families now exist. More is to be said on this topic, so let us highlight it as a special concern.

The Church's Role in the Poverty Crisis

Not too long ago, visitors to the United States were impressed with the spirit of voluntarism they observed in this country, whether it came from society at large or from local churches. Alexis de Tocqueville made this observation during his highly reported visit in 1830 (*Democracy in America*, 1835, 1840), claiming that private citizens carried out a major part of necessary charity work in America. In recent years, however, government approaches to aid have grown massively in comparison to private alternatives.

The "Robin Hood" approach (i.e., permanently borrowing from Peter to pay Paul, or more bluntly: taking from the rich to distribute to the poor) to solving the problem has never proven consistently effective. In all economies where such forceful redistribution of wealth has occurred, the standard of living for all has dropped.

In many places in the world today, as has been true from earliest of times, the church is in the forefront of poverty relief, freely giving her financial aid to the poor, caring for the widows, taking in the destitute orphans, rescuing abandoned babies, as well as serving as tutors for parentless children, visiting the sick, and caring for the dying. Despite this long and often appreciated legacy of support for the poor and the needy, the evangelical church slowed in providing such ministry in the years that followed 1925. This was probably due to the emphasis on the "social gospel" in liberal theology, which many evangelicals began to view with deep suspicion as evidence of attempts to procure salvation by works rather than as evidence of social concern in the church.

This turn of events is regrettable, for, historically, evangelicals have supported the oppressed. William Wilberforce in England, and those in the Clapham Sect, led the long fight for the abolition of the slave trade. Others, with just as impeccable evangelical credentials, such as George Mueller and Charles H. Spurgeon, were known not only for preaching the gospel, but also for supporting large orphanages. This work by evangelicals has continued, but mainly through parachurch ministries such as World Vision and similar agencies. The Salvation Army, founded by William Booth, was one of the most effective evangelical ministries to the poor; very few ministries have reached as many poor and needy persons as the Salvation Army or as rescue missions in major cities in the United States.

The poor have also suffered from those in the church who have, without warrant, preached the health, wealth, and prosperity gospel, incorrectly stating that God wants everyone to be equally rich.[33] Proclaiming this false gospel, more often than not, turns out to be a get-rich-quick scheme for those who lead the movement, but rarely if ever for those at the bottom of the pile—and this is done in the name of the Almighty!

A biblical foundation for the concept of work exists: the dominion mandate of Genesis 1:28. Mortals were to "fill the earth" and exercise dominion over all the created order as a stewardship for which each must give an account to God on the final day. All concerns about upward mobility are strongly linked to one's concept of work, view of the family, and the view each has of faith in the living God.

Conclusion

Christians are called to exhibit special care for the poor, the sick, the elderly, the widow, the orphan, the resident alien, and the oppressed. Those who address poverty and the struggles of the poor cannot afford to ignore the centrality of the home, the family, and the church in favor of considering purely economic factors. The biblical principles of stewardship of time and resources, along with a high view of the value of the family, the people of God in the church, and the concept of work, need to play a key role in addressing poverty. Also, the concept of private property must be defended. Giving our money in a generous and liberal way must characterize the people of God, to be sure. Moreover, the necessity of saving in order to provide for our children and ourselves in the long run is part of the future-oriented nature required of all who answer to God. The poor may always be with us, but therein lies both the challenge and the opportunity to demonstrate the power of the gospel.

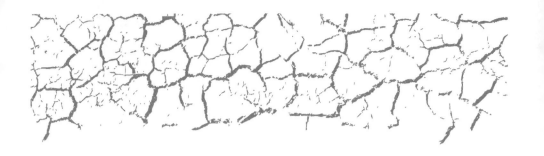

Remember the Poor: A New Testament Perspective on the Problems of Poverty, Riches, and Redistribution

By David Kotter, M.Div., M.B.A.

Though poverty has afflicted people throughout history, people in daily life respond to the poor in different ways. Some people are wired for compassion and have hearts that burn to help others in need. Other people tend to grow calloused after seeing impoverished people begging every day, perhaps in a subway station on a daily commute into a big city. Some might blame the poor for their poverty and spell out personal initiative and self-reliance as the remedy. Others argue for a political response and hope for a state-centered solution to poverty. Yet others in developing nations can be overwhelmed into inaction by the staggering numbers of destitute people. Local churches may have a desire to help but lack a plan about where to begin. Even though most agree that poverty is a serious problem, few agree on the origins of poverty or what solutions will actually help more than hurt poor people.

In this situation the New Testament provides helpful illumination of the causes of poverty, the responsibilities of Christians and local churches for serving people in need, and requirements for those who receive aid from others. A concern for the poor is an integral part of Christian life and gospel ministry. Individual Christians should actively participate in helping others in need. The effective advance of the gospel itself changes hearts and lives in ways that should lead to the alleviation of poverty. Nevertheless, caution is in order to correctly diagnose problems and implement solutions from a biblical perspective. Humility is required because poverty is an enduring problem that must be battled on earth until it is ultimately eliminated in the kingdom of God. Armed with biblical teaching as a guide, individual Christians and local churches should be better equipped to accurately and faithfully carry out this mission of caring for the poor. Thorny problems of specific application in a fallen world will be addressed by later chapters in this volume.

This chapter is devoted to drawing out New Testament teachings on the poor as a building block for the essays in the rest of this volume. The first half examines the causes of poverty from a New Testament perspective. The second half will highlight how the gospel brings solutions to the problems of poverty, riches, and redistribution through changing the hearts and lives of both poor and rich people. The creation of wealth is included as the means to alleviate scarcity until poverty is cured in the new heavens and the new earth. At that time God himself will be with his people and shelter them with his presence so that they shall not hunger or thirst ever again (Revelation 7:16).

How Jesus Christ Embodied Compassion for the Poor

Jesus Christ incarnated the love of God toward the poor throughout his personal ministry, and he impressed this concern on his disciples and the leaders of the early church. At the outset of his ministry in his home town of Nazareth, Jesus intentionally turned to a passage in Isaiah to read, "The Spirit of the Lord is upon me, because he has anointed me to proclaim good news to the poor. He has sent me to proclaim liberty to the captives and recovery of sight to the blind, to set at liberty those who are oppressed, to proclaim the year of the Lord's favor" (Luke 4:17-18, quoting Isaiah 61:1-2). Then, with every eye in the synagogue riveted upon him, Jesus announced: "Today this Scripture has been fulfilled in your hearing." Proclaiming good news to the poor was at the forefront of Jesus's announcement, and this attentiveness to the poor continued throughout his earthly ministry.

For example, when John the Baptist despaired in prison, he sent two disciples to inquire whether Jesus was truly the Messiah from God. Jesus verified that he was sent from God by encouraging the disciples to inform John that "the blind receive sight, the lame walk, those who have leprosy are cleansed, the deaf hear, the dead are raised, and the good news is proclaimed to the poor" (Luke 7:22-23). In other words, his care for the poor and afflicted served as confirming evidence that his mission originated with God.

Jesus's concern for the poor evidently left a deep impression on his disciples. The apostle John thus informed his readers, "If anyone has the world's goods and sees his brother in need, yet closes his heart against him, how does God's love abide in him?" (1 John 3:17). To John it was inconceivable that anyone who had experienced the gracious and generous love of God toward sinners could then refuse to extend help to a brother in need. Stated another way, John might have said that when the love of God abides in a believer through the gospel, it leads Christians who have the goods of the world to open their hearts toward others in need.

James, an early church leader, wrote more explicitly that concern for those in need was important evidence that a Christian truly possessed saving faith in Jesus. He asked believers, "If a brother or sister is poorly clothed and lacking in daily food, and one of you says to them, 'Go in peace, be warm and filled,' without giving them the things needed for the body, what good is that?" (James 2:15-16). In other words, James contended that when a believer had been changed fundamentally by the gospel, it necessarily resulted in tangible and practical actions directed toward meeting the needs of poor brothers and sisters.

When the key leaders of the church in Jerusalem considered the apostle Paul's gospel ministry to the Gentiles, they specifically asked him to remember the poor. Far from being a burden, Paul reported that this was "the very thing I was eager to do" (Galatians 2:10). Along with his tireless travels to bring the gospel of Jesus Christ to unbelievers, Paul also coordinated a multi-city, multi-year relief mission to address the needs of the poor in Jerusalem. This provides an example that should encourage all believers not only to care for others in need, but to eagerly pursue this as an integral part of a broader gospel ministry. Indeed, the gospel provides solutions for the poor because it is the only means of changing hearts and lives in a way that will meaningfully alleviate the underlying causes of poverty.

This consensus among Jesus, John, James, and Paul demonstrates that believers should be keen to address the problem of poverty as an aspect of the advance of the gospel. Generous and sacrificial service to others should characterize the lives of believers because Jesus himself set the ultimate standard of generosity and self-sacrifice. He freely gave to his disciples with the expectation that they would freely give to others on earth (Matthew 10:8).

Jesus did something even greater for the poor, though: he sacrificed his life on a cross so that both the rich and the poor could be forgiven and enter the kingdom of God. This gets to the heart of Jesus's compassion for the poor. In the first beatitude, Jesus declared, "Blessed are you who are poor, for yours is the kingdom of God. Blessed are you who are hungry now, for you shall be satisfied" (Luke 6:20-22). In this way, Jesus treats poverty and hunger as problems that have specific solutions and need to be solved. The problem of hungry people can be addressed now with food; but the ultimate solution to poverty is the full realization of the kingdom of God, where hunger will be no more.

Historically, caring for the poor has been one important aspect of the church's mission, but it should not displace preaching the gospel as the functional center of the church's ministry. Also, the means and methods for remembering the poor evolve with each generation as the nature of poverty and the ability to create wealth progress over time. For this reason, it will be helpful to revisit the New Testament understanding of the causes of poverty, followed in the subsequent section by a discussion of how the gospel makes a difference in alleviating poverty. This chapter will end with practical application of the gospel solution to poverty for churches, individual believers, and the poor.

Defining Wealth, Riches, and Poverty

Developing effective solutions requires a thorough and precise understanding of a specific problem, because knowing that something needs to be done and knowing what to do are often two different matters altogether. For this reason, it is important at the outset of this study to develop a biblical understanding of the nature and causes of poverty. This section will begin with a clear definition of terms that will be used consistently throughout the rest of this chapter.

Though "wealth" and "riches" are commonly considered synonyms and are often used interchangeably, it will be helpful for this discussion to draw a conceptual distinction between them based on the physical objects that constitute wealth or riches, the heart attitudes of the people who possess wealth or riches, and the means by which wealth or riches are obtained.

First, most people have a mental image of the lifestyle of the rich that includes large amounts of money, expansive houses, fine clothes, and gold jewelry. Such an impression is consistent with the definition of riches that will be used in this chapter for an ostentatious display of income and assets. Wealth, on the other hand, will be defined as "a suitable accumulation of resources and possessions of value." Under this simple definition, one is wealthy to the extent that one has sufficient food of good quality, clothing appropriate to keeping cool or warm, and shelter for protection from the elements. In a modern economy, this definition is often extended to include access to safe and reliable transportation and communication that enables one to work. Wealth includes adequate physical possessions to live and flourish as a human being created in the image of God, and it also requires a specific heart attitude toward the purpose of possessions.

Second, riches and wealth can also be distinguished by the heart attitude of their owners. The term "riches" is often used by translators of the New Testament to denote people who have both an abundance of physical assets and also self-indulgent hearts. This combination leads to wearing gold rings and fine clothes (James 2:1-7), feasting sumptuously every day (Luke 16:19), and relying on luxurious possessions for enjoyment and security (Luke 12:16-21). The New Testament also provides examples of rich people who turn away from obvious opportunities to care for others in need, such as Jesus's parables of the rich man and Lazarus (Luke 16:19-31) and the self-indulgent farmer (Luke 19:16-20).

This aspect of the heart is an essential part of the discussion of poverty and riches in the New Testament, because riches are inherently deceitful. Poor people are tempted to believe that all their problems would melt away if they could obtain riches, but they need to deeply comprehend that "those who desire to be rich fall into temptation, into a snare, into many senseless and harmful desires that plunge people into ruin and destruction" (1 Timothy 6:9).

On the other hand, rich people are tempted to believe they are secure, superior to others, and even blessed by God because of their riches. But Jesus wanted rich people to see from the parable of the sower that "the cares of the world and the deceitfulness of riches" (Matthew 13:22) choke off any fruitfulness from hearing the gospel. Indeed, Paul warned that, because of a craving for money, "some have wandered away from the faith and pierced themselves with many pangs" (1 Timothy 6:10).

In sharp contrast to this deception of riches, wealthy persons will—in their hearts—consider themselves stewards entrusted with managing assets that actually belong to God. This stewardship is often manifested as a generous heart toward others in need. Just as Peter wrote: "as each has received a gift, use it to serve one another, as good stewards of God's varied grace" (1 Peter 4:10). In the same way, Paul knew that stewards were required to be trustworthy (1 Corinthians 4:1-2) and that, in Christ, there was a way to view wealth in the world such that possessions were not one's own (1 Corinthians 7:29-31).

A third distinction would be the way in which a coin, clothes, or a house is obtained. Riches in ancient times were often obtained at the expense of other people by defrauding workers or oppressing the weak. In such zero-sum exchanges, one person became richer exactly by the amount that another person grew poorer. In this way, rich people were appropriately condemned in the New Testament for arrogantly obtaining abundant possessions through oppressing and impoverishing other people and using these riches for self-indulgence. Riches could also be inappropriately obtained by other sinful pursuits. For example, Demetrius the silversmith of Ephesus became rich from manufacturing idols of Artemis (Acts 19:23-28).

Wealth, on the other hand, was created by people rather than taken from others. Wealth in the first century was primarily created from the providential increase in grain from the labor of farming, from the increase of herds through careful shepherding, and from quietly working with one's hands to serve others. In times of favorable weather in an agricultural community, every farmer could have more grain to eat, and no family needed to have less. Likewise, two shepherds could both grow wealthy from burgeoning flocks without causing harm to one another. Even Paul, who was a tentmaker by trade (Acts 18:3), fashioned tents from raw materials and traded the tents with others for money. Wealth was created through trading because both parties were better off as a result of the exchange. In the same way, Lydia was a wealthy merchant whose expensive purple goods did not distract her from hearing the gospel message from Paul (Acts 16:14).

Along these lines, money or gold should not necessarily be confused with wealth. Money stores wealth, but only to the extent it can later be traded with other people to obtain suitable resources and possessions of value. Discovering a chest of gold coins on a desert island, for example, is of little value to a stranded sailor who is hungry or thirsty. In the same way, simply observing a coin in a person's hand is not sufficient to determine whether it constitutes wealth or riches. It is necessary to understand whether the coin was acquired through honest work or obtained by some sinful means. Further, a coin in the hand of a person with a heart full of gospel-driven generosity constitutes wealth that is pleasing to God. A coin in the hand of a person with a self-indulgent heart would fit the definition of riches and be abominable to God (Luke 16:12).

Ultimately, wealth is created as people obey the cultural mandate to subdue the world and make it useful for human beings (Genesis 1:28). In this way, wealth is produced when boards, nails, and other materials are assembled into a house, because this builds an environment that can be managed and protected from the weather. Wealth is created when cotton is spun into thread, woven into cloth, and sewn into clothes that are comfortable, durable, and aesthetically pleasing. Conversely, wealth is destroyed if a storm blows a house over or as clothes wear thin over time from use.

While poverty can also include a mindset of helplessness and despair, low education, and other sociological factors, for brevity this chapter will limit the definition of poverty to "a sustained lack of suitable resources and possessions of value." Poverty can be understood as a lack of wealth, i.e., inadequate access to food, clothing, and shelter for life, and perhaps also transportation and communication. Poverty has been the usual state of mankind in a fallen world from the beginning of recorded history.

The creation of wealth, then—including the creation of physical goods that are useful for producing food, clothing, and shelter—is a significant part of the solution to meeting the needs of people in poverty. Increasing the wealth of anyone is part of the solution to poverty for everyone because more useful goods are available to share or trade. However, increasing the riches of some is often the cause of poverty for many others through the oppressive transfer of physical goods. How those goods are distributed among people in various states of need is a question of generosity and redistribution that will be addressed later in this chapter.

Before continuing with an examination of the causes of poverty in the New Testament, it is important to note that, according to these definitions, essentially everyone was poor in the first century. Careful studies by Bruce Longenecker suggest that four out of five people (82%) during the time of Christ lived at a subsistence level that barely sustained life during the best of times.[34] He estimates that only 15% of the urban population consisted of traders, artisans, and military veterans who lived with a moderate surplus above subsistence. Only 3% of elite people were rich or wealthy. Even among the wealthy, however, no amount of money at that time could purchase air-conditioning, anesthesia, or a cell phone. To put this in perspective, an average individual living at the poverty level in the United States in the twenty-first century has a better life than 97% of the people who lived in the first century.

This radical discontinuity between the standard of living during the first century and the previously unimaginable wealth of contemporary society should caution against jumping to conclusions based on the surface meaning of biblical texts. Even answering the question "Who are the poor?" is a significant challenge that will be addressed in a separate chapter of this book. That not all poverty is rooted in the same cause is clear from the New Testament; it is sometimes caused by oppression and external circumstances, and can also be caused by poor people themselves.

The Causes of Poverty

The New Testament still provides helpful categories to understand the causes of poverty, though in recent centuries technology has advanced exponentially and society has benefited dramatically. Nevertheless, the eternal truth of Scripture and the fundamental nature of the human heart have not changed since the first century. Since poverty has several different causes, different methods are required to address the problems of people in need. For this reason, the next section of this chapter will survey the causes of poverty found in the New Testament and as summarized in the diagram below:

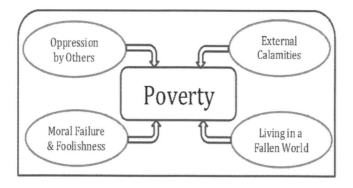

One cause of poverty is oppression by those who become rich by taking advantage of the poor or by hoarding riches in the face of obvious needs. A second cause of poverty occurs when an individual is sinfully lazy or morally foolish and fails to create wealth through honest work. A third cause is sudden disaster that destroys wealth, including calamities such as droughts that inhibit workers from creating wealth.

The state of society and technology that made it difficult to create wealth in the first century made it more difficult to recover from such disasters, which contributed to this cause. Problems associated with living in a fallen world—such as old age, infirmities, and loss of family members—constitute a fourth cause of poverty. Along with the discussion of each cause of poverty in this section, New Testament solutions for alleviating poverty are also provided. The ultimate gospel solution to the problem of poverty is discussed in the section that follows.

Poverty from Oppression

In the first century, creating wealth was difficult because the vast majority of the population was employed in subsistence farming. The most common way of accumulating riches was through oppressing the weak, leveling heavy taxation, and exploiting slaves. For this reason, it is not surprising that the New Testament contains many denunciations of rich people from that time but still encourages honest work and diligent labor.

The New Testament explains how some people wrongly became rich at the expense of the poor. For example, James describes the case of landowners who grew rich from holding back wages that rightfully should have been paid to subsistence day-laborers working in their fields. James warned such fraudulent people, "Come now, you rich, weep and howl for the miseries that are coming upon you," indeed, "the wages of the laborers who mowed your field, which you kept back by fraud, are crying out against you, and the cries of the harvesters had reached the ears of the Lord of hosts" (James 5:1-4). James also describes how righteous people were murdered so that rich people could live "on the earth in luxury and self-indulgence" (James 5:5-6), and this illustrated both the sinful means of obtaining riches and the sinful heart issues associated with hoarding riches.

Jesus warned against the evil of those who "devour widows' houses and for a pretense make long prayers." For obtaining riches in this way, Jesus declared that "They will receive the greater condemnation" (Mark 12:40). Jesus specifically pronounced woes upon hypocritical scribes and Pharisees who appeared religious but inside were "full of greed and self-indulgence" (Matthew 23:25). In a parable Jesus described a person blessed by God with abundant possessions, who hoarded riches and overlooked the suffering of the poor. He said, "There was a rich man who was clothed in purple and fine linen and who feasted sumptuously every day. And at his gate was laid a poor man named Lazarus, covered with sores, who desired to be fed with what fell from the rich man's table" (Luke 16:19-21). The rich man had no regard for the poor in this life or even in the afterlife, where he expected Lazarus, like a servant, to ease his suffering with a drop of water (Luke 16:22-31).

Jesus warned people to "Be on your guard against all kinds of greed, for one's life does not consist in the abundance of his possessions" (Luke 12:15). To underscore this point he told a parable of a farmer whose lands produced abundant crops. In this situation the farmer's wealth was produced legitimately as a gift from God through the productivity of his lands. Though his means of obtaining wealth were acceptable, God called the farmer a fool for hoarding the grain to support a self-indulgent lifestyle and telling himself to "relax, eat, drink, be merry" (Luke 12:19). God ended his life that very night (Luke 12:20). Jesus said that a similar fate would befall "the one who lays up treasure for himself and is not rich toward God" (Luke 19:21). In other words, simply obtaining possessions legitimately does not give one the right to dispose of them at will. Believers are stewards of God's possessions and accountable to him for individual choices.

Poverty from Sinful Laziness

Sinful oppression of others was only one cause of poverty in the New Testament, as people were also poor because of their own sinful choices. For example, Paul heard that some of the believers in Thessalonica were walking "in idleness, not busy at work, but busybodies" (2 Thessalonians 3:11). Others at Ephesus were thieves (Ephesians 4:28), which, according to this chapter's definitions, could be poor people who oppressed others to gain riches. The prodigal son of Jesus's parable famously wasted a fortune through foolish choices and moral failures (Luke 15:11-24). Paul encouraged the Thessalonians to admonish the idle (1 Thessalonians 5:14) and even instructed Titus to sharply rebuke people who were lazy in the church at Crete (Titus 1:12-13). Paul's expectation of believers was that they would "aspire to live quietly, and to mind your own affairs, and to work with your hands, as we instructed you, so that you may walk properly before outsiders and be dependent on no one" (1 Thessalonians 4:11-12). Paul knew that poverty could not be cured until people were fundamentally changed.

Poverty from Sudden Calamities

People in the time of the New Testament were continually exposed to loss from sudden calamities. This ranged from the loss of a valuable coin (Luke 15:8-9), to the loss of a sheep, to the loss of an entire city sacked by a marauding foreign army. Droughts destroyed harvests, and even large catches of fish could be lost if nets broke. Jesus also discussed how some were unjustly put to death by Roman authorities (Luke 13:1-5), a tragedy that also resulted in an economic loss to their families. Essentially anyone could be precipitously plunged into poverty with little warning.

Wealth was difficult to create in the first century because of the state of society and technology. Markets were quite limited, with fewer opportunities for work, trade, and the specialization needed to create wealth. Poverty was widespread, not only because catastrophic losses were more common, but also because recovery was difficult. A farmer could plant only one crop each year. A shepherd could expect an increase to his flock only in the birthing season. Recovering from a catastrophic loss was a difficult challenge that would require help from others and might take several years. In more advanced economies today, farmers share the risk of loss with others by purchasing crop insurance. Irrigation is used to mitigate the effects of drought, and electronic bank deposits protect people from losing valuable currency. By contrast, a manufacturing plant that employs three shifts of workers can create wealth around the clock, and a second plant could even be constructed to increase production and wealth creation further yet.

Poverty as Part of Living in a Fallen World

Even if they were spared sudden disasters, people in ancient times could expect to become poor simply from living in a fallen world. Blindness and other infirmities prevented many from working to create wealth. Women were frequently widowed and children were orphaned by disease or violence. The New Testament considers such individuals as a separate category and recommends generosity to alleviate their poverty. Widows are explicitly named as worthy of honor, and Paul expected that their children or even grandchildren would care for their needs (1 Timothy 5:3-4). James likewise considered visiting orphans and widows in their affliction as a necessary expression of a true "religion that is pure and undefiled before God" (James 1:27). Accordingly, the early church intentionally developed a plan and appointed people to distribute food daily to widows (Acts 6:1-6). In the same way, people who were unable to work, including the aged, blind, and paralyzed, received care. On the other hand, Paul made a significant distinction for people who were able to work but who were simply unwilling . He wrote bluntly, "If anyone is not willing to work, let him not eat" (2 Thessalonians 3:10). Having a surplus or even an abundance from which to live has been an exception in most societies.

The Root Cause of Poverty

The previous section demonstrated four general causes of poverty from the New Testament. Understanding the different categories is important because specific solutions need to be crafted to address the significantly distinct causes of poverty. Even so, it is especially important to grasp that each of the four categories of poverty have the same fundamental root cause. Sin is the root cause of poverty in the world, as illustrated in the diagram below.

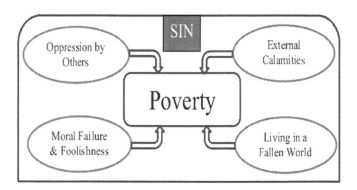

In the Garden of Eden, the first man and woman experienced an abundance of food and joy, walking with God in the afternoon and freely eating from every plant and tree with exception of one (Genesis 1:29; 2:9, 16). In the new heavens and the new earth, those who come through the great tribulation will not hunger or thirst anymore, and once again will experience the pleasure of the presence of God (Revelation 7:15-17). The combination of material abundance and hearts purified of sin will bring an end to poverty.

At present, however, sin still troubles the world, and the ground has been cursed (Genesis 3:17). Thorns and thistles have transformed productive work into toilsome labor, and scarcity exists because bread comes only with great sweat and effort. Rather than creating wealth according to the cultural mandate, it is easier to collect riches by oppressing other people and devouring their possessions. Laziness now competes with ambition and impedes work rather than spurring it onward. Moral foolishness makes speculating about riches more attractive than laboring to create wealth by serving others. The very creation itself groans in bondage to corruption, which causes calamities and disasters that destroy wealth and subject people to poverty. Finally, death itself is a result of sin and leaves widows and orphans destitute. Sin, in summary, is the root cause of poverty in this world, and the bad news is that all solutions that ignore this reality are destined to fall short from the outset. But the good news is that Jesus Christ came into the world to save people by conquering both sin and death. This good news is the gospel, and its advance will necessarily alleviate poverty on earth and eventually end poverty in the new heavens and the new earth.

The Gospel Solution to Poverty

At the outset of his ministry in Nazareth, Jesus announced that he had been empowered by the Holy Spirit to "proclaim good news to the poor" (Luke 4:17). This pronouncement of a specific solution to a specific problem was more than a sentimental expression of solidarity. In his message to John the Baptist, Jesus expected him to understand that the solution to the problem of blindness was to receive sight, the solution to lameness was to be able to walk, the solution to deafness was to be able to hear, the solution to death was to be raised up, and most importantly in this discussion, the solution that poor people most needed was to have the good news preached to them (Luke 7:22-23). This important gospel message was good news for poor people because the advance of the gospel would alleviate poverty and suffering on earth. Just as Jesus directly cured some blind people, restored hearing to some deaf people, and directly raised up some from death to life, he intended to explicitly address the poverty of some poor people. This embodiment of the love of God toward the poor was taken to heart by Jesus's followers, as demonstrated in the opening section of this chapter.

During his earthly ministry, Jesus did not heal every blind or deaf person, and those he raised up from the dead eventually died again. In the same way, Jesus was calling poor people to focus on spiritual realities that were more important than the suffering and deprivation of this world. Jesus was pointing them to a greater reality: that life on earth is short and eternity is long, and that poor people who trusted in him would be blessed to receive the kingdom of God (Luke 6:20). It is important to see that riches in themselves are not the solution to the problem of poverty, but Jesus says the blessing of the poor is instead to receive the kingdom of God. In fact, he said, "Fear not, little flock, for it is your Father's good pleasure to give you the kingdom" (Luke 12:32). He encouraged them to not repeat the mistake of the world in worrying and seeking "what you are to eat and what you are to drink," rather than seeking the kingdom of God and anticipating that these things will also be provided in the generous, yet complex, planning of God (Luke 12:30-32). Therefore the gospel is good news for all people, especially for poor people on earth and in the world to come.

In addition, the gospel is good news for rich people as well. Jesus's unequivocal declaration should be soberly considered by everyone who lives above subsistence level: "Truly, I say to you, only with difficulty will a rich person enter the kingdom of heaven. Again I tell you, it is easier for a camel to go through the eye of a needle than for a rich person to enter the kingdom of God" (Matthew 19:23-24). In other words, Jesus said that it was not impossible for rich people to be saved. When asked, Jesus replied, "With man this is impossible, but with God all things are possible" (Matthew 19:26).

What rich people need more than anything else is to hear the gospel of Jesus Christ, because there is no other means of salvation. Poor people likewise need more than anything else to receive the kingdom of God by hearing the gospel and trusting in Jesus Christ for salvation. It is worthwhile to specifically review the message of the gospel, and then note specific ways in which the advance of the gospel will alleviate poverty on earth and eventually eliminate poverty in the full realization of the kingdom of God.

The Heart of the Gospel

The heart of the gospel is that God is the wise creator of the world and the loving king who made all people to live in a perfect relationship with him. Unfortunately, everyone has rejected the authority of God, pursued self-interest apart from him, and rebelled against the created order. The biblical word for this rebellion is "sin," and the infinite justice of God requires that all sinful rebels should be punished with death. Nevertheless, the unending love of God caused him to send his only son, Jesus, into the world to pay the penalty instead. Though he was without guilt, Jesus voluntarily laid down his life by dying on a cross. He was able to bear the just punishment that sinners deserved so that all who trusted him could be forgiven and have everlasting life. Through his death, Jesus Christ broke the power of sin.

The good news of the gospel is that sinners can be saved by grace through faith in Jesus Christ. Not only do those who trust in him receive forgiveness of sins, but they also experience peace with God, are adopted into the family of God, and receive the gift of the Holy Spirit. This Spirit, over time, increasingly transforms believers to be more like Jesus Christ through a process called sanctification. Among other things, this process of transformation will necessarily alleviate poverty in the world until Christ returns and poverty ends in the new heavens and the new earth. This overarching centrality of the gospel is illustrated in the final diagram below:

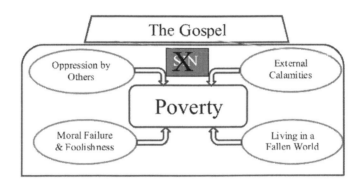

How Gospel Transformation Alleviates Poverty

Zacchaeus provides a helpful illustration of how the transforming process of sanctification can alleviate poverty. When this rich tax collector encountered Jesus Christ, the gospel brought about a fundamental change in his heart. Accordingly, he said to Jesus, "Behold, Lord, the half of my goods I give to the poor. And if I have defrauded anyone of anything, I restore it fourfold" (Luke 19:1-10). Before his conversion, Zacchaeus valued riches highly and had little regard for people. His forceful collection of excess taxes for the Roman government oppressed Roman subjects, inflicting poverty on them (Luke 19:8). When the gospel changed his heart, Zacchaeus was delighted and immediately took steps to rectify his prior fraud. The sanctifying process of the Spirit further moved his heart toward dramatic generosity to the poor.

Not only does the gospel bring an end to oppression, it causes laziness to be replaced with diligent work. Christians are instructed: "whatever you do, work heartily, as for the Lord and not for men," because more than an employer or even a customer, "you are serving the Lord Christ" (Colossians 3:23-24). Poverty is primarily alleviated by wealth created through diligent work. Such work was intended to produce more than subsistence living; it was intended to generate a surplus. Such a surplus, according to our earlier definition, could be either wealth or riches, depending on the heart attitude of the owner.

Paul recognized the temptation for wealth to become riches when he wrote, "As for the rich in this present age, charge them not to be haughty, nor to set their hopes on the uncertainty of riches, but on God, who richly provides us with everything to enjoy" (1 Timothy 6:17). He encouraged Timothy to charge such people to "do good, to be rich in good works, to be generous and ready to share" (1 Timothy 6:18). Part of God's goal in creating wealth is to enable believers to be generous toward others. Specifically, Paul writes, "You will be enriched in every way to be generous in every way, which through us will produce thanksgiving to God" (2 Corinthians 9:11). The gospel transforms, making those who were self-indulgent by nature radically generous. The clear expectation of the New Testament is that a surplus or abundance should be created and available to generously serve others. Paul specifically stated his expectation that a believer should do "honest work with his own hands, so that he may have something to share with anyone in need" (Ephesians 4:28). A long history of Christian philanthropy has flowed from this biblical expectation.

This followed from the teachings of Jesus, who encouraged his followers to be rich toward God and to be cautious of riches on earth, saying, "Do not lay up for yourselves treasures on earth, where moth and rust destroys and where thieves break in and steal, but lay up for yourselves treasures in heaven, where neither moth nor rust destroys and where thieves do not break in and steal." (Matthew 6:19-21). He explained that the process was to "sell your possessions, and give to the needy. Provide yourselves with moneybags that do not grow old, with a treasure in the heavens that does not fail, where no thief approaches and no moth destroys" (Luke 12:33). Most importantly, this process illuminated the character and faith of the giver, because "for where your treasure is, there your heart will be also" (Matthew 6:21; Luke 12:34). This attention of the heart is critical because people either serve money in their hearts or serve God in their hearts with money. Jesus was clear: "No servant can serve two masters, for either he will hate the one and love the other, or he will be devoted to the one and despise the other. You cannot serve God and money" (Luke 16:13).

The gospel fundamentally changes the hearts of believers. Therefore, the advance of the gospel should bring a decrease in oppression that makes some rich and others poor. It should also change attitudes toward work that will create more wealth, more independent people, and surpluses that can be shared. Critically, the gospel changes the hearts of rich people who would otherwise hoard a surplus into hearts that imitate the generosity of Christ toward the poor by sharing wealth. A thorough understanding of grace inevitably leads to a desire to feed those who are hungry and clothe the unfortunate, as Jesus made clear in his description of the separation of the sheep and goats (Matthew 25:31-46).

Such radical changes in the hearts of people alleviate the suffering of the poor but are not sufficient to bring an end to poverty because the creation is still subjected to futility and in bondage to corruption as a result of sin. For this reason, Jesus told his disciples, "For you always have the poor with you, and whenever you want, you can do good for them" (Mark 14:7). Though Christians increasingly transformed by the gospel can and should battle against poverty, there will be no end of poor people as long as sin persists on earth. As a further result of sin, the processes of aging and infirmity will continually inhibit the productivity of workers in creating wealth, and death will continue to plague widows and orphans with hardship. Nevertheless, the battle is worth fighting because greater wealth assuages these privations caused by sin.

Practical Steps for the Alleviation of Poverty

In light of this New Testament perspective of caring for the poor, it would be profitable to summarize some general points of application for local churches, individual Christians, and people who find themselves in poverty. These recommendations would be true for local churches and believers at any point in history, and subsequent chapters in this book will provide specific points of application for Christians in the industrialized economies of Western societies. This final section will begin with an examination of problems associated with redistribution of wealth to alleviate poverty, followed by other specific areas of application.

The Problem of Redistribution

One might conclude that since poverty is a problem of scarcity, and riches can pose temptations associated with abundance, the simple solution would be to redistribute money to make everyone equal. The New Testament demonstrates inherent problems with redistribution, however.

First, redistribution through charitable donations can tempt rich people to pridefully attract attention to themselves. Therefore, Jesus warned, "Beware of practicing your righteousness before other people in order to be seen by them, for then you will have no reward from your Father who is in heaven...But when you give to the needy, do not let your left hand know what your right hand is doing, so that your giving may be in secret. And your father who sees in secret will reward you" (Matthew 6:1-4). Therefore, just as there are right and wrong ways to obtain possessions, there are right and wrong ways of redistributing possessions. Using the poor for a pretentious show is inherently sinful, but private gifts are pleasing to God.

Second, redistribution can tempt poor people to grumbling and laziness. Jesus spoke to this concern through a parable about a landowner who hired laborers for his vineyard. Some worked all day, some only part of the day, and a few only about an hour. When the employer paid everyone equally, he paid some appropriately for their work and redistributed wealth generously to others, and grumbling arose among those who worked longer for the same compensation. They said, "These last worked only for one hour, and you have made them equal to us who have born the burden of the day and the scorching heat" (Matthew 20:12). But the master, who fully honored his agreements with all of his workers, replied, "Am I not allowed to do what I choose with what belongs to me? Or do you begrudge my generosity?" (Matthew 20:15). Jesus recognized a universal temptation toward laziness when something could be obtained for less work and toward grumbling in the face of seeming inequity of redistribution. Yet this parable also illustrates the important principle that the landowner had rights to his own property and was responsible for his own generosity, and this leads to another problem with redistribution.

Third, any redistribution must be performed voluntarily rather than through coercion. Depriving a person of personal property, even for a good cause such as poverty relief, is inherently stealing, and as such is forbidden in the New Testament. To this point, Paul wrote, "Everyone must give as he has decided in his heart, not reluctantly or under compulsion, for God loves a cheerful giver" (2 Corinthians 9:7). Thus, compulsory governmental programs of redistribution seem to be fundamentally inconsistent with the example of the New Testament.

Another problem with redistribution is the temptation to corruption among those who serve as middlemen between the rich and the poor. For example, Judas objected when Jesus was anointed with expensive perfume instead of selling the ointment for a year's wages. The apostle John pointed out that Judas only pretended compassion in this situation, "not because he cared about the poor, but because he was a thief, and having charge of the moneybag he used to help himself to what was put into it" (John 12:6). Paul recognized this inherent temptation when he was organizing the collection of a large charitable gift for the poor believers of Jerusalem, and specifically brought honorable men appointed by donor churches to travel with him. He explained, "We take this course so that no one should blame us about this generous gift that is being administered by us, for we aim at what is honorable not only in the Lord's sight but also in the sight of men" (2 Corinthians 8:20-21).

In summary, generous acts are fundamentally good and pleasing to God but inherently bring accompanying temptations. Redistribution also brings temptations of envy and grumbling to the poor. Even the early church struggled to fashion a redistribution program that would minimize complaints between different groups (Acts 6:1).

Responsibilities of Local Churches toward the Poor

Local churches can best alleviate poverty by keeping the gospel at the very center of their preaching and teaching, and every other ministry of the church. At the close of his first letter to the Corinthian believers, Paul was emphatic about reminding the troubled church about the gospel: "For I delivered to you as of first importance what I have received: that Christ died for our sins in accordance with the Scriptures" (1 Corinthians 15:1-2).

The gospel is the only means by which people receive forgiveness of sins, experience peace with God, are empowered by the Holy Spirit, and begin the lifelong transformation of sanctification. This transformation of the heart converts riches as a means of self-indulgence into wealth that is stewarded before God and can be generously used for the benefit of the poor. Further, this transformation also develops the heart attitudes required to diligently obey the cultural mandate to create wealth by serving others and subduing creation. The gospel is also the center of the local church, which is best positioned to effectively transfer the world's goods from wealthy Christians to those in need. The creation of wealth in the hands of gospel-changed people with generous hearts is thus a strategic means of the church for alleviating poverty.

In addition to maintaining the centrality of the gospel, churches should also develop wise programs to help believers give generously to the poor. When the early church received complaints about an ineffective program for serving destitute widows with food, the leaders called the church to "pick out from among you seven men of good repute, full of the spirit and of wisdom, whom we will appoint to this duty. But we will devote ourselves to prayer and to the ministry of the word" (Acts 6:1-4). Though the specifics of such programs in local churches will change with time and culture, all can follow the same basic principles. Programs for the poor should maintain financial accountability and a good reputation. They should be grounded deeply in both wisdom and compassion to actually help rather than hurt or tempt the poor. All local church leaders should in some way benevolently help people in need without detracting from their devotion to prayer and the ministry of the word.

A significant advantage of such programs administered through local churches compared to governmental programs is that relief is voluntarily provided and personally administered. Paul was clear: "Each one must give as he has decided in his heart, not reluctantly or under compulsion, for God loves a cheerful giver" (2 Corinthians 9:7). Indeed, Paul expected believers to abound in every good work, and wrote with confidence, "You will be enriched in every way to be generous in every way, which through us will produce thanksgiving to God" (2 Corinthians 9:8, 11). A more personal approach to administration follows Paul's personal example of working long hours when necessary in order to not "eat anyone's bread without paying for it" (2 Thessalonians 3:8).

Such local church ministries will necessarily depend on Christians with the world's goods for the means of serving the poor, and the gospel encourages believers to this end. As Paul wrote, "If we have sown spiritual things among you, is it too much if we reap material things from you?" (1 Corinthians 9:11). Indeed, Paul understood that when some have shared in spiritual blessing, "they ought also to be of service to them in material blessings" (Romans 15:27). The spiritual transformation that the gospel produces in believers also brings the heart attitudes that are committed to the creation of wealth and generosity toward the poor.

Responsibilities of All Christians toward the Poor

The gospel does not simply save people from sins; it transforms believers to be more and more like Jesus Christ. This transformation includes changed attitudes toward work and possessions that should result in an increasing creation of wealth. This fundamental change brought by the gospel should also result in contentment and generosity that serves the poor and avoids temptations associated with riches. Indeed, all Christians are called to imitate God as children learn from following a parent. This includes mirroring God's ingenuity in creation through obedience to the cultural mandate to subdue the earth (Genesis 1:28). This imitation should also embrace God's pattern of working six days each week, with a day of rest (Exodus 20:9; Deuteronomy 5:13), though such diligence should extend beyond working professionally to include domestic work and serving others. Impoverished people around the world would suffer less if they worked with this diligence.

The effect of this individual initiative is magnified in institutional settings that support enterprise and restrict corruption. As believers are increasingly transformed by the gospel, they should work vigorously. Paul wrote, "Whatever you do, work heartily, as for the Lord and not for men, knowing that from the Lord you will receive the inheritance as your reward. You are serving the Lord Christ" (Colossians 3:23-24). Neither riches nor fame were to be motivations for such work, as Paul encouraged believers to "do their work quietly and to earn their own living" (2 Thessalonians 3:12). All such business needs to be conducted with an attitude of dependence on God and gratitude to God. James warned people in business that saying, "Today or tomorrow we will go into such and such a town and spend a year there and trade and make a profit" would be presumptuous without remembering that

God ultimately governs the outcome of such plans (James 4:13-15). Indeed, James was consistent with Moses's earlier admonition, "Beware lest you say in your heart, 'My power and the might of my hand have gotten me this wealth.' You shall remember the Lord your God, for it is he who gives you power to get wealth" (Deuteronomy 8:17-18). Paul declared that "there is great gain in godliness with contentment," so that believers would generate a surplus through their vigorous and diligent work and avoid self-indulgence with the excess (1 Timothy 6: 6-11). While God "richly provides us with everything to enjoy" (1 Timothy 6:17b), he also graciously provides a surplus so that believers will "have something to share with anyone in need" (Ephesians 4:28). Indeed, believers are admonished "to do good and to share" what they have, "for such sacrifices are pleasing to God" (Hebrews 13:16). Paul encouraged believers to regularly link such prosperity from God with generosity by preparing in advance to give to the poor: "On the first day of every week, each of you is to put something aside and store it up, as he may prosper..." (1 Corinthians 16:2).

From another perspective, the Holy Spirit indwelling believers also helps them increasingly put off sin over time, such as the sin of laziness (Proverbs 10:4, 10-11, etc.). This would also include working at pursuits that give only the appearance of accomplishment, such as achieving ever-higher ranks on video games or competitively accumulating friends on social networks, because "he who follows worthless pursuits will have plenty of poverty" (Proverbs 28:19). Therefore the preaching of the gospel serves to alleviate poverty by simultaneously enabling people to turn from sins that cause poverty and turn toward pursuits that both develop hearts of generosity and create wealth to share.

Responsibilities of the Poor

People who are poor are under the same obligation to work toward creating wealth as are all other believers. Everyone should work diligently; but calamities, oppression, and life in a fallen world may render even a diligent worker's income insufficient to meet the needs of life. However, receiving aid when it is not absolutely required is equivalent to taking money from other people under fraudulent conditions or even stealing. If one is in need because of catastrophic or unusual circumstances, an attempt to repay generous people is commendable. While it is admirable for wealthy believers to lend to those from whom they expect no repayment, it is even better for the poor to repay them over time, if possible (Luke 6:34-35). Paul gave specific instructions to Timothy to provide aid only to widows who were "really in need" and included criteria for those worthy of receiving aid such as being "well known for her good deeds, such as bringing up children, showing hospitality, washing the feet of the Lord's people, helping those in trouble and devoting herself to all kinds of good deeds" (1 Timothy 5:3-16). In other words, everyone should contribute as much as possible, whether working independently for a living or serving others while receiving aid.

People in poverty are called to be generous toward others with even greater needs. Paul cited the Macedonian church as an example to inspire others because "their overflowing joy and their extreme poverty welled up in rich generosity," such that they "gave as much as they were able, and even beyond their ability. Entirely on their own they urgently pleaded with us for the privilege of sharing in this service to the Lord's people" (2 Corinthians 8:1-5). Jesus similarly commended as an example to others a poor widow who donated two very small copper coins and "out of her poverty, put in everything – all she had to live on" (Mark 12:43-44). Another requirement of receiving aid is gratitude toward individuals, a local church, and, ultimately, to God. Paul expected that service to the poor would not only supply needs, but also overflow in many expressions of thanks to God. He wrote, "Because of the service by which you have proved yourselves, others will praise God for the obedience that accompanies your confession of the gospel of Christ, and for your generosity in sharing with them and everyone else" (2 Corinthians 9:12-14). Most importantly, Paul ended with a reference to the gospel and the generosity of God, who gave his own son for sinners: "Thanks be to God for his indescribable gift!" (2 Corinthians 9:15). Finally, Jesus knew that the presence of sin in the world would ensure the existence of poverty and provided the most profound form of encouragement when he said, "Blessed are you who are poor, for yours is the kingdom of God" (Luke 6:20). Jesus also declared that in his own presence and ministry, "The kingdom of God has come near. Repent and believe the good news!" (Mark 1:15). The poor can even take comfort in this life, knowing that the full consummation of the kingdom will bring an end to sin and poverty.

Conclusion

Throughout his personal ministry, Jesus Christ incarnated the love of God toward the poor, and he impressed this concern on his disciples and the leaders of the early church. Jesus made it clear that the poor need the gospel to enter the kingdom of God. Jesus was also clear that rich people need the gospel because it would be otherwise impossible for them to enter the kingdom of God. The gospel breaks the power of sin, which is the root cause of poverty on earth. The gospel not only saves people, it transforms them in ways that increase wealth creation and develop generous hearts to share with others in need. The gospel alleviates poverty in the present and will bring an end to poverty in the culmination of the kingdom of God. As the church carries out its mission of preaching and teaching for the advancement of the gospel, it is simultaneously working to alleviate the suffering of the poor and to bring an end to the sin that causes poverty. The apostle Paul could therefore declare that remembering the poor was the very thing he was eager to do in his ministry of the gospel.

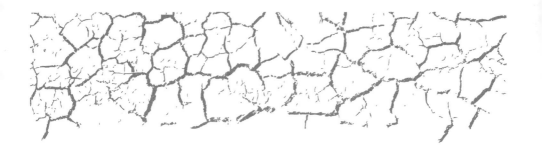

Does God Require the State to Redistribute Wealth? An Examination of Jubilee and Acts 2–5

By Art Lindsley, M.Div., Ph.D.

The simple answer to the question, "Does God require the state to redistribute wealth?" would be "No." However, there are a number of people who think that God does require the state to distribute wealth from those who have to those who have not. What could possibly make these scholars think that this is the case? While there are a number of lines of argument that they pursue, the recurring refrain always centers around two biblical passages: Leviticus 25 on Jubilee, and Acts 2-5 on the early Christian community. These passages have been used to teach that the Bible mandates socialism or at least a substantial government involvement in caring for the poor. This chapter intends to examine these two passages and see what a deeper look into Scripture might reveal about their real meaning. First, we will look at "Five Myths about Jubilee;" second, we will examine whether, as some claim, Acts 2-5 teaches socialism.

Five Myths about Jubilee

Those who advocate for the state redistribution of wealth have certain assumptions about the biblical passages on Jubilee—particularly that it involves forgiveness of debt and redistribution of land. A study of biblical passages on economic themes (Jubilee included) reveals otherwise. If an argument is going to be made for the forgiveness of debt, it is better to do so on solid biblical grounds rather than believing myths or half-truths.[35]

The sabbatical years occurred every seven years, and Jubilee was celebrated at the end of seven cycles of sabbatical years—the fiftieth year (or forty-ninth, as some argue). During the sabbatical years the Israelites rested from their labor and allowed, among other things, the land to rest.

While there is some evidence that sabbatical years were observed, it seems that, according to 2 Chronicles 36:21, it happened only sporadically. This text says that the number of years for the captivity in Babylon corresponded to the number of sabbatical years that were not observed. If sabbatical years were infrequently observed, then there is a question as to how often, if ever, Jubilee was observed.[36] But whether Jubilee was observed or not, Jubilee was God's law for his people and needs to be taken seriously by all who believe in biblical authority. Even if God's people were disobedient to these laws, they could still teach us valuable principles.

When the Israelites reached the Promised Land, God distributed land to the twelve tribes (Joshua 13:7; 23:4), and the purpose of the Jubilee law was to keep the land in the hands of the tribes and families to which God had given the land in the first place. With this context in mind, we will examine the five common myths about Jubilee that seem to be contradicted by the text of Leviticus 25.

Myth #1: Jubilee Meant a Forgiveness of Debt

It is clear in the Old Testament text and to many commentators that, in Leviticus 25, Jubilee does not involve forgiveness of debt, at least in the way we normally use the term. There is no debt forgiven because it has already been paid. The key verses missed (or not read at all) are Leviticus 25:15-16. In verses 8-10, a ram's horn is to be blown on the Day of Atonement of the fiftieth year (or forty-ninth), and each family is to return to their property. Verses 15-16 tell how this process is to work:

> Corresponding to the number of years after the jubilee, you shall buy from your friend; he is to sell to you according to the number of years of crops. In proportion to the extent of the years you shall increase its price, and in proportion to the fewness of the years, you shall diminish its price; *for it is a number of crops he is selling to you* [emphasis added].

So if an Israelite family member owed a debt, he could go to someone and ask for a lump sum payment priced according to the number of years before the Jubilee. The price would be determined by the projected amount of crops to be yielded prior to the Jubilee. To put it in modern terms, if you have a debt of $250,000, there are five years prior to the Jubilee, and each crop is worth $50,000, then the lender (or "buyer") would give you $250,000 for the rights to farm the land, and at the time of Jubilee you would receive your land back because the debt had been paid off. So the "buyer" does not really own the land but leases it. The debt is paid off by the land (crops).[37] The buyer or leaser would be paid according to the terms of the lease. We do not know exactly how the price was determined for each year of crops, given the uncertainty due to bad weather or other factors that could lead to a poor or lost crop. Perhaps the price took into account that some years would be more profitable than others.[38]

Now at the time of Jubilee you would, of course, rejoice that your debt had been paid and your land returned to your full use, but you would likely not thank the leaser for "forgiving" your debt. The Jubilee declaration might be analogous to a "mortgage burning party." You would celebrate with friends that this significant debt was paid, but you would not thank the bank for "forgiving" your debt. The debt is not "forgiven" or "cancelled" because it is paid. I would love for someone to pay off my mortgage or cancel my debt, but that is not what happened at Jubilee.

This understanding of Jubilee as the payoff of a lease is common in Old Testament commentaries. Here are some scholars and commentaries that have made this observation:

Matthew Henry (1710):
Thus it was provided that the lands should not be alienated from their families. They could only be disposed of, as it were, by leases till the year of the jubilee and were then to return to the seller or his heir.[39]

The Interpreter's Bible:

In the year of Jubilee all indentured labor, in regard to Hebrews, was to come to an end, all leases were to expire; the Hebrew might not alienate his agricultural land, but he might lease the right to farm it, the sum to be paid being the estimated value of the crops up to the year of Jubilee, when the lease would automatically end.[40]

R.K. Harrison:

Land could not be sold in a conventional sense, and any payments for property amounted to the purchaser taking a lease on it until the next Jubilee year...since only the produce of the land could thus properly be bought or sold.[41]

Gordon Wenham:

Leviticus 25 prohibits anyone from selling himself or his land off permanently. In effect he may only rent out his land or his labor for a maximum of forty nine years. The rent is payable in one lump sum in advance, as if there was a sale, but in the Jubilee year the land reverts to its original owner and the slave is given his freedom.[42]

Derek Tidball:

Purchasing land was like purchasing a lease.[43]

Ron Sider:

Before and after the year of jubilee land would be "bought" or "sold." Actually, the leaser purchased a specific number of harvests.[44]

Walter Kaiser:

Verses 13-17 of Leviticus 25 go on to spell out the financial implications of this transaction, for what appeared to have been the sale of the land was in fact only the sale of the *use* of the land. Therefore, as the year of Jubilee approached, and the years were few, it diminished the value and the cost of the land to the purchaser, depending on the number of harvests the land could produce until the Jubilee.[45]

There is thus significant consensus among Bible scholars that Jubilee actually entailed the completed payment of a debt, not its forgiveness.[46]

If the debt exceeded the value of the crops that would be harvested before the next Jubilee, the one leasing could supplement the amount of the lease by selling his labor for those years as an indentured servant.[47] At any time the lease could be paid off by a family member or the original person leasing the land with no early payment penalty. The price would be the number of years' worth of crops remaining on the lease.[48]

Even though Jubilee is not a "forgiveness of debt," there are other biblical grounds for the idea. In the parable of the "unmerciful slave" (Matthew 18:23-35), Jesus portrays a king who has a slave brought to him who owes him 10,000 talents (about $10,000,000 or more). Since the slave has no means to repay the debt, the king commands that he, his family, and his goods be sold. The slave pleads for mercy and receives it from the king. His debt is forgiven. Later that same slave meets someone who owes him 100 denarii (a denarius is a day's wage), and when this debtor cannot repay, the slave has him thrown into prison. Other slaves observe this scene and report what he has done to the king. The king says, "You wicked slave, I forgave you all that debt because you entreated me. Should you not also have had mercy on your fellow-slave, even as I had mercy on you?" Jesus here commends the voluntary and merciful act of the king and holds that one who is shown such mercy over a very large debt should be merciful to one with a much smaller debt. Forgiving debt is not here a matter of justice but of mercy. Although the context of this parable is a chapter that wrestles with the importance of forgiving sin, we certainly see that forgiving a debt is a merciful, though not mandatory, option. It is also possible to pay off another's debt. This is certainly encouraged by stories in the early church about some Christians who sold themselves into slavery in order to get money to buy others out of slavery.[49] Leviticus 25 encourages family and friends of the debtor to pay off his debt so that the use of the land returns back to the original family's hands (Leviticus 25:47-55).

Michael Harbin, in a thorough academic paper on "Jubilee and Social Justice" (available on IFWE's website: http://www.tifwe.org), concludes that "Jubilee does not involve forgiveness of debt ... since there was no debt, there was nothing to be forgiven ... Jubilee is then really a semi-centennial national expiration of land leases."[50]

Certainly there is a biblical basis for voluntary debt forgiveness. But there is a significant difference between a debt that is paid and the mandatory forgiveness of debt. Jubilee is clearly an example of the former and not the latter. Jubilee is not a celebration of forgiveness of debt but of freedom from debt now paid.

Myth #2: Jubilee Involved a Redistribution of Wealth (Land)

I've heard it said that Jubilee is the paramount example of legal, government mandated redistribution of wealth. Whether the Jubilee was ever practiced or not, the argument goes, God required by law that land be redistributed every fifty years.

It should be clear from the previous section (Myth #1) that if Jubilee does not involve the forgiveness of debt but the celebration of a debt paid by leasing the land (crops), then there is no redistribution of wealth. There is no redistribution of wealth because the land (legal title) never left the ownership of the original family to which God had given the land. Michael Harbin concludes, "Jubilee did not entail the forgiveness of debt and nor did it require a periodic redistribution of wealth … Actual ownership of the land really did not change hands, but remained with the family who had inherited it from God."[51]

Other passages in Leviticus 25 indicate that some property could change hands permanently. In other words, there are some biblical "footnotes" or "asterisks" to this leasing process. Jubilee applied only to land in the country, outside the city. Inside a walled city, a house that was sold could be redeemed for a full year after the sale, but after that it was the permanent property of the one who bought it. Since the Levites had no permanent land, they could sell, or "lease," their homes in Levitical cities, but could redeem the house at any time or wait till the year of Jubilee when the house would be returned to their use (Leviticus 25:29-34). There was no redistribution of permanently owned houses in the cities, and there was no redistribution of wealth gained through leasing the land. If there were bountiful harvests each year, then the profit remained in the hands of the one who had leased the land. So only land in the country was returned to the original owners of the land.

Far from being an argument for redistribution of land and wealth, Jubilee keeps the distribution in exactly the same place as where it started. It is not redistributed to a different family, but returned to the same one according to God's original distribution.

Myth #3: Jubilee Shows the Relative Nature (Relativization) of Private Property

According to this myth, since God owns the land (Leviticus 25:23) there are no absolute rights to private property. Therefore, this provides warrant for government to take private property (land or wealth) and redistribute it. If you have been following the argument of this article, you will see that Leviticus 25 argues the exact opposite. God owns the land, but he has given the Promised Land to the tribes and families of Israel with the condition that private property cannot be sold, squandered, or permanently given away. The property rights remain in the hands of the tribe or family who were given the land in the first place. Jubilee underlines the value and importance of private property for the tribes of Israel. The family farm cannot be taken away from them permanently. No matter how tragic the circumstances, no matter how immoral a family member becomes, or how unwise they are in maintaining their property, the family is not permanently deprived of their land. John Schneider in his paradigm-altering book *The Good of Affluence* writes the following:

> To the extent that Jubilee involved the legal distribution of property, the shares were unequal to begin with. The Levites got no land; first-born sons received twice the land given to the other sons (Deuteronomy 21:17); daughters neither owned nor inherited anything. And non-Israelites had no share in the land. They could perhaps lease land and use it for a while, but they could not really buy and own it. For Jubilee would actually take it back from them and return it to the natural owners...The people whom the Jubilee helped were not the poor but the families of original affluence. The Jubilee

(if practiced) guaranteed that they endured in their landed affluence regardless of whether they wanted (or deserved) it... What the jubilee did was restore property and power to old landed families, the true Israelites, and there is no condition relating to whether they needed it or not... For by limiting the property rights of non-Israelites or other buyers to a form of leasing, rental, or temporary investment, it literally prohibited the liquidation or sharing of assets for ethical purposes.[52]

Far from being relativized, private property rights in Israel were established permanently.

Myth #4: Jubilee Leads to Income Equality

Some argue that the periodic "redistribution" of land at Jubilee kept the rich from getting richer and the poor from getting poorer. Jubilee certainly did prevent any one person or small group of people from buying up most, or all, of the land. It did stop those "who add house to house and join field to field, until there is no more room" (Isaiah 5:8). But it did not prevent some from becoming wealthier than others. Lenders who leased the best land available before Jubilee and diligently worked to make it productive could accumulate significant assets prior to each Jubilee. That would allow them to lease even more properties during the next fifty years. So some individuals or families could, over time, accumulate effective control over large amounts of land even though they did not have permanent ownership. The accumulated assets could also allow these individuals or families to buy up unlimited numbers of houses in walled cities, which after a year (unless redeemed) would be their permanent property. So while the Jubilee law did prevent all the land from being permanently owned by one family or a few families, it did not prevent some from becoming much wealthier than others.

One commentator says that "Jubilee sets ... limits on the rich getting richer and the poor getting poorer."[53] This is true only with regard to the permanent acquisition of land. But there is nothing in the passage that would necessarily prevent income inequality. The primary intent of the law is not economic equality at all. God wanted to prevent Israelite families from losing their ability to enjoy the Promised Land. God had promised his people freedom from slavery and a land flowing with milk and honey—a land where they could prosper and enjoy life with their family, using their creativity (Genesis 1:26-28) to farm the land and enjoy the fruits of their labors. Micah 4:4, which says, "Each of them will sit under his vine and under his fig tree," is a verse that has captivated many authors, including the founders of America. This verse communicates safety, security, productivity, and enjoyment of God's creation. John Schneider argues that the theme of the Old Testament from the Garden of Eden through Noah and the patriarchal narratives is the "promise of God to bring his people quite deliberately into conditions of material prosperity."[54] This is particularly true with regard to the Promised Land (Deuteronomy 8:7-10):

> For the Lord your God is bringing you into a good land, a land of brooks of water, of fountains and springs, flowing forth in valleys and hills; a land of wheat and barley, of vines and fig trees and pomegranates, a land of olive oil and honey; a land where you will eat food without scarcity, in which you will not lack anything; a land whose stones are iron, and out of whose hills you can dig copper. When you have eaten and are satisfied, you shall bless the Lord your God for the good land which He has given you.

God's intent, argues Schneider, is material delight, great affluence, and a lack of scarcity. There are of course spiritual dangers to this wealth, and God warns his people about the dangers of forgetting the giver (Deuteronomy 8:11-15) or boasting in themselves as the source of the wealth (Deuteronomy 8:17-18). The Israelites were also to share their wealth with those in need. They were not to harvest around the margins of their fields but allow the poor and sojourner to glean (Leviticus 19:9-12; 23:22). No collateral was to be required of the very poor and no interest charged on loans (Exodus 22:25-27). Just weights and measures were to be used (Leviticus 19:35-37). Israelites were to love strangers and sojourners as they loved themselves (Leviticus 19:33-34).

However, the main purpose of Jubilee seems to be not "forgiveness of debt," "redistribution of land," or "income equality," but the preservation of the prosperity in the Promised Land that God had promised his people. Schneider argues:

> It seems the main purpose of the jubilee was rather to preserve the original integrity of the land as God had apportioned it in the beginning. And in that way its aim was to preserve the substance of the promise of delight to the people of Israel too. In sum, the jubilee made it harder for people to ruin the basic structures that God had created to secure their prosperity.[55]

This approach has the advantage of avoiding the debates about capitalism or socialism that we might put forward and places Jubilee firmly in a redemptive-historical context. The purpose of Jubilee was not income equality but that no Israelite would permanently lose the enjoyment of sitting under "his vine and under his fig tree" (Micah 4:4). Cal Beisner sums up the message of Jubilee on income equality:

The law of jubilee was designed not to promote income equality, but to prevent one family member's destroying an entire family's means of productivity, not only in his own generation but also in generations to come, by contracting huge debts and selling, permanently, the family's means of production.[56]

Jubilee was also designed to perpetuate the family's enjoyment of the fruit of their labors as they used their creativity to turn their land into an approximation of the Garden of Eden.

Myth #5: Jubilee is a Universally Applicable Principle

Actually, Jubilee applied only to Israelites, not to aliens and sojourners (non-Israelites). This is another significant "footnote" almost entirely omitted from the normal narrative about Jubilee. Even though aliens (sojourners or strangers) might be able to "lease" land or hire an indentured servant, they could not permanently own land or slaves (Leviticus 25:47-48). Only Israelites could own land or own foreign slaves (Leviticus 25:44-46). There was no "redistribution" or return of the land to foreigners, and foreign slaves were not freed at Jubilee. The poorest people of the land (aliens, widows, and orphans) were to be included in feasts, but they did not have property (land) rights, except to houses in walled cities. Schneider says:

> Writers on the subject almost universally miss the point that its provisions applied only to members of the original Israelite tribes. The poorest people in society were unaffected by it. For aliens, sojourners, non-Israelite debtors and slaves possessed no land in the first place and thus had no share in its repossession on the day of jubilee. Their economic need, however dire, played

no role in the redistribution. Strange as it may seem, given the function of these texts in modern theologians' discourse, the people whom the jubilee helped were not the poor, but the families of original affluence.[57]

In his commentary on Jubilee, Calvin notes Jubilee's exclusive benefits for Israelites and its place in God's history of revelation:

Thus the land of Canaan was an earnest, or symbol, or mirror, of the adoption on which their salvation was founded. Wherefore it is not to be wondered at that God was unwilling that this inestimable benefit should ever be lost; and, lest this should be the case, like a provident father of a family, He laid a restraint on His children, to prevent them from being too prodigal; for, when a man has any suspicions of his heir, he forbids him to alienate the patrimony he leaves him. Such, therefore, was the condition of the ancient people; yet it cannot be indiscriminately transferred to other nations who have had no common inheritance given them.[58]

There are of course many biblical passages on the importance of caring for the poor. The Bible also stresses that the gospel is for people of every tribe, tongue, people, and nation (Revelation 5:9). Because of the gospel message, the nations will be glad.

Certainly the gospel does go out to all nations, and there are hints that may point to Jubilee being fulfilled in the preaching of Jesus.[59] But present day application of the Jubilee laws are not immediately clear and not as easy as those who perpetuate these myths want to maintain. The Jubilee law certainly cannot be used to defend redistribution of wealth by the state.

Now let us move to the second central passage we want to examine: Acts, chapters two through five. We will look at five key points that counter the contention that this text teaches socialism.

Does Acts 2-5 Teach Socialism?

Two articles in *The Washington Post* "On Faith" blog explicitly state that Christianity is socialist and anti-capitalist. The central argument given by the authors of both articles is that the description of the early Christian community in Acts 2-5 as having "all things in common" (Acts 2:44) mandates socialism (or communism). Is this true? What can be said to such a claim?

Some scholars offer an alternative argument: that the Bible's central principles are consistent with a market economy (commonly called capitalism) and contradict a centrally-planned economy (commonly called socialism). To begin, let us define capitalism and socialism. Both economic systems claim to best advance human flourishing, but they make different claims concerning how resources should and can be rationed.

Capitalism is an economic system that largely allows markets to allocate scarce resources through prices, property rights, and profit/loss signals. Socialism is a system under which the government owns the means of production, and, through coercive taxation and wealth redistribution, allocates resources and makes decisions concerning property, prices, and production. Incidentally, communism, a progression from socialism, is both a political and economic system, which would abolish private property and give to individuals based on need.

But what about this claim that Acts 2-5 teaches socialism (or communism)? First of all, what do the passages say? Acts 2:44-45 says that immediately following Pentecost, "all those who had believed were together and had all things in common; and they began selling their property and possessions and were sharing them with all, as any might have need." In Acts 4:32-35, it says of the early congregation that "not one of them claimed that anything belonging to him was his own; but all things were common property to them .... For there was not a needy person among them, for all who were owners of land or houses would sell them and bring the proceeds of the sales and lay them at the apostles' feet, and they would be distributed to each as any had need."

A superficial reading of the text may indeed lead one to conclude that the language of socialism is here; however, a closer look at the text reveals otherwise.

The Early Believers Did Not Sell All their Possessions

Even though it may seem that the phrases "had all things in common," "selling their property," and "all things were common property" mean that the early believers sold everything and had a common pot, the context immediately qualifies these general statements. The believers continued to live and meet in their own homes. Craig Blomberg, in his study *Neither Poverty nor Riches,* says:

> [Chapter 2] Verses 43-47 are dominated by highly marked imperfect tense verbs, whereas one normally expects aorists [once-for-all actions] in historical narrative. There is no once-for-all divestiture of property in view here, but periodic acts of charity as needs arose. [60]

This is even clearer in Acts 4-5. The NIV translation of Acts 4:34b-35 says: "From *time to time,* those who owned land or houses sold them, brought the money from the sales and put it at the apostles' feet" [emphasis mine]. Blomberg comments:

> Again we have a rash of imperfect verbs here, this time explicitly reflected in the NIV's "from time to time." The periodic selling of property confirms our interpretation of Acts 2:44 above. This was not a one-time divesture of all one's possessions. The theme "according to need," reappears, too. Interestingly, what does not appear in this paragraph is any statement of complete equality among believers. Presumably, there was quite a spectrum, ranging from those who still held property which they had not sold ... all the way to those who were still living at a very basic level.[61]

John Stott affirms Blomberg's conclusions about property in the early church, also underscoring Luke's use of the imperfect tense: "Neither Jesus nor his apostles forbade private property to all Christians... It is important to note that even in Jerusalem the sharing of property and possessions was voluntary... It is also noteworthy that the tense of both verbs in verse 45 is imperfect, which indicates that the selling and giving were occasional, in response to particular needs, not once and for all."[62] N.T. Wright agrees that private property was not abandoned: "These early believers seem not to have sold the houses in which they lived, since they went on meeting in individual homes (2:46). Rather, they sold extra property they possessed."[63]

Note the positive example of Barnabas (Acts 4) and the negative example of Ananias and Sapphira (Acts 5). Barnabas "owned a tract of land, sold it and brought the money and laid it at the apostles' feet" (Acts 4:37). It does not say that this giving comprised all his possessions or that it was the only tract of land he owned. It provides a positive example of what was going on in Acts 2-4. When Barnabas saw that there were needs he could meet, he was generous with what he owned. Perhaps, some have speculated, he was the first person of substantial wealth to donate to the cause.

Then there is the negative example of Ananias and Sapphira in Acts 5. Ananias "sold a piece of property" (Acts 5:1) (similar to Barnabas) and, with his wife's knowledge, kept part of the proceeds for himself. The problem with this was not that they had not sold all their possessions or that they needed to give all of the proceeds of their land to the apostles, but that they lied about it. They pretended to be more generous than they were. Ananias, then later Sapphira, came before Peter and died, presumably as a divine judgment. Peter explicitly said that "While it remained unsold, did it not remain your own? And after it was sold, was it not under your control?" (Acts 4:4). The problem, as Peter pointed out, was that Ananias had lied to the Holy Spirit (v. 3); he had lied not to men, but to God (v. 4).

So there is good reason to believe that the early believers did not sell all they had, but were generous and, as occasion demonstrated, they sold part of their possessions and gave the proceeds to the apostles for distribution. But even if we, for the sake of argument, grant that all believers sold all their possessions and redistributed them among the community, does that prove socialism or communism is biblical? No, there would have to be state-coerced taking of property and forced distribution of it for this to be the case. But here the state is not the one selling (or giving) property to those that had need.

The Early Christians' Sharing Was Totally Voluntary

Karl Marx, co-author with Friedrich Engels of *The Communist Manifesto*, viewed the ownership of private property as oppressive.

Marx wanted the workers to revolt against the owners of the means of production and to take control of private property. He wanted the state to own the means of production and private property to be abolished. Again, in this passage from Acts, there is no mention of the state at all. These early believers contributed their goods freely, without coercion, voluntarily. Elsewhere in Scripture we see that Christians are even instructed to give in just this manner, freely, for "God loves a cheerful giver" (2 Corinthians 9:7). There is plenty of indication that private property rights were still in effect (remember Barnabas, Ananias, and Sapphira). This is neither communism (abolition of private property) nor socialism (state ownership of the means of production). This is not even socialism as defined as a community-owned or regulated system. Even if we grant, for the sake of argument, that it was socialism of some sort, why is it seen only here (in Acts 2-4) and not throughout the rest of the New Testament?

This Was Not a Permanent Practice but a Temporary Measure

As we have seen, this early sharing was voluntary, without state coercion, and did not necessitate that believers give up their rights to private property. Certainly this early sharing was noble, indicating a generosity of spirit. It is a beautiful example of love. While this type of generous giving is a permanent norm, the particular situation in Acts 2-5 seems to have been a temporary response to a particular need. We do not see a recurrence of this scenario throughout the rest of Acts, in Paul's letters, or in the rest of the New Testament. So what was going on here?

In short, Pentecost had just happened. People of many nations were in attendance (thus the necessity of speaking in tongues). After the initial preaching by Peter and others, there were, that first day, three thousand new believers (Acts 2:41). More and more were being added to their number each day (Acts 2:47). Should these new believers immediately return to their homes in other parts of Israel or elsewhere? Would they not want to continue in the apostles' teaching, worship, fellowship, and prayers (Acts 2:42-46)? But then how could these visitors provide for themselves? How would they have enough to eat and a place to stay for an extended period?

The answer is that those who had gave to those who had not. Eventually, most of these new believers returned home. There was no longer an extraordinary need for food and shelter. The attitude of "what's mine is yours if you need it" continued, however. In Acts 6, the widows were being neglected in the "daily serving of food" (Acts 6:1), so seven men were appointed to oversee that process. There was a famine relief effort undertaken by the disciples in Acts 11:27-30. There was always a concern that the needs of the poor be met (Galatians 2:10). There were often communal meals (1 Corinthians 11:20). There also were many who were wealthy and gave generously (but had not given everything away): Joseph, called Barnabas (Acts 4:36-37), Dorcas (Acts 9:36), Cornelius (Acts 10:1-2), Sergius Paulus (Acts 13:6-12), Lydia (Acts 16:14-15), Jason (Acts 17:5-9), Aquila and Priscilla (Acts 18:2-3), Mnason of Cyprus (Acts 21:16), Philemon (Philemon 1), and many others. The spirit of Acts 2-5 remained, but there was no push to abolish private property and establish socialism in any form. There was a concern for equitable distribution of goods to the poor but not an egalitarian communism (2 Corinthians 8:13-15—the Greek word *isotes* means "equitable" or "fair"). In any case, the communal sharing that retained some private property in Acts 2-5 was not the practice of the early church in the rest of Acts or the rest of the New Testament. But even if you think that the model of Acts 2-5 was socialist, which it was not, you have to still go further to prove your point. You have to show that the early example constitutes a mandatory command. There is a fundamental problem with this contention.

You Cannot Get "Ought" out of "Is"

You cannot get the imperative out of the indicative. In his *Treatise* on moral philosophy, David Hume famously argues that "an unremarked transition from premises whose parts are linked only by 'is' to conclusions whose parts are linked by 'ought'... [is] altogether inconceivable."[64] In the same way, you have to show that the historical precedent in Acts 2-5 is a mandatory prescription for all later Christians. Can you get the imperative (*all Christians should do this*) from the indicative (*some early Christians did this*)? You can try with all your might, but you will never cross the divide. The fact that some Christians shared all things (with some qualifications) does not constitute a command that all Christians should follow their example. C.S. Lewis outlines this distinction in *The Abolition of Man*:

> From propositions about fact alone no practical conclusion can ever be drawn. *This will preserve society* cannot lead to *do this* except by the mediation of *society ought to be preserved*. *This will cost you your life* cannot lead directly to *do not do this*: it can lead to it only through a felt desire or an acknowledged duty of self-preservation. The Innovator is trying to get a conclusion in the *imperative mood* out of premises in the *indicative mood*; and though he continues trying to all eternity, he cannot succeed for the thing is impossible.[65]

The only way you could cross this divide is by showing that other biblical passages command socialism.

Interpreting Narrative by Didactic Passages

You can't make a universal command from something that was practiced in the first century unless it is clearly taught elsewhere in Scripture. For instance, the fact that Jesus wore a seamless robe does not mean that all future believers must do likewise, unless it is commanded elsewhere. Or does the fact that Jesus had "nowhere to lay his head" (no home) mean that all believers thereafter must be homeless? R.C. Sproul explains how Christians must interpret biblical narratives through the lens of broader Christian teaching: "We must interpret the narrative passages of Scripture by the didactic or 'teaching' portions. If we try to find too much theology in narrative passages, we can easily go beyond the point of the narrative into serious errors."[66]

Unless a command makes mandatory a historical precedent in the teaching of Jesus's life or of the early church, then it is not binding on later believers. Thus, even if Acts 2-5 was socialism, which it was not, it would hold nothing other than historical interest to later believers. It would have no binding power on the later church. So in order to show that Acts 2-5 teaches socialism, you would have to show that:

1. All believers in Jerusalem sold all their possessions and put them in a communal pot, which was then controlled by the state (the distinctive mark of socialism).
2. Private property rights (upheld through the rest of Scripture) were abolished or discouraged by this passage.
3. The voluntary giving demonstrated by individuals in this passage gives the state the right to coerce people to give up their property or redistribute it (socialism).
4. The pattern shown here was not temporary but permanent. It was the rule in the rest of the New Testament.

5. You can get "ought" out of "is," the imperative from the indicative, a necessary mandate from a historical example.

6. There is clear teaching that entails government ownership of the means of production, coercive taxation and wealth redistribution (socialism) in the rest of Scripture.

Wise teachers have maintained that it is not good to base an important doctrine on a single passage of Scripture. But if you do so, surely in that passage the doctrine should be taught, not just mentioned by way of narrative. Not only is socialism not taught in Acts 2-5, it is impossible, without meeting the above conditions, to show that it does so.

Conclusion

So we see five myths commonly taught about Jubilee and five arguments demonstrating that Acts 2-5 does not teach socialism. If these are the two passages that are most referenced to uphold state redistribution of wealth, then the case is weak indeed.

Of course, just because the Bible doesn't require the state to redistribute wealth doesn't entail that the state can't do so. Whether the state is the best vehicle to meet needs of poor people is a separate issue. Certainly the believer must be concerned about the poor, the stranger, the widow, and the orphan because God requires us to do so. Jesus says that whoever serves one of the "least of these" serves him (Matthew 25:45). There is a case to be made that the state (by law) provides a safety net for the poor. But state involvement does not absolve believers of responsibility individually or corporately as the church. The biblical commands are not given to the impersonal secular state but to us to care personally for those in need with our time and treasure.[67]

Scripture quotations taken from the New American Standard Bible®, Copyright © 1960, 1962, 1963, 1968, 1971, 1972, 1973, 1975, 1977, 1995 by The Lockman Foundation. Used by permission. (www.Lockman.org)

CHAPTER 5

Evangelicals and Poverty: the Voluntary Principle in Action

By Richard Turnbull, M.A., Ph.D.

iccadilly Circus in central London is surrounded by neon lights, high-end hotels, exclusive shops, theatres, and the trappings of tourism. Around 150 years ago it was also a short distance away from one of the most extensive slums in London, some 30,000 people living in appalling conditions of poverty with open sewers, gin shops, and prostitution. Criminality was rife. Today in Piccadilly Circus there is a fountain with a statue, usually referred to, erroneously, as Eros, the Greek god of love. The figure is actually that of Anteros, the Angel of Christian Charity. The name of the fountain, the Shaftesbury Memorial Fountain, and the nearby street, Shaftesbury Avenue, are the clues.

"I Want Nothing but Usefulness to God and My Country"

A year after the veteran anti-slavery campaigner, William Wilberforce, left Parliament in 1825, the future leader of Evangelicalism in England entered the House of Commons.[68] Anthony Ashley Cooper, known as Lord Ashley until his succession as the Seventh Earl of Shaftesbury upon his father's death in 1851, was a very different character from Wilberforce.[69] Although less well known, he is potentially of greater importance. Shaftesbury's evangelical Christian vision of society was remarkable. He faced up to the challenge of poverty with a passion and with a Christian vision built upon Scripture and the voluntary principle. He understood the role of government but also that it was a limited role. He believed in both the conversion of the soul and the transformation of society. He viewed trade unionism and socialism as threats to freedom and indeed to the very fabric of society itself. Socialism was anathema to him.[70] For Shaftesbury, the appropriate response to poverty was achieved primarily though the adoption of the voluntary principle: Christians working together in voluntary societies. This was at the heart of his vision for both economy and society. He was driven by a sense of a deep calling from God, though he also suffered from introspection that bordered on the depressive. Yet he was offered cabinet office by both political parties of the day—three times in 1866 alone—and he declined on each occasion (though not without some anguish). Thousands of people lined the streets of London for his funeral. He was associated with hundreds of Christian voluntary societies. His motivations were profoundly theological. With an acute sense of the duties implied by a belief in the Second Advent of Christ, Shaftesbury successfully negotiated his way through the minefield of eschatology to produce a rounded, dynamic, and biblical understanding of Christian responsibility in a free society. His vision is one we would do well to recover.

This chapter is a historical examination of the evangelical approach to understanding and implementing the biblical call to care for the poor. The competing paradigms within evangelical thought on poverty alleviation can best be distinguished by the voluntary principle versus the principle of redistribution. These paradigms and their implications for political economy and the proper organization of society could not be in starker contrast. Evangelicals have historically embraced the voluntary principle, which relies on the interworking of free market competition, which promotes and encourages the biblical doctrine of work and fosters massive wealth creation. This has dramatic, positive implications for a long-term escape from material poverty. The voluntary principle was led by Chalmers and Shaftsbury and later taken up by others. This chapter examines the historical tradition of evangelicals in both the voluntary school and the redistributive school, and concludes that the redistributive tradition that has taken in so many evangelicals lacks a moral, theological, and religious basis from an *evangelical* standpoint.

In Matthew 26:10, Jesus told the disciples, "The poor you will always have with you." This statement produces differing responses amongst evangelical Christians.[71] Some Christians have responded to this statement with complacency in the face of social evil. Jesus's point is taken at face value; his words should not be contradicted but serve as reassurance, a reminder that Christians cannot fully eliminate poverty. This has left the field open for a very different approach from some other evangelicals. This group does not take the words of Jesus in a literal sense but, instead, grounds its claims in the trajectory of Scripture that sheds light on divine love for the poor, but which, in this approach, is interpreted as a "bias" or "preferential option" for the poor. Indeed, an entire methodological approach has emerged from this perspective, which might be described as the evangelical "redistributive tradition." This outlook makes certain assumptions about the perceived benefits of (high) taxation, an enhanced role for the state, and a negative view of the market and competition.

The contrast between these two approaches (the voluntary principle and the redistributive tradition) could not be starker. Historically, evangelicals have, generally, held a positive view of wealth creation and enterprise, and have adopted the voluntary principle in how they have sought to deal with poverty and disadvantage. Market principles and virtuous compassion have defined this approach. Indeed, because the market is part of God's provision, behavior, compassion, and responsibility are crucial components of a Christian vision for society. The evangelical thus views the market not simply as a system of resource allocation, but also as a place where discipleship is exercised or even learned. When the creativity, innovation, and dynamism of the market are combined with the voluntary principle, the result is a dynamic yet conservative approach to the challenges of poverty. This position is characterized by enterprise (Exodus 35:30-32 — "See, the LORD has chosen Bezalel ... and he has filled him with the Spirit of God, with wisdom, with understanding, with knowledge and with all kinds of skills—to make artistic designs for work in gold, silver and bronze, to cut and set stones, to work in wood and to engage in all kinds of artistic crafts"), compassion (Zechariah 7:10 — "Do not oppress the widow or the fatherless, the foreigner or the poor"), and cheerful giving (2 Corinthians 9:7 — "Each of you should give what you have decided in your heart to give, not reluctantly or under compulsion, for God loves a cheerful giver"). We need to explore this vision and assess what has happened to it in the face of the critique of the evangelical redistributive tradition.

As well as the Earl of Shaftesbury, a Scottish Presbyterian minister, Thomas Chalmers (1780-1847), was another representative of the voluntary tradition. As we will see, whereas Shaftesbury operated on the national stage, Chalmers put the principles into action in his local parish in Glasgow.

The Building Blocks

The history of economics and commerce is as complex as that of theology. To understand the link between the evangelicals of the eighteenth and nineteenth centuries and the market economy, we need to reflect upon both Adam Smith and John Calvin.[72]

The publication in 1776 by Adam Smith of *An Inquiry into the Nature and Causes of the Wealth of Nations* marked the origin of the modern investigation of the science of economics. The work has been described as "the fountainhead of classical economics."[73] Smith not only defined the essential concepts of a market economic model—value, price, cost, and exchange—but also advocated a minimalist approach to government intervention in the workings of the market.[74] Smith's basic aim was to produce a model for economic growth. The idea of the division of labor, leading to greater productivity, was at the heart of his approach.[75] Smith, though, went further. He also divided labor into two further categories. Productive labor was deployed in the production and manufacture of goods. Unproductive labor included not only the clergy (for which there was, regrettably, more than ample evidence) but also, more significantly, the government.

Adam Smith's worldview shaped his economic model. This view was essentially deist. The iron laws of Newtonian mechanics were translated into equally rigid laws of economics. This "natural law" view of the world emphasized that nature was ordered and harmonious. In the classical economic model, this harmonious order was reflected in the principles of equilibrium. Theologically, this suggested that a God of order meant an ordered economic system that functioned for the common good through its mechanism.

These ideas in the economic world actually built upon Smith's philosophical views set out in his earlier work, *The Theory of Moral Sentiments* (1759). According to Smith, man was composed of three sets of motives: self-love and sympathy, freedom and propriety, and labor and exchange. He applied these couplets to man's economic activity. He assumed a natural propensity to barter together with an essential selfishness in humanity. Crucially the effect of the economic mechanism is to bring about, not only the satisfaction of others, but indeed the welfare of all, by each serving their own interests. In this way a greater public good is achieved. In addition, principles of natural compassion are implanted in man, "which interest him in the welfare of others and make their happiness necessary to him."[76] Although this view is essentially optimistic, Smith was more than aware of the negative impact of greed. The economic system represents a self-regulating mechanism; interference should be resisted. To summarize:

> Smithian man, then, is roughly equal by natural abilities and equipped with a propensity to exchange; he is also motivated principally by self-interest in his economic dealings, and he is provided by nature, slowly and spontaneously, with a system which perfectly suits him and one which naturally makes his inherent self-seeking fit him for society. And from this desire of every man to seek his own advantage and to improve his condition arises all public and private wealth.[77]

The paradox in the classical model between the pursuit of self-interest on the part of individuals and the overall achievement of the public good could be explained only by the providential design of those laws of economics that brought this about. This "natural theology" links evangelicals and the market. Natural theology refers to those natural laws or provisions in creation that determine the workings of the created world. Among evangelicals there has been more dependency on this approach than is sometimes acknowledged, although, of course, evangelicals have always been particularly concerned about the disruption to the model caused by sin, to which we will return.

The way in which this theology of order has influenced evangelicalism is best appreciated though the insights of the Geneva Reformer John Calvin. Although there is an extensive scholarly debate over the extent to which Calvin allowed for a natural theology, Calvin's influence on later developments means it is crucial to consider his theology.[78]

Calvin believed that God had planted clear marks in the universe. Hence no one can plead ignorance. God "daily discloses himself in the whole workmanship of the universe. As a consequence, men cannot open their eyes without being compelled to see him."[79] Calvin used both astronomy and the human body as evidence of God's glory manifest in both the order and variety of the universe. However, Calvin did not stop there. For him, sin and the fall disguised the wonderful ordering of God from our understanding. Hence man can now only discern God as redeemer. This is in line with David Bebbington's view of the link between the Enlightenment and Evangelicalism, although others, especially Anthony Waterman, have noted that the problem with the natural theology approach and its essential optimism was "a widespread reluctance at that time to grasp the nettle of original sin."[80] In a sense this summarizes the evangelical approach to the market; it is part of

God's ordered universe, but participants in the market are infected by original sin. It is not the market that is the problem but the sinful behavior of individuals. Hence the need for ethics and values.

Several Christian theologians had significant influence on economic thought in the eighteenth and nineteenth centuries, including William Paley, John Bird Sumner, Richard Whateley, and Edward Copleston. Thomas Chalmers is the example par excellence. Chalmers stands out as the prime example of an evangelical who adopted political economy as a set of theoretical principles and sought to put them into practice in a parish context—to which example we will shortly return. Chalmers's worldview was that of natural theology but with a personal deity. He was closely linked to Malthus and, like him, viewed poverty as inevitable and redistribution as powerless.[81]

In the second volume of his *Natural Theology*, Chalmers considered in detail how the natural order affected both the economic and political well-being of society. There was, he asserted, a natural law of property. In addition to that, he appealed to the law of self-preservation (individuals acting in their own interests), which led to both industry and what he termed the law of relative affection. In other words, we are back to the paradox of self-interest leading to the common good. The law of relative affection followed Smith's theory of moral sentiments in maintaining that a natural seed was implanted in humanity that gave the individual compassion for the distress and destitution of others. So Chalmers argued that "the philosophy of free trade is grounded on the principle, that society is most enriched or best served, when commerce is left to its own spontaneous evolutions," and that the "greatest economic good—or, in other words, a more prosperous result is obtained by the spontaneous play and busy competition of a thousand wills, each bent on the prosecution of its own selfishness." It "is when each man is left to seek with concentrated and exclusive aim, his own individual benefit—it is then, that markets are best supplied."[82] This was not just theory for Chalmers, but for evangelicals it also reflected their understanding of the scriptural material on, among other things, enterprise and creativity (Exodus 35:30-35), work (2 Thessalonians 3:10), property (Exodus 20:15; Proverbs 19:14), trade (Acts 16:14), and responsibility in giving (2 Corinthians 9:7).

This has very strong resonances of Adam Smith and the "invisible hand," a hand which, in the view of Chalmers, was clearly that of the Almighty himself. As Chalmers said, this "strongly bespeaks a higher agent, by whose transcendental wisdom it is that all is made to conspire so harmoniously and to terminate so beneficially."[83]

Two particular problems arose from the classical model and its adoption by evangelicals; the impact of sin and the possibility of inequality. Sin, as we have noted, distorted the market through the sinful acts of the market's participants. In economic terms this led to disequilibrium; in Christian terms it led to poverty and suffering. The classic evangelical view saw life on earth as a probation or test for the life to come. Hence the market functioned as a field in which to exercise—a school of discipleship—to bring values into the functioning of the market. Only by participating in the market can the redeemed individual bring values and behaviors to bear in a transformative way; ultimately, this is how to deal with poverty and suffering.

The Voluntary Principle

How then did these early evangelicals respond to poverty? The answer lies in the acceptance of the classic economic model alongside the voluntary principle, which involved both the rejection of state intervention and the development of voluntary organizations, which in turn provided an appropriate setting for the exercise of philanthropy—the market plus the voluntary principle. What subsequently changed was an elevated role for the state, which most evangelicals viewed as disastrous but which became formative for the "redistributive tradition."

The voluntary principle means the rejection of a determinative role for the state in economic intervention in favor of the voluntary action of Christian people, both individually and acting together, reminding us once again of the biblical principles of enterprise, work, and cheerful giving.

For Chalmers, government intervention was not only unnecessary but also arrogant, as it sought to usurp the Creator from his rightful position. In addition, any extensive role for the state had the effect of taking over those things that truly belonged in the heart—the moral sentiments. Chalmers's appeal to property, industry, and compassion for others was the beginning of an evangelical economic ethic. As he put it, "we cannot translate beneficence into the statute-book of law, without expunging it from the statute-book of the heart."[84] Compulsion would lead to the "extinction of goodwill in the hearts of the affluent and of gratitude in the hearts of the poor."[85] Chalmers shows great Christian insight at this point. He understood that the nature of the human person not as a depository of "rights" but as an individual with a will, a conscience, indeed, a moral personality. The intervention of the state had led to duties being replaced by rights, to dependency rather than freedom. Edward Copleston went on to suggest, articulating the voluntary principle in his own words, that "an action to be virtuous must be voluntary."[86]

In the changing industrial landscape of nineteenth-century Britain, a wide spectrum of voluntary societies developed, ranging from visiting societies, savings clubs, loan societies (an early example of micro-finance), and poor relief societies, to schools and both social and evangelistic missionary societies. These organizations were neither new nor exclusive to the nineteenth century, but there was then a significant expansion of them. They were characterized by local control and independence from state aid—important characteristics for our discussion. Later, critics often viewed these societies as having more to do with an elite middle-class identity and a place for working out guilt about poverty than a genuine response to poverty and social welfare.[87] As well as being unfair, this criticism underplays the significance of these voluntary societies. These societies were the main means of responding to needs at a local level. Certainly among the many evangelical societies these were places for "voluntary work for God." Women were especially prominent among the volunteers.

The attraction of the voluntary society for the advocates of political economy (the market) was that it enabled the proper provision of social welfare to be kept separate from state intervention. It also allowed a distinction to be drawn between deserving and undeserving poverty. The voluntary visitor operating in a local area was quickly able to ascertain the degree to which applicants themselves were at fault. For both Shaftesbury and Chalmers, the essentially local nature of voluntary societies was crucial because it allowed for the relationships between families, donors, recipients, and so on, to be maintained. This more easily enabled relief to be temporary rather than becoming enshrined as a legal right; state aid depersonalized poverty relief. The increase in the power of the state in Victorian Britain was partly due to the fragmentation of the voluntary attempts to relieve poverty. There is persuasive evidence that there was a remarkable increase in the voluntary charity sector after 1850. Evangelical societies were central to this picture. Indeed, "as many as three-quarters of the total number of voluntary charitable organizations in the second half of the nineteenth century can be regarded as Evangelical in character and control."[88]

The critics viewed the voluntary society as a place of social control and power, but these societies provided an important contribution to the genuine search for solutions to poverty in accordance with the theological and economic worldview of most evangelical practitioners.

Chalmers and Glasgow

Chalmers, partially due to his opposition to compulsory welfare relief for the poor (the Poor Laws), was a pioneer of urban mission activity through his social experiments in his Glasgow parish of St. John's in the period of 1819-1823. Chalmers denounced all forms of "legalized charity" (i.e. government instituted) in articles in the *Edinburgh Review* in 1817 and 1818. He set out to show that even the poorest of communities could achieve self-help without government compulsion. He advocated the linking of rural and industrial parishes and teams of clerical and lay workers in each area. Crucially, the foundation of such care lay in the family and the home. This, combined with a degree of self-restraint, ensured that voluntary care and relief was provided; there was no need for the state to intervene. He set out his views in his *Christian and Civic Economy of Large Towns (1821)*.

Chalmers became the minister of St. John's parish in September 1819. There were some two thousand families in the parish, and many of them had no connection with the Christian church. Chalmers was determined to establish a system of pastoral care and social welfare that reflected biblical principles. He began by establishing schools, but the heart of his pastoral system lay in the division of his parish into manageable portions for social care. The parish was divided into 25 districts, each with somewhere between 60 and 100 families. His team established oversight over these districts, each district having an elder responsible for spiritual matters and a deacon concerned for social welfare. Chalmers not only oversaw the entire system but was himself closely and personally involved, visiting families as well as holding evening meetings. Chalmers was determined to demonstrate that voluntary relief was more effective than compulsory assessment and that this was possible in large cities. The system was based on personal relationships and self-help—all founded upon the principles set out in Scripture. The deacons spent an hour each week with their families, which meant that they knew them individually and were thus better placed to support them and encourage them and also to properly assess any request for assistance. This was the first major large-scale attempt to put the voluntary principle into action in a local area. We now turn to the broader and wider advocacy of the voluntary principle.

Shaftesbury
Birth and Upbringing

Anthony Ashley Cooper was born on April 28, 1801, into a family of English aristocrats with landed estates, which he would in due course inherit. The family's politics were Tory.[89] Ashley's childhood was less than congenial, and he was often at loggerheads with his parents. The key influence in his early years was the family housekeeper, Maria Millis. She showed him the love that his parents lacked towards him; also, as a committed Christian, she introduced the young aristocrat to evangelical devotion. The effect was to be long lasting. Maria prayed with Ashley and read him the Bible. Shaftesbury later recalled that it was to Maria that he owed his first memories of prayer and piety.[90] Ashley hated school but eventually emerged with a first class honors degree in Classics from Oxford.

The natural course for Ashley was to enter politics. He was duly elected the Tory Member of Parliament for Woodstock, near Oxford, in the general election of 1826. In October 1825, Ashley, looking to the forthcoming election, wrote in his diary, "I have a great mind to found a policy upon the Bible."[91] He was influenced by Philip Doddridge, a noted nonconformist writer of the previous century, and also by the evangelical Thomas Scott's renowned commentary on the Bible. All of this came together in the clear call of God on Lord Ashley's life, an essential prerequisite to a life of Christian service. In 1827, he wrote in his diary, "I desire to be useful in my generation, and die in the knowledge of having advanced happiness by having advanced true religion."[92] He had earlier declared, "I want nothing but usefulness to God and my country."[93]

Theological Convictions

Shaftesbury's application of classic evangelical and Protestant doctrine was powerful and dynamic. In the context of the advancement of Enlightenment rationality, the power of the state, and even the secular narrative, Shaftesbury stood firm. Christian theology was to be applied to society, not submerged beneath it. Evangelical belief, according to Shaftesbury, provided a template for the life of discipleship. His theological motives had three strands: first, the principle of the Bible and its teaching; second, the voluntary worker principle expressed across denominational boundaries; third, the implications of the end-times.

Shaftesbury's starting point with the Bible could not have been clearer. He told the annual meeting of the Church Pastoral Aid Society in 1862:

> There is no security whatever except in standing upon the faith of our fathers, and saying with them that the blessed old Book

is 'God's Word written,' from the very first syllable down to the very last, and from the last back to the first.[94]

Scripture should be read and digested privately and devotionally, guiding the whole of life, and was equally applicable in both private and public domains. He argued that 2 Chronicles should be studied, prayed over, and weighed by every person in public life. The Bible was its own missionary, accessible to the ordinary person. He told the Bible Society in 1860:

> Tens of thousands have thrown off their corrupt and ignorant faith, not in consequence of the efforts of preachers, or teachers, or lecturers, but simply and solely from reading the Word of God, pure and unadulterated, without note or comment, without any teaching except the blessed teaching of God's Holy Spirit.[95]

Shaftesbury's commitment to both interdenominational unity and the voluntary worker principle (the use of lay people—lay agents—in the Lord's work) was central to his vision. He described the Bible Society as "a solemn league and covenant of all those who 'love the Lord Jesus Christ with sincerity.'" This is what he told the annual meeting of the London City Mission in 1863:

> Put all that aside, and let all establishments and all distinctive churches sink into the ground, compared with the one great effort to preach the doctrine of Christ crucified to every creature on the earth, to every creature that can be reached on this habitable globe.[96]

The voluntary Christian society was the great place where all Christians could come together for service. He saw this particularly with his work with the London City Mission and with ragged schools. He told the Ragged School Union that "all who care for the advancement of Christ's kingdom, to whatever church they belong, must join together, heart and soul, for the purpose of bringing to completion this great, this mighty undertaking."[97] Shaftesbury was driven by the Christian vision of the unfinished task of bringing the gospel to the un-evangelized, especially the poor and marginalized, and its transforming power to bear upon a society that claimed to be Christian. The lay-agency principle was the most effective way of the gospel penetrating even into the darkest depths of London's slums. Shaftesbury was scathing about the Victorian passion for building churches—"we want men, not churches."[98] In his view, the lay workers employed in the voluntary societies, whether paid missionaries, volunteer teachers, Scripture readers, or parish visitors, were in by far the best position to assess social need. The advance of the state rather led to the collapse of the voluntary principle, as so many social functions were taken over by government.

The third important aspect of Shaftesbury's theological concern was eschatology.[99] For the present purpose it is sufficient to note that he gave a priority to faithful discipleship in the light of the Second Advent of Christ. This position turned on its head evangelical obsessions with chronology and timing and replaced them with a call to discipleship. He urged constant attention to the responsibilities of the present and the dynamic of living in constant, yet unknown, expectation of the second coming. He set it out clearly:

I am now looking, not to the great end, but to the interval. I know, my friends, how great and glorious that end will be; but

131

while I find so many persons looking to no end, and others rejoicing in that great end, and thinking nothing about the interval, I confess that my own sympathies and fears dwell much with what must take place before that great consummation.[100]

Shaftesbury and the Voluntary Societies

Shaftesbury illustrates how moral values can be brought to the market. He believed that it was entirely appropriate for government to legislate for the protection of the vulnerable. So he campaigned in Parliament for the protection from exploitation of young people in particular, from danger in factories and mines, seeking to hold the owners to their responsibilities. He campaigned against prostitution and poor housing, and in support of those who suffered the ravages of mental health breakdown. However, he never viewed the state as the solution; rather, he saw the role of government as extremely limited and potentially damaging to the wider Christian and social cause. This was the reason why the Christian voluntary society came to play such a significant role in his thinking, and why he lamented—particularly around 1870—government taking over functions previously undertaken by such Christian societies.

The London City Mission

The London City Mission was formed on May 16, 1835. The City Mission was founded on the principle of taking the gospel to the urban poor of London, primarily through home visitation. The work grew into reaching out to particular employment groups (such as flower girls and cab drivers), and many missionaries were also involved in founding schools. The City Missionaries met poverty on a daily basis and were often the only people who could penetrate a London slum containing perhaps 20,000 people living in cramped, damp, and dangerous conditions. Shaftesbury walked the streets of London with the City Missionaries, gathering evidence for his Parliamentary campaigns, encouraging the Christian workers and preaching the gospel. Hence, we see that personal relationships, personal responsibility, and localism through voluntary societies lay at the heart of this vision.

Shaftesbury strongly advocated the City Mission's program of systematic home visiting and allocating missionaries to special interest groups such as the cabmen. The force of home visiting was that it was an individual encounter, "carrying the Gospel to men's hearts from house to house, from heart to heart, from man to man, from soul to soul, from individual to individual."[101] The use of lay agents, Shaftesbury said, was essential to gain access to the dens and alleys of London. Not only were these representatives of the mission "living agents," but many of them were drawn from the very ranks of those they were enlisted to serve—essentially the principle of incarnation. The City Missionary was in a unique position to watch for and counteract the rise and progress of evil, whether physical or spiritual. A significant amount of the evidence gathered by Lord Shaftesbury for use in his campaigns for social reform was gathered in cooperation with the City Missionaries.

> My experience of their value dates back over half a century. In all the operations in which I have been engaged, these men were my companions and fellow-laborers, and I derived unbounded assistance from them in the matter of Ragged Schools, Common Lodging-Houses, Special Services, and in every effort for the improvement of Society. . . . In all difficulties of research, our first resource was to the City Missionaries, because we knew

that their inquiry would be zealous and immediate, and their report ample and trustworthy.[102]

By way of illustration, there is the most remarkable story of Lord Ashley, as he then was, encountering some of the hardest criminals of London. Crucial to Ashley's approach, as with Chalmers, was the combination of self-help, social provision, and spiritual salvation. In 1848, Ashley was invited by a London City Missionary named Thomas Jackson to accompany him to a meeting of London's convicted felons. It must have been a quite extraordinary scene for this English aristocratic gentleman to accompany Jackson into the heart of one of London's most notorious slums. In fact, three meetings were held altogether, and a total of 394 convicts attended. Ashley had two aims: to preach the gospel and to assist these individuals in finding a new life. Ashley was a supporter of various schemes of emigration, which were designed to help those who had perhaps fallen into criminal ways and to enable them to make a new start. Standing next to Jackson, Ashley preached the gospel of eternal salvation to his hearers and then sought to persuade them to help themselves and to lift themselves out of the quagmire in which they found themselves.

The Ragged Schools

The name seems rather quaint and old fashioned. The title "ragged" would be an unlikely choice in the contemporary age. However, this should not distract us from the impact of this movement in Victorian England. Shaftesbury was associated with the ragged school movement for over forty years, and it represented one of the main ways in which he expressed his commitment to Christian social welfare on the ground. The rapid decline, even collapse, of ragged schools following the

Education Act of 1870 (which introduced compulsory state education) was a real blow to Shaftesbury. Indeed, that particular piece of legislation was a significant milestone in seeking to understand the loss of an evangelical vision for society after that date.

In the period up to 1870 there was spasmodic provision of schooling by various charitable societies. Often, due to appearance, general condition, and clothing, the poorest children were excluded from the charity schools. Many of the early ragged schools came into existence through the offices and efforts of individual City Missionaries. The umbrella body, The Ragged School Union, came into being on July 5, 1844. Lord Ashley became the president. The basic aim was the education of the poor so as to enable them to read the Bible, an essential prerequisite, of course, to salvation. The Ragged School Union, however, also had wider educational and social objectives.

Crucial to the purposes of the RSU was the idea of reaching those excluded from the other educational provisions of society. The second annual report referred to the aim of "removing every ragged, destitute child from our streets, and to the placing of that child in the path of industry and virtue."[103] These aims found their outworking in the establishment of schools of industry attached to the ragged schools. Similarly the ragged school movement led directly to the founding of the Shoeblacks Brigade to provide direct employment. At Old Pye Street school in Westminster, a Juvenile Refuge and School of Industry was established with the RSU financing a tailor and a shoemaker as teachers of their trades—an apprenticeship model.

The extent and influence of the movement upon the poor grew rapidly. The first annual report noted twenty schools, 2,000 children, and 200 teachers. The twenty-fourth report, in 1868, reported 257 schools with 31,357 scholars. The tenth report, in 1854, reported on RSU activities covering industrial classes, Shoe-Black Brigades,

Refuges, placing scholars in employment, emigration, mothers' meetings, libraries, Penny Banks, and Clothing Funds. By 1870 the list had expanded to cover meals societies, sanitary associations, libraries, flower shows, rag collecting, Shoe Clubs, Coal Clubs, Provident Clubs, and Barrow Clubs. The last of these was a form of micro-finance, with individuals contributing to the club, which then enabled loans to be made for barrows (or perhaps a potato oven), thus empowering individuals to make a living from selling vegetables. The impact of the RSU on the poor and as part of the evangelical Christian response to urban poverty and deprivation should not be underestimated.

Lord Ashley occupied the chair for the first annual meeting of the RSU in 1845, and did so every year up to 1884. Shaftesbury's links and connections with the myriad of organizations that arose out of the activities of the RSU were extensive. He had a particular concern for the well-being of the costermongers. This was a proud, close-knit group of barrow-holders (vegetable sellers) and flower girls, all of whom were always struggling to make ends meet. He was committed to giving every possible aid and assistance in his power to helping the poorest in London. Shaftesbury chaired not only national meetings but also gatherings of individual schools. Ragged schools were not glamorous. They often met in crowded and inadequate conditions, perhaps a room fifteen feet square accommodating fifty to sixty children and eight to ten teachers. Ashley's own description of one particular ragged school revealed the extent of the problems. There was an average Sunday evening attendance of 260, aged from five to twenty years. This number included forty-two who had no parents, seven children of convicts, twenty-seven who had been imprisoned, thirty-six who had run away from home, nineteen who slept in lodging houses, forty-one who lived by begging, twenty-nine who never slept on beds, and seventeen who had no shoes or stockings.[104] He was also closely involved with the refuge movement, often associated with ragged schools. He became president of The Reformatory and Refuge Union, involved as well in their connected work of "training ships."

Another area that grew out of the ragged school movement was that of the Shoeblack Brigades, founded in 1851 under Shaftesbury's patronage. The purpose was the combined aims of providing employment and encouraging disciplined lives. The boys' earnings were split three ways. A third was banked for the future, a third went to the mission to cover costs, and a third was retained by the boys themselves. One year after foundation, there were thirty-six boys employed and 150,000 pairs of boots and shoes had been cleaned.[105] By 1856, the number of boys had increased to 108. The Shoeblack Brigades were criticized for providing no long-term employment, but Shaftesbury was more concerned with personal formation rather than cleaning shoes. He always linked such schemes to others, especially emigration proposals (a new life elsewhere). Perhaps there was too much of the romantic in Shaftesbury, but his aim was to enable those less fortunate than others to be lifted out of the social quagmire they found themselves in. Learning, discipline, and thrift would equip them for a better life, a life he always hoped would be dependent in a personal way upon God.

Shaftesbury viewed his work with voluntary Christian schools with especial care and favor. They became places where education was shaped by the Bible. Food, even lodging, was often provided for those in need, but faith and education were not seen as separate. He believed the movement was for nothing less than the glory of God. This helps explain Shaftesbury's utter despair at the increased role of government in education from 1870 onward, when compulsory state education was introduced. Quoting his diary entry on the matter at length illustrates both his passion and his commitment to the Christian voluntary society. He viewed the prospects of state intervention as disastrous.

> The godless, non-Bible system is at hand; and the Ragged Schools, with all their divine polity, with all their burning and fruitful love for the poor, with all their prayers and harvests for the temporal and eternal welfare of the forsaken, heathenish, destitute, sorrowful, and yet innocent children, must perish under this all-conquering march of intellectual power. Our nature is nothing, the heart is nothing, in the estimation of these zealots of secular knowledge. Everything for the flesh, and nothing for the soul; everything for time, and nothing for eternity.[106]

He noted with regret the inevitable fact of the sinking of the ragged schools, though his heart could still be lifted by the atmosphere at the annual ragged school prize giving. Shaftesbury had great foresight; in the following quarter of a century the number of voluntary Christian societies fell substantially. For Shaftesbury and others like him, however, the voluntary society was essentially local and relational, neither of which could be said of government interventions.

Evangelicals and the Redistributive Tradition

So what happened to this vision and how did the redistributive tradition gain the upper hand amongst evangelicals? There are two reasons. First, with the onset of the power of the state, evangelicals weakened in their vision for society and retreated into a private view of the faith. The conversion of the individual and the transformation of society through those individuals became separated. Welfare was abandoned to the state. The consequence was not only the loss of the impact of faith in the public square but the loss of freedom itself. Second, an intellectual Christian socialism gained the upper hand.

The name of R.H. Tawney is inextricably linked with the development of this "redistributive tradition." *Religion and the Rise of Capitalism* originated in the lectures given in 1922 in memory of the prominent Christian socialist, Henry Scott Holland (1847-1917). Holland and Charles Gore (1853-1932), who wrote the book's forward, founded the Christian Social Union in 1889 to investigate the social disorder of society. In the 1920s, perhaps in the aftermath of war, explanatory metanarratives seemed to be the order of the day, with Tawney's work and Max Weber's *Protestant Ethic and the Spirit of Capitalism* both appearing in these early decades of the twentieth century. Essentially, Tawney drew socialist conclusions. He criticized the "naïve and uncritical worship of economic power."[107] The interests of the individual must be "submitted to the control of some larger body of interests."[108]

Weber saw the modern spirit of capitalism as embodied in the idea that the acquisitive spirit was now "the ultimate purpose of life."[109] The source of this spirit he traced primarily to Calvinism. Due to Calvin's doctrine of predestination, the elect were certain of their salvation. The natural inclination to good works, therefore, had to be worked out elsewhere—for example, in the market. The consequence was what we now know as the Protestant work ethic.

These two sociological meta-narratives of Tawney and Weber have been deeply influential. What is more remarkable is the extent to which these broad worldviews exerted such influence on *evangelical* opinion. The means by which this occurred was through the observation that one strand of radical Protestantism—the Anabaptists and Mennonites—displayed the work ethic and yet rejected capitalism. This teaching, with its unspoken undergirding in Christian socialism, has been embraced by wider sections of the evangelical community in a relatively unthinking manner.

The main proponents of this view are generally associated with the Mennonite tradition. John Howard Yoder (1927-1997) represented this outlook at a more academic level in his book *The Politics of Jesus,* first published in 1972. Early in his book, Yoder states, "Jesus is according to the biblical witness, a model of radical political action."[110] This understanding takes the form of a social ethic, of a challenge to the political authorities and, as Yoder puts it, "the beginning of a new set of social alternatives."[111] Yoder goes on to claim that Jesus accepted voluntary poverty for the sake of the kingdom and instructed his disciples to redistribute capital. This ignores, among other things, not far short of twenty years of business enterprise in Jesus's earthly father's carpentry business, not only making the usual products of the business but also the necessary profits to sustain it.

This sort of approach was popularized through Ronald J. Sider's *Rich Christians in an Age of Hunger,* first published in 1977. This work takes the shared Tawney and Weber thesis that the objective of economic affluence has taken center stage, combines that worldview with Yoder's politicization of Jesus, and builds an economic and social ethic that has deeply influenced evangelical thinking on both sides of the Atlantic. Sider was an early critic of a growth-based economy. The objective, he argued, was not just a simpler lifestyle but "to reduce total expenditures…to the point where you enjoy a standard of living which all persons in the world could share."[112] This argument has been reappearing in the light of the most recent financial crisis.

> [S]trategies of growth…have reached a point of diminishing returns…[the] backstop provided by government spending and central bank debt acquisition is the only thing keeping the

system from hurtling into a deflationary spiral....The picture is bleak; rising poverty, disappearing social services, and general strikes and protests.[113]

Unfortunately for its proponents, no (or insignificant) economic growth undermines the very basis of their own analysis of world need. A lack of growth will mean falling incomes, falling employment and indeed, even for the most dedicated socialist, a falling tax base. It is remarkable that so many evangelicals fell for the plot.

Sider's starting theme in his biblical analysis is unsurprisingly that of liberation followed by incarnation, the classic themes of Christian socialism. Sider's prescription included the redistribution of capital, the denunciation of sinful structures on trade—consumption and profits—the rejection of consumption and the hint of a subsistence life style—living in community. This lifestyle would in fact bring more poverty. Sider acknowledges, "Eating less beef or becoming a vegetarian will not necessarily feed one starving child. If millions of Americans and Europeans reduce their beef consumption, but do not act politically to change public policy, the result will not necessarily be less starvation in the Third World."[114] Hence, the demand must be for socio-political and structural change.

The same theme was struck in another, later work from the same tradition, Donald Kraybill's *The Upside-Down Kingdom*. In describing the kingdom of God as upside-down economically in "stark contrast to the prevailing Western economic philosophy," Kraybill produces the familiar prescriptions of the redistributive tradition.[115] He says we "can begin by consuming less," adding that this is "the beginning of responsible stewardship of the God-owned non-renewable resources."[116] This, however, is a category confusion where acquisitive materialism is conflated with economic growth.

This perspective arrived in Britain through two channels: a hugely popular pietistic work, *Celebration of Discipline*, written by Richard Foster, and Bishop David Sheppard's *Bias to the Poor*, the authors both being prominent evangelicals. The former, reflecting Mennonite teaching, advocated lifestyle issues; the latter dealt with the so-called divine bias to the poor. The consequence has been a long-term loss of perspective in Britain on economic matters among Christians in general and evangelicals in particular.

David Sheppard's book *Bias to the Poor* was published in 1983. Sheppard was a prominent evangelical and Bishop of Liverpool, a city that had suffered significant economic depression (as well as a long tradition, at least post Second World War, of left-wing political representation). Sheppard wrote from experience and in an engaging and sympathetic manner. He attacked the voluntary principle under the guise of power.

> [B]oth charity and paternalism are concepts which are rightly criticized; both offer help, but frequently retain control in the fatherly or charitable hands of someone else, and therefore may then be said to strengthen rather than weaken dependence.[117]

The replacement of the voluntary principle by the state principle (Sheppard made no mention of dependency on the state and the power of the state) has been one of the key reasons why evangelical approaches to poverty and economics have become so confused, and why so many have, perhaps unwittingly, embraced socialistic solutions. Sheppard's writing is extremely appealing and winsome. It does, however, lack serious depth in both economics and theology. A re-reading of the book is a reminder of how many were taken in by it. Christians, he argues,

...should take a lead in a public campaign to change the assumption that everyone pays their taxes grudgingly and unwillingly. Taxation is a proper way by which wealth is distributed more fairly and by which the poor and the whole of society are given better opportunities. A scheme of international taxation is needed, if the enormous gap between rich and poor nations is to be lessened.[118]

But if those taxes lead to wasteful and excessive government expenditures, or in fact do not enhance fairness and opportunity, but stifle innovation and enterprise, which can lead to growth, employment, and increased national income, then perhaps there is a better moral case for a campaign against excessive and ineffective taxation rather than in favor of it. The point is how the redistributive tradition makes assumptions about its superiority, assumptions that are open to serious challenge.

The impact of *Celebration of Discipline* was more subtle. This was a book of discipleship that embraced the pietistic approach of much of the earlier Mennonite teaching we have mentioned. Hence themes of sacrifice, community, simplicity, and lifestyle come to the fore. It is the combination of this personal piety alongside the more redistributive tradition that led to evangelicals' embracing this methodology.

To summarize, we can say that the redistributive tradition is characterized by a distinctive analysis and a particular prescription. The common observations are these:

- Theological assumptions that build on the themes of Christian socialism.
- An analysis that displays a simplistic approach to economics, especially in matters of growth and enterprise.

143

- An interpretation that sees redistribution as the central theme.
- Policy prescriptions that assume a prime role for government, the morality of high taxation, and an uncritical commitment to inter-governmental international aid.

All Christians will share a concern about the reduction of poverty. The unforeseen consequences of the redistributive tradition, however, are that wealth creation is ignored, growth denied, philanthropy strangled, and the voluntary principal lost.

Conclusion

The evangelical response to poverty depends upon a dynamic understanding of God's providential provision of the market, together with the practical application of the moral sentiments of compassion as implanted in the heart. The need for compassion and care is a result of sin, which leads to behavior that distorts the market. So evangelicalism's embrace of the "invisible hand" is neither an unthinking nor an unlimited adoption of the free market. Rather, it is an acceptance of the nature of divine provision with the application of Christian moral values. The voluntary principle lies at the heart of the thesis because, without it, government becomes all-powerful, the opportunity for Christian morality and discipleship in the market place is lost and, hence, God's good and gracious provision is denied. What is more, government fails on account of locality and relationships, both of which evangelicals have viewed as essential. Indeed, government may induce poverty and increase dependency rather than reduce it; hence self-help is also an evangelical principle. In addition to that, government, or perhaps we should say, excessive government and centralization, are, in fact, dangerous, not only to economic freedom but also to the very

Christian voluntary societies that lie at the heart of the response to poverty. This has been well articulated by Professor Roger Scruton:

> The first act of totalitarian governments is to abolish the charities through which people help themselves, and which are the main obstacle to creating the total dependence of the citizen on the State.[119]

Thus, the threat is not only to economic and religious freedom, but in essence to freedom itself. The redistributive tradition, which has taken in so many evangelicals, lacks a moral, theological, and religious basis from an *evangelical* standpoint. The threat of socialism and socialist solutions is a real one and the attraction is illusory. So, for the evangelical, there will be a real emphasis on the market, on self-help, and on incentives to work; but alongside that lies compassion on the ground through the voluntary principle. In this way, innovation flourishes, philanthropy is encouraged, compassion is exercised, and the gospel is maintained. The fact that this was recognized by the Earl of Shaftesbury so comprehensively some 150 years ago simply illustrates that he was a most remarkable man.

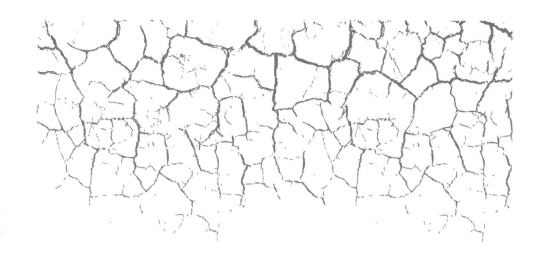

PART 2

MARKETS AND THE POOR

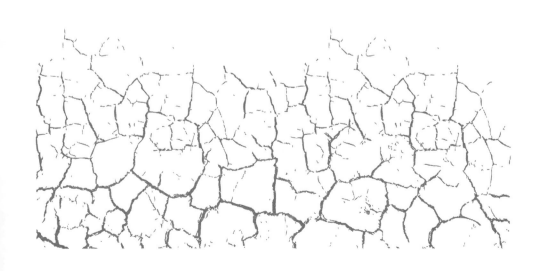

CHAPTER 6

Markets and Justice

By R. Mark Isaac, Ph.D.

Introduction: Fear and Trembling

The invitation to contribute to this volume addressing the issues of markets and justice from the perspective of a Christian economist is an awesome (in the traditional sense of the word) prospect. The goal of this chapter is to work from a few important parts of economic theory (the structure and function of markets, property rights, voluntary exchange, and voluntary association) toward the implications of these economic concepts with regard to biblical concepts of justice, broadly defined, and more specifically for addressing the needs of the poor.

Before beginning this journey, the concept of the total depravity of mankind serves as a double warning. For those outside the Calvinist community, the phrase "total depravity" is often mistakenly identified with the idea that people can do no good in their lives or in the lives of anyone else. Not so. Total depravity refers to how our fallen nature seeps into every part of our lives, including our spiritual lives, and also including our professional lives. That also must include the process of an economist putting words to paper, even for a noble purpose. "The human mind receives a humbling blow when all the thoughts which proceed from it are derided as foolish, frivolous, perverse, and insane."[120] Moreover, the task of this chapter is to discuss the role of some very human institutions (property rights, freedom of exchange, and voluntary association) in the light of God's justice and his command for how we are to live our lives.

Any human institution is subject to the effects of sin, but that does not mean that we can shun all human institutions. Indeed, the Bible depicts "markets" in a variety of lights. In some passages of Scripture, markets can be seen as participating in the divine. For example, Abraham offered to pay the market price for his burial ground (Genesis 23); the woman who anointed Jesus's feet did so with an ointment described as "expensive," indicating a market price (Mark 14:3-9). But markets are also associated with the sinful. Slaves were bought and sold (Exodus 21); more specifically, Amos chastises those who would "buy the poor for silver and the needy for a pair of sandals" (Amos 8:5). Perhaps most significantly, markets are also depicted in passages about the mundane. "When one man's ox butts another, so that it dies, then they shall sell the live ox and share its price" (Exodus 21:35). The excellent wife of Proverbs 31 "considers a field and buys it" and "perceives that her merchandise is profitable." In Jesus's parables, the characters buy, sell, and hire workers. From the viewpoint of an economist, there is power in the ordinariness of the story of Jesus and the Samaritan woman at the well, where Jesus was alone because he sent his disciples ahead to purchase supplies (John 4:8). We are told in several places that the disciples had a common purse. That it was "common" to them is a statement of the power of voluntary agreements and the freedom that such voluntary arrangements provide. This is a topic that will be addressed at some length below. It was, nevertheless, their purse. From the "Woman of Samaria" story above, we know that they must have used the money in it to buy goods in a market setting. Luke 8:3 tells us about two women who funded the ministry, and the author of John seems notably upset over the rumors that Judas was stealing from the common purse (John 12:13).

But alongside these opening caveats, one must note that we are to be a people of hope, and one can still hope that the task of interpreting economic principles in the light of justice is the Lord's work. The flip side of the total depravity of mankind is the fullness of God's grace and of his sovereignty. As Dutch theologian Abraham Kuyper said, "There is not a square inch of the entire world of which Christ does not rightly say, 'That Is Mine.'"[121] As Craig Bartholomew quotes Bernard Zylstra, the gospel is "the healing power which redirects fallen creation, in line with God's original design, and towards its originally intended consummation."[122] And Bartholomew himself charges Christians, as part of their cultural mandate, to do their best to judge cultural creations (think of markets, central planning, etc.) and "to oppose misdirection away from the glory of God."[123] How then can we not turn our attention to evaluating and judging the various economic modes or organizations that have emerged in human society, whether monarchical absolutism, multi-layered feudalism, communism, corporatist fascism, or the free exchange of goods and services?

The purpose of this chapter is to use the tools of economics to examine three essential components of what might be broadly called a market economy: well-defined property rights; voluntary exchange and contracting; and voluntary agreements for collective action. All three of these will be discussed in the next section. The manner of analysis is intended to do three things. First, I will offer an introductory presentation of these critical components of the market economy to non-economists and discuss why economists think they are important. Second, I will point from the "hows and whys" of the market to the implications of property rights, free exchange, and free association, to the prospects for justice and concern for the poor. Third, I will briefly map these components to a select number of instances in the Bible to show that the contemporary issues and applications are also relevant to the broad sweep of time and space of the stories in the Bible. These examples are not intended to be an exhaustive biblical analysis, but rather to point toward the theme of the concluding section: how can economists and theologians engage in complementary analysis of these human institutions in the light of a divine hope for Christians to participate in making a better world?

Structure and Function of Markets with Implications for Justice and the Poor

This section is structured around a basic analytic model, namely that the essence of the market economy consists of three parts. First, there are meta-market institutions in the society that provide a system of well-defined property rights and likewise provide for relatively costless enforcement of those rights. Second, the market social system allows for the voluntary exchange of that property and of associated forms of voluntary bilateral exchange and contracting for control of that property. Third, what is commonly called a "free market" economy actually has a much broader implication: the freedom to contract to form voluntary associations. Each of these will be addressed, in turn, in this chapter.

Well-Defined Property Rights

The first requirement for a market economy is the existence of well-defined and enforced property rights. Property is not necessarily owned by an individual alone but can also be owned by a partnership, a congregation, and so forth. Similarly, property rights do not need to be defined in reference to an individual alone, although whatever rights exist must be well defined and enforceable for all participants.

What is an example of a wedge between property rights defined in isolation for a single individual (this is "my" house) and property rights defined with reference to multiple individuals? An easy case is that "my" house may actually be held in something called "joint tenancy" with my wife. In addition, consider the case of the common law of rights-of-way. Imagine that Mr. Jones owns land that completely surrounds a parcel of land owned by Mr. Smith. In other words, Mr. Jones's land surrounds that of Mr. Smith like a doughnut surrounds a hole. Mr. Smith would like to be able to access his land by traversing across Mr. Jones's land. In my mind, it makes little difference in the grand scheme of things whether the common law or statutory law says that Mr. Smith does or does not have the aforementioned right-of-way. What is important in my definition is that whichever right society deems to be proper, it must be well-defined, stable and expected, and enforceable (thus the nature of the rights-of-way will be appropriately incorporated into the market prices for the two pieces of land). If Mr. Smith has no right of access without paying Mr. Jones, then I require that it be relatively costless for Mr. Jones to prevent Mr. Smith from trespassing, unless Mr. Jones sells that right to Mr. Smith. Conversely, if the bundle of rights owned by Mr. Smith includes the right to traverse Mr. Jones's land, then I require that it be relatively difficult for Mr. Jones to be able to obstruct Mr. Smith.

Another interesting aspect of property rights is that, in some circumstances, rights to what appears to be the same piece of property can be separated. For example, in some societies the water rights to a piece of land can be traded separately from the land itself. Is one of these two approaches superior? From an economic point of view, there is a presumption, subject to refutation in special circumstances, that the unbundling of rights forms a superior system. But if I could choose, I would rather have a world with my less preferred outcome (no unbundling) than a world in which there was constant jockeying to rearrange property or danger that the enforcement of the property rights would be jeopardized by political intervention.[124] There are numerous Old Testament prohibitions against exactly these dangers: for example, moving land markers (Deuteronomy 19:14; Proverbs 22:28) and the palace intrigues of Ahab and Jezebel designed to defraud Naboth of his vineyard.

A well-known biblical example of this idea of creative but well-documented property rights is seen in the Levitical rules about ownership of land and the so-called Jubilee, which is discussed at greater length below, and which constitutes a central part of chapter four in this volume.

A second part of my definition of the institutions of property rights is the allowance for creative, voluntary institutions of collective ownership, something that I fear some libertarian-minded readers may resist. But I offer this obvious example of how a market-based economy can create a useful model of collective ownership: the equity stock corporation. Who owns the assets of a corporation? Outside of bankruptcy court, the stockholders do; and in laws that vary in the United States depending on the state of incorporation, well-defined rules prescribe how this collective governs issues of ownership as well as control. I was the holder of stock in a corporation whose board of directors (a legally constituted body) recently proposed merging the corporation with another. How was this accomplished? By collective action: a voting process of one share, one vote. My side lost, and I exercised my legal right to exit this collective agreement by selling my shares in the new corporation.

This approach, although coming at the story from a different direction, is nevertheless instructive for the debate of the "held in common" discussion of Acts 4—5 (see chapter four in this volume). Left-leaning Christians never seem to tire of arguing that this passage indicates hostility to the protection of private property. It does nothing of the sort, as the interchange between Peter and Ananias makes clear (Acts 5:3-5). It is also true that, as a human institution, sin was not absent, as the later discussion of a distributional dispute (Acts 6:1)—an example of what economists call "rent-seeking"—makes clear.[125] Rent-seeking is a process of expending resources to influence the purely distributional outcomes of a non-market process. In Acts 6, the dispute is over the division of the charitable resources. Why was it necessary for some in the Christian community to waste time and resources arguing about whether the Greek widows were getting their "fair" share compared to other widows? Was there indeed some ethnic discrimination, or were the Greek-speaking members simply trying to get "more"? I have identified this type of squabbling as an indication of sin. To an economist, rent-seeking behavior in a purely distributional contest is also viewed as wasteful—in other words, poor stewardship.

Having noted the shortcomings of the early (Jerusalem) church's system, I will nevertheless argue below that some market-oriented commentators may be too quick to try to apologize or explain away this institution. The early Christians were attempting to engage in institutional adaption, and they acted voluntarily, which is likewise made abundantly clear in the discussion between Peter and Ananias

(Acts 5:4). As good stewards, the early Christians would need to modify their approach to communal ownership if it failed. And modify it they did. In Acts 6, they modified the process through the creation of the deacons.

A discussion about the modification of property rights must be approached on different levels. One can imagine numerous research papers or dissertations on the subject of "optimal" definitions of property rights. The eastern United States typically defines water rights differently from the western United States. Which definition is superior? According to what criteria? Could a talented graduate student propose a system different from either of them that we could argue was superior to both? Almost certainly, although it is an empirical question whether or not such a newly proposed system would, in fact, be superior to the two existing systems that have been refined for hundreds of years in light of local knowledge and conditions. Either of the current systems can be broadly compatible with the functioning of a market economy as long as the "rules of the game" are well known and enforced. For example, in riparian ("eastern") water rights, owners of land have specific common law rights to the use of water from bordering streams. In this form of water rights, the rights to the water typically cannot be unbundled from the right to the land itself. If this form of water rights is well defined and expected, then property values in the region will reflect the embedded property rights. In my judgment, the biggest difference exists not between these two systems ("eastern" and "western") but rather between them and a society in which water is distributed by whichever local thug marches the biggest army into the valley—only until he is displaced by a rival thug with a bigger army.

Does this mean that any property rights system that exhibits stability—in the sense of existing for a long period of time—also necessarily embodies the second concept that the property rights therein are well-defined? Not at all. A good counter-example is the long-standing poor definition of property rights to onshore underground deposits of oil and natural gas in the United States. Drawing by poor analogy to the "rules of capture" of small animals on British lands, American courts instituted a property rights system that lacks well-defined property rights where the stock of oil or natural gas underground is concerned. The owner of surface mineral rights establishes a property right only to the oil and natural gas produced from a well on his property. This has led to continual problems in over-drilling throughout the history of American petroleum production, with documented losses in economic efficiency. Movie fans among the readers will recognize this as the "I drink your milkshake" issue from *There Will be Blood*, and the problem can be visualized in any of a number of photographs available online, such as the one at the Pasadena *Star News,* depicting oil derricks in the Los Angeles area packed so tightly that "It is no uncommon thing to see three, even four wells on a lot 50 by 150 feet."[126]

Economic analysis illustrates numerous advantages to a system of well-defined property rights:

First, well-defined property rights put a damper on resource-destroying fights over rights to resources. Such fights could be physically violent in some cultures, or they might play out with well-heeled lawyers and lobbyists maneuvering in the corridors of government. Regardless of the manifestation, resources expended simply on taking property rights away from Tweedledum to give to Tweedledee are wasteful, and thus can be viewed as disregarding the biblical mandate to good stewardship (Genesis 1:28).

Secondly, well-defined and stable property rights encourage such activities as investment in capital and durable goods. Why bother to invest in factories, facilities, or equipment that can be stolen as soon as its profitability becomes evident? Why invest in something that will be stolen? Well-defined property rights lead to additional investment in capital and durable goods, spurring economic well-being.

Thirdly, well-defined property rights encourage owners to be good stewards of their property because they can be confident of owning it in the future. One clear illustration of this involves the disastrous results of many open-loan bicycle programs at colleges across the country. In these programs, an organized group buys many bicycles (typically painted a bright color) and simply leaves them around campus for people to borrow and return. The people who borrow the bicycles do not have to be members of the organization that owns them, which divorces usage rights from ownership rights. Because the users of the bikes have no ownership stake in them, the result is often that, after several months, a large portion of the loaned bicycles are trashed beyond repair.[127] Such a program encourages poor stewardship, and stewardship of the world is an inherently positive biblical principle. This is not meant to criticize the motives of those who set up such bicycle-loan programs; but it is an example of the concept of total depravity: even a well-intentioned program organized by well-meaning individuals can end up distorted by the operation of sinfulness.

Finally, well-defined property rights minimize the problems of involuntary benefit or harm to third parties during voluntary transactions. (Economists call these "costs and benefits externalities.") Although extended discussion of solutions to the problem of externalities is of great interest to economists, it is beyond the scope of this chapter.

What do we see about the arguments for well-defined property rights in Scripture? Two of the Ten Commandments directly support the existence of well-defined property rights: the prohibitions against theft and against covetousness. On the other hand, the gleaning requirements (Leviticus 19:9; 23:22) are examples of a well-specified prior constraint on the use of the land by an owner. The owner of a field is directed not to harvest to the very edges or to the bareness of the stalks or vines; that product is to be available to the "poor and for the sojourner."

Indeed, land is a special and complicated case in the Old Testament. There are parts of the story of "the land" that are troublesome, and these are addressed in other chapters of this volume. Upon returning to the Promised Land, the Israelites waged relentless warfare, at the direction of the Lord, to seize control of the land from indigenous populations. However (or perhaps because of this) the Lord was recognized as the ultimate owner of the land, and he made the post-conquest assignments through his prophets by tribe and clan. As hard as it may be for us to come to grips with this land assignment by warfare, it must be noted that the Lord, nonetheless, laid out limits. For instance, the tribe of Dan was condemned for waging unapproved land-acquisition warfare against an illegitimate target (Judges 18).

As Lindsley documents in chapter four, land continued to have a special place in the Old Testament system of property rights. In this largely agrarian society, the Levitical code of the Jubilee served as a type of social safety net.[128] In the Jubilee system, the Lord proclaimed to Moses: "The land shall not be sold in perpetuity, for the land is mine" (Leviticus 25:24). If an Israelite became poor and sold his land, it could be redeemed for the purchase price by a "redeemer" relative or by the man himself if he returned to sufficient means. Furthermore, in the absence of redemption, the land was to be returned to the original owner in the year of Jubilee (in a cycle of seven consecutive periods of seven years, the Jubilee was the fiftieth year). Notice the special status accorded to the land. By contrast, a house inside a walled city could be sold in perpetuity (following a one-year redemption period for the original owner) (Leviticus 25:29).

The Levitical code of the Jubilee ensured that the implications of this special set of property rights were well understood by persons who might engage in what was essentially a sale and purchase of long-term land leases: "You shall pay your neighbor according to the number of years after the jubilee, and he shall sell to you according to the number of years for crops. If the years are many, you shall increase the price, and if the years are few, you shall reduce the price, for it is the number of crops that he is selling to you" (Leviticus 25:15). What was not specified was that the poor person selling the land retained a valuable property right: an option to repurchase. The price presumably would also reflect the retained optional value to the original owner. It is somewhat amusing that modern skeptics of the market who decry derivative and synthetic contracts miss the fact that the text in Leviticus spells out something that resembles a classic "American option" contract.

Bankruptcy laws play a similar and interesting role in contemporary economic times. A declaration of bankruptcy is one way in which it is possible for a freely negotiated contract to be voided. But, by and large, the consequences of bankruptcy for contract negation are understood by contracting parties in our economic system. A consequence of bankruptcy laws is likely to be that people thought to be at risk of bankruptcy are either shut out of contracting or are accommodated at more unfavorable terms. Bankruptcy laws can thus protect or harm the people they are intended to protect. If one puts on the hat of an economist, a similar evaluation could be made regarding the Jubilee provisions prohibiting someone from being able to sell "their" land in perpetuity (of course, the biblical point was that it was not really "their" land). But it is one thing to argue whether or not the Jubilee code of ancient Israel or the bankruptcy code of the contemporary United States creates a utopian ideal or falls short in some economically meaningful ways. It is a different argument instead to show that, if these laws are well defined, they gave the people an expectation that their property rights are stable and ought to be protected from violent attack or confiscation by corrupt police officers, political establishments, or court systems.[129]

Do we not clearly see this point of view expressed by the prophets of the Old Testament? Contrary to what one might hear in some sermons, the prophets are not attacking a system of private property rights. In fact, I assert that the opposite is the case. I believe that the prophets are attacking the violation of the property rights of the poor people of that time. We can see that what they repeatedly condemn is injustice in the court system of the Kingdom Era. "For I know how many are your sins—you who afflict the righteous, who take a bribe, and turn aside the needy in the gate" (Amos 5:12). In chapter eight, Amos likewise condemns dishonest business practices such as perverted weights and measures (Amos 8:5) and, by the language of "[trampling] upon the needy and [bringing] the poor of the land to an end" (Amos 8:4), what can be interpreted as the illegal expropriation of land from the poor. The same chapter likewise condemns the wanton sale of the poor into slavery "even for insignificant debts" (see the interpretive footnote at Amos 2:6).[130]

Having made the case for a system of well-defined and stable property rights, is that all that anyone can say regarding this part of the market system and justice? I think not. A Christian may draw upon moral reasoning from the Scriptures to argue that some well-defined systems of property rights are not just. The most obvious case is that of the abusive chattel slavery in early America in which individuals, by accident of their birth and through no voluntary contractual decisions of their own, did not possess the right to control their own labor. This is an extreme, but very real, example in which stopping our moral reasoning as to what is "just" with merely a statement about well-defined property rights runs the risk of legitimizing any status quo, as long as that status quo satisfies the requirement that property rights be well-defined and individuals are thus able to contract with appropriate expectations that those rights will be preserved.

On the other hand, Christians should, I believe, nevertheless remain careful when entering into overly broad conversations about "just" and "unjust" systems of property rights. If a Christian should conclude that an existing system of property rights violates some external concept of morality, then we suppose that person might resolve to change those property rights. From the perspective of microeconomics, the Christian with such a resolve should first recognize three dangers:

First, attempts to change property rights will very likely introduce a regime of property rights uncertainty, with all of the costs that have been discussed above. For example, suppose that a group of Christians announced that they intended to lobby for an expansion of federal powers to condemn private property for the construction of federal dams. (This is not an absurd or hypothetical example; many Christians supported the New Deal policies of Franklin Roosevelt that did exactly this.) Simply the announcement of such a campaign—even if it did not, in fact, succeed—could, by introducing uncertainty into the integrity of private property rights in that area, lead to the neglect and poor stewardship of the property, as owners would no longer trust that they had the long-term horizon of secure property ownership.

A second caution that a Christian should consider is the fact that a rearrangement of property rights may benefit some people but leave other people worse off; the Christian cannot simply walk away from a consideration of the costs imposed upon others by the process of changing property rights. I am not at all suggesting a biblically-based tyranny of the status quo. In the case of American slavery of Africans, it is easy to side with the perspective of Christian abolitionists that restoring the rights of slaves to their own labor trumped any loss to the slave-holders. But consider instead a more difficult example such as the land in the path of flooding from a government dam. Should Christian supporters of the New Deal have been more concerned about the costs imposed on the people being displaced, particularly noting that many of the people displaced from their land were poor? Isn't the abuse of government power to the detriment of the poor one of the central themes of the condemnations in the book of Amos? It is interesting that as the environmental movement (which counts many Christian supporters) has moved away from Progressive and New Deal policies on construction of dams as an exercise in what used to be called "water conservation," a recognition of the human costs of property expropriation has returned to center stage.[131]

A third danger is that an opening up property rights for redefinition could make the Christian an agent of "rent seeking," through which scarce resources are expended in the resulting scramble to benefit from the reassignment process. Even in the most noble of examples, redefining property rights can require significant direct costs of the process of reassignment. Who cannot help but shudder at the ravages of over 600,000 combat deaths (on top of civilian deaths) in the bloodiest war in American history, the end result of which was to reassign to slaves the property rights to their own labor.

In summary, I am not suggesting that Christians should never support a rearrangement of property rights. But the costs described above are very real, not hypothetical. It would be irresponsible for a Christian to ignore the costs of such an initiative, and is sinful to act without a great deal of humility and dependence upon divine guidance.

Finally, there is a further moral caveat regarding the reassignment of property rights. I believe that a Christian should constantly ask the question: "When does one person's perceived moral imperative for a more 'just' assignment of property rights actually serve as an excuse for simple theft from the moral lens of the Eighth Commandment?" Andrew Jackson successfully voided the property rights of Native Americans in their own land when he forced them to leave the American southeast on the Trail of Tears, but I hope that most Christians recognize that program as little more than simple, reprehensible theft.

In summary, there may be moral arguments about particular systems of property rights that are beyond the economist's ability to evaluate, but that does not make the lessons of economics irrelevant to such a debate. The rearrangement of property rights in productive resources from corrupt regimes in Eastern Europe was one in which economists played central roles in attempting to design reallocation schemes that were as bereft as possible of the dangers of property rights instabilities. There were greater successes in some countries than in others, but it remains a perfectly valid economic exercise, though beyond the scope of this chapter, for economists to evaluate mechanisms for reallocating property rights viewed as unjust, as was the case at the fall of the communist regimes of Eastern Europe in the 1980s.

Freedom of Exchange and Bilateral Contracting

Let us turn now to the second major attribute of a market system: freedom of exchange. It is this attribute that many non-economists may mostly directly associate with the idea of markets, particularly if that exchange is carried out within a monetary system. (Although the fundamental idea to an economist is freedom of exchange, money is a useful social invention that solves the so-called "double coincidence of wants" problem.)

To an economist, the fundamental idea behind freedom of exchange is that voluntary exchange between two people occurs when each believes he will benefit from a transaction. If you have gathered grain and I have a basket of fish, we might exchange some fish for some grain because we each believe the transaction would make us better off. From a strictly biological point of view, the gain is obvious: A balanced diet of both grain and fish will be healthier than a diet of a single commodity. The social implications of that transaction show us that the exchange moved resources to higher value use through the mutual agreement of both parties.

The "money" part of the equation comes in where some of the mutually beneficial exchanges in society may be paired in bilateral exchanges. Suppose the farmer holds wheat, but the fisherman needs to add fruit to his diet; money allows the fisherman to sell his fish for cash to the grain dealer and then use the money to purchase grapes.

The grain-for-fish exchange process described above is typical of what is often taught in undergraduate economics courses as a "pure exchange" economy. Such simplicity does have advantages. An advantage is that it demonstrates that wealth is created even when the stock of goods being exchanged remains unchanged; in other words, *trade itself creates wealth*. Or, in different words, trade takes us out of a zero-sum society. In this case, the exchange of grain for fish allows both people to consume a more balanced and hence healthier diet. That mutual improvement in health represents the wealth that is created from exchange itself. The disadvantage of an example such as this is that stopping our discussion with pure exchange economy examples can lead quickly into the nefarious idea that the earth's resources are in fixed supply, and hence all of economics is about dividing up a fixed set of those goods. This ignores the possibility of exchange creating wealth, not only in the exchange of final goods themselves, but also in two other ways:

First, the farmer and fisherman understand that exchange can improve their diets, and thus have an incentive to become more productive in their activities. This channel illustrates how a market economy is not simply about exchanging a fixed set of goods, but rather about creating a more abundant earth.

The second channel to increased productivity occurs in exchange in the production process itself and the specialization of labor. If Simon is a farmer and Joseph is a carpenter, Simon and Joseph can enter into a mutually beneficial exchange in which Simon obtains farm implements that make his land more productive, and Joseph can obtain new tools to make him a better carpenter, either through multilateral exchange or through money as a medium of exchange. In both of these ways, freedom to exchange moves society out of a zero-sum situation in which one person is wealthy only because another one is poor.

Here the theological and economic paradigms part ways and traverse different paths. The economist says that voluntary exchange is mutually beneficial, as indicated by how much each individual values the goods exchanged. The economist shows that mutual exchange moves resources to their highest value, again as determined by subjective value. Does this mean that all mutually beneficial trades are just? An economist who argues "yes" simply uses a reductionist definition of justice as mutually beneficial exchange, since mutual benefit is a purely private construct in the value systems of the two traders.

Let's suppose that a pastor or theologian understands the economic argument that mutually beneficial trade destroys the "zero-sum society" argument that is too often heard from the pulpit. Nevertheless, the pastor or theologian can bring under the microscope our individual values per se: Money exchanged for sex; diamonds purchased for millions of dollars; tens of millions of dollars paid for the labor of a Hollywood star, an athlete gifted by genetic factors, or a Fortune

500 CEO. One of the ways for an economist to become unpopular at a cocktail party is to defend, upon the basis of mutual benefit, the merchant who sells gasoline for $20 a gallon following a hurricane. Although I am one of those economists who would do so, as a Christian can I really argue that mutual benefit by itself is just? Yes, although to make this argument convincingly (if that is possible at such a cocktail party) requires a discussion beyond the bare bones of mutual benefit. The transaction is beneficial to the person paying the high price, not simply because his valuation of the gasoline has gone up dramatically, but because the valuation of many consumers has gone up dramatically at the same time; and the successful buyer is obtaining a resource that is at a new level of scarcity, as represented by the higher price.

Furthermore, exactly as in the grain and fish example earlier, the higher price serves as a signal for either this seller or others to begin to move more gasoline into the afflicted area and thus to benefit those in the path of the hurricane. While to a non-economist these arguments may seem tortuous, for an economist to argue for an external concept of justice that stands against the principle of mutual benefit is to race headlong towards the slippery slope of "just price" theology, price controls, and all of the bad economics those views entail.

But what about the numerous verses in the Bible that seem to go beyond simply condemning dishonest business practices and directly address our orientation for dealing with the poor? Examples include the Psalms (Psalm 9:18): "The needy shall not always be forgotten, and the hope of the poor shall not perish forever;" Proverbs (Proverbs 22:2): "The rich and poor meet together; the Lord is the maker of them all;" the warnings of Amos (Amos 2:7) against "those who trample the head of the poor into the dust of the earth and turn aside the way of the afflicted;" and, likewise, Amos's forceful warnings (Amos 6) against those who revel in luxurious consumption. And without a doubt these examples include Jesus himself, reading from the scroll of Isaiah in his hometown (Luke 4:18): "The Spirit of the Lord is upon me, because he has anointed me to proclaim good news to the poor."

To me, as both an economist and as a Christian, the way to reconcile these points of view is through the argument that has been made forcefully by Deirdre McCloskey.[132] If a Christian revival swept the country tomorrow and a hundred million people changed their values about their houses, cars, cocktails, clothes, toys, and so forth, the market economy would still function. It would continue to move resources to higher values, but it would also reflect new, biblical values. If anything, the occurrence of such a lightning-stroke change in values would make a well-functioning market system extraordinarily valuable as people reordered their lives. If Joe D. Yuppie no longer values his BMW as a symbol of pride and accomplishment and decides he would rather take the subway to work, somewhere there is someone who would value that car (perhaps now at a significantly reduced price) as an essential aid in providing two adults with transportation to work to support a family.

As extraordinary as it may seem to non-economists, I find that Jesus himself describes a worldview consistent with what I have just proposed. I find one of the most powerful indications of how Jesus viewed markets in the story of the rich young man (or ruler). Now it may (and probably has) appeared to some Christians that this multi-layered story of Jesus's meeting with a rich and godly young man must constitute an attack on the market economy because worldly possessions bar a right approach to the kingdom of God. One of the most important distinctions for studying a biblical view of markets, however, is to distinguish between teachings about how Christians value wealth and possessions as opposed to judgments made on the market process. What does Jesus tell the rich young man in all three versions of the story (Matthew 19:16; Mark 10:17; Luke 18:18)? "Go, sell all that you have and give to the poor and you will have treasure in heaven; and come follow me." Jesus specifically directs the young man to use the market to unload his possessions. Most strikingly, Jesus could have said, but did not say, "Go, give all of your possessions to the poor." What is the difference? To an economist there is all the difference in the world.

Imagine for a moment the rich young man entering a village and going to the household of a poor farmer. "Here," the young man might say, "I am giving you this gold-leafed vase for your expensive spices." Do we expect the poor farmer to say "How lovely, it goes so well with the china and the silverware over in the corner of my mud hut"? No, whatever the farmer might be polite enough to say, he would probably think, "I can barely raise my own grain and afford some oil and salt; I have no use for a gold-covered vase for expensive spices I can never afford." And so it might proceed. The rich young man gives away his possessions haphazardly. Perhaps in some cases the poor person on the receiving end is lucky enough to be a good match. Maybe a household that can afford to support one horse has just watched that horse die, making the gift of a horse most welcome. But how does the rich young man undertake the process of executing a string of such appropriate matches? The answer is that it would be almost humanly impossible to do so, and Jesus recognized this. He instructed the young man to sell his possessions and then give to the poor. Jesus's astute instructions encourage well-being on both sides. Back in Jerusalem, the young man could perhaps auction off his stable of horses. He could find a good mutually beneficial price for his collection of gold-leafed vases. After the entire process, he could then distribute money to the poor, who would use the money as is best for them.

A Further Manifestation of the Freedom of Contract: Voluntary Association

The previous subsection described the freedom of exchange as a paradigmatic example of the market economy. From my perspective, this is fine as an introduction and example, but it has limitations if not viewed in a broader context. To stop here risks supporting the syllogism that the opposite of government coercion in the economic sphere is market exchange, when more correctly the opposite of government coercion is freedom to exchange and contract.

What do we gain from this expanded concept of the market? Freedom of contracting allows for voluntary wealth-creating institutions that do not function as bilateral exchange narrowly defined. This has both process and form implications.

When governments allow individuals the freedom to contract, it also means that individuals are free to experiment with new institutions, taking advantage of local conditions and expertise. Elements of this process can be found in such concepts as Friedrich Hayek's idea of decentralized knowledge, Vernon Smith's concept of ecological rationality, and Elinor Ostrom's models of polycentrism in institutional evolution.[133]

By recognizing the broad nature of voluntary arrangements in a free market economy, we look beyond simple bilateral trade to a wealth of human voluntary contracting institutions. Included in this list would be the limited liability equity corporation, the partnership, the nonprofit (non-equity) corporation (a common arrangement of many congregations), the "club" organization, the foundation, the homeowners' association, and of course the family.[134] By such voluntary associations, Christians created monasteries, universities, denominations, the Salvation Army, and countless hospitals and orphanages. And, at the risk of introducing a topic that cannot be explored fully in this chapter, the "progressive" branch of the social-gospel orientation of the mainline Protestant denominations in the late nineteenth and early twentieth centuries promoted the substitution of coercive government programs for the voluntary associations and institutions that Christians had so carefully created over prior centuries. But that is a topic for another day.

There are a couple important things to notice about these voluntary institutions:

First, the successful functioning of these institutions requires us to rely significantly upon our topic of discussion above: the existence of well defined property rights. In fact, one reason I used the term "freedom of contract" is because virtually all of these institutions rely upon a stable set of well-defined property rights embedded in a low-risk legal system. Investors in a public corporation are promised that they will not be held personally liable for liabilities of the firm in bankruptcy or in tort cases. Residents who purchase a home in a neighborhood with restrictive covenants that prohibit putting a car on blocks in one's front yard rely upon the courts to allow enforcement action against agreement violators. Marriage carries with it a bundle of property rights that vary by state but include communal property, the ability to title with rights of survivorship, expectations of child support in a divorce, and an ordered process of transfer of assets upon death.

Second, focusing on voluntary contracting forces economists to confront some of the most important questions of the so-called "New Institutional Economics." These questions include:

- Why do market systems produce firms, which are not spot markets but operate through hierarchical contractual relationships?

- What are (and what should be) the boundaries between the hierarchy or a firm and its participation in traditional markets?[135] Similar questions about the boundaries between different types of organizations can be a fruitful area of inquiry for nonprofit charitable organizations.

Third, adopting this broader view of the market economy as freedom for voluntary contracts for exchange allows advocates of the free market to become less defensive about the passage in Acts 4-5. The members of the church were voluntarily (that is, with no government coercion whatsoever) selling their property to participate in a collective process of aiding the less fortunate. Yes, without a doubt we see that, like many politically-governed institutions, there existed dangers of what economists call rent seeking (the costly contesting for resources from a non-market allocation), as Greek-speaking and non-Greek-speaking communities disputed whose widows received less than their fair share. The apostles' creation of the order of deacons can be viewed as attempting, with apparent success, to put a halt to this discord (Acts 6:1-7). Likewise, it appears that the ad hoc response in Acts 4 and 5 never became a system, but deacons did become a Christian system that was transferred to the broader Mediterranean community by Paul and the other apostles. Rather than apologizing or attempting to explain away their practice, advocates of free markets and free contracting should say "more power to them." Obviously they did not create a perfect institution at their first attempt; as argued in the opening of this chapter, no such perfection is possible in a world where sin taints all our endeavors. Sinful arguing about whose widows should receive more led to a wonderfully inspired new institution: the order of deacons. How many years was it before the American limited liability company was perfected? If the system relied too much on collective decision making and too little on taking advantage of the incentives of individual decision making, then one may also realize that the Jamestown settlers likewise suffered a bleak existence until they recognized that private land ownership would provide for a more bounteous harvest and a more just distribution of the rewards of effort.[136]

To reiterate, the opposite of government coercion is not simply "the market" but is instead freedom of contracting, exemplified both in bilateral exchange and in voluntary association. To an economist, freedom of exchange and voluntary group action are obvious arenas of human action. Human beings exchange. They produce. But they also join together for group action. Institutions that advance well-being will survive, while those that do not can be modified or abandoned.

Nevertheless, one must be careful along three dimensions in arguing for the moral equivalence between freedom of voluntary association and justice:

The first problem that arises stems from sin. As human institutions are infected with sin, voluntary associations may unjustly affect other parties. Take the homeowners association as an example. I am willing to argue that anyone who voluntarily joins a homeowners association that prohibits putting a car on blocks in the front yard is treated justly if neighbors enforce that agreement. But neighborhood covenants created out of racism have denied Jews, blacks, Latinos, and others from living in particular neighborhoods. Jesus's view of such agreements should not be hard to figure out by referencing his parable of the Good Samaritan.

Second, asserting that voluntary exchange and institutional evolution exemplify wealth creating activities should not be confused with a Panglossian statement that institutional evolution is perfect. Mancur Olson's classic *The Logic of Collective Action* presents a theoretical argument that some wealth-improving institutions may stay unorganized because of the divergence between individual and group incentives.[137] He also lays the groundwork for understanding that group creation may not be wealth creation when the group is formed to seek monopoly rents from the government (again, economists refer to this as "rent seeking"). The work that I have done with many co-authors over the years, most especially with James Walker, shows that individual, voluntary behavior in collective action captures more economic benefits than the most pessimistic economic view of "free riding," but free riding is a real phenomenon nevertheless.[138]

Third, a voluntary association must be truly voluntary both in its form and in its purpose. A voluntary association of residents of a community that steals the property of people of a different race or religion may be voluntary in form, but it is formed for a most involuntary purpose: to violate the Eighth Commandment.

Just as we looked at some snapshots of property rights in the Bible, I will review here some of the biblical illustrations of markets and contracts for voluntary association. I do not intend for this section to compete with a theologian's exhaustive interpretation of references to markets in the Bible, but rather to provide a quick overview—from the perspective of an economist —of the many references to trade markets, buying, selling, prices, voluntary action, and related topics in the Bible in order to provide some examples to serve as a touchstone for developing a biblical understanding of the functioning of markets and the implications for justice

The first use of the terms "buy" and "sell" in the Bible appears to be in Genesis at the end of the story of Abraham (Genesis 23), where Abraham seeks to purchase a burial plot for Sarah. More specifically, the transaction takes place not as a pure barter exchange, but rather for cash. Abraham is a righteous man and rejects his host's offer to receive the plot as a gift. "But if you will, hear me: I give the price of the field. Accept it from me that I may bury my dead there....So the field of Ephron in Machpelah, which was to the east of Mamre, the field with the cave that was in it and all the trees that were in the field, throughout its whole area, was made over to Abraham as a possession in the presence of the Hittites, before all who went in at the gate of his city....The field and the cave that is in it were made over to Abraham as property for a burying place by the Hittites."

Later in Genesis (chapter 25), Esau sells his birthright to Jacob. The medium of exchange in that transaction is not clear, although the birthright may have been traded for bread and lentil stew. A commentary on the transaction explains that the phrase "Thus Esau despised his birthright" was perhaps an indication of a condemnation of Esau's values that led him to make the transaction.[139]

In Genesis 37, Joseph is not only sold into slavery by his brothers in return for silver coins, but he is sold to people involved in long-distance trading ("gum, balm, and myrrh"—Genesis 37:25-28). Although Joseph was sold before the Ten Commandments were revealed, it is clearly depicted as a sinful act (Genesis 42), one that stole Joseph's right to his labor, and of which his brothers later repented. This story illustrates that the right of voluntary action must be voluntarily engaged in by all involved parties in order to operate justly. A voluntary association whose purpose is to enact an unjust act on another is itself unjust. We are also reminded that Joseph's brothers were reunited with him when during a famine in Canaan they received word that grain was for sale in Egypt (Genesis 42).

The Decalogue requires, "Thou shalt not steal," clearly indicating the existence of private property and suggesting that voluntary exchange of property is preferable to theft. By the time the Law of Moses was prescribed, numerous references to the process of buying and selling were given. We can also see the effect of sin in the institutions. Despite the condemnation of the enslavement of Joseph and the provisions of the Eighth Commandment, we can see that slaves were bought and sold anyway (Exodus 21:2, 16). The first passage puts limits on the exploitation of Hebrew slaves; the second prohibits the initiation of slave trading ("Whoever steals a man and sells him, and anyone found in possession of him, shall be put to death").

On a more mundane level, people are clearly referred to as owners of oxen and of houses, again pinpointing private property (Exodus 21:29; 22:8). A market in livestock existed, as we can see from Exodus 21:35, which discusses sharing the price of a live ox. There were obviously credit market s, as the Mosaic law sets out standards regarding interest allowed to be charged to the poor (Exodus 22:25)

The Mosaic commandments for the construction of the Tabernacle (Exodus 35:10) make reference to "skilled craftsmen," indicating specialization of labor beyond a subsistence economy. Exodus 36 indicates that the craftsmen were most likely paid for their work out of *voluntary contributions* raised for the construction of the Tabernacle ("And they [the craftsmen] received from Moses all the contribution that the people of Israel had brought for doing the work on the sanctuary" (Exodus 36:3). One of the craftsmen was Oholiab, "an engraver and designer and embroiderer in blue and purple and scarlet yarns and fine twisted linens" (Exodus 38:23).

In Leviticus the Law of Moses addresses some of what we might call baseline conditions for the security of contracts in trade. "You shall not deal falsely" (Leviticus 19:11b); "The wages of a hired servant shall not remain with you all night until the morning" (Leviticus 19:13b).

There are markets for land, and Leviticus 25 requires sophisticated pricing related to the optional values of the Year of Jubilee. It likewise makes reference to the sale of houses, which, if inside non-Levitical walled cities, were exempt from the Jubilee provisions. In very much this spirit, Naomi was reported to be "selling the parcel of land that belonged to our relative Elimelech" (Ruth 4:3).

As was mentioned earlier, Jesus and the disciples had a common purse of cash. We know from John 4:8 that they used the cash to buy provisions. Jesus's parables are stories that speak to the everyday world of his listeners, and they are full of stories of markets. In Jesus's parables, people buy, sell, and lease land, purchase jewels, hire laborers, and even have opportunities for investment with bankers. Contracts are enforced, in that people who fail to pay debts are imprisoned. But Jesus repeatedly preaches on the values that correspond to the kingdom of heaven. "Do not lay up for yourselves treasures on earth, where moth and rust destroy and where thieves break in and steal, but lay up for yourselves treasures in heaven, where neither moth nor rust destroys and thieves do not break in and steal. For where your treasure is, there your heart will be also."

After Jesus's resurrection and ascension, the new Christian religion, so painstakingly documented by Stark, expanded not just among "the poor" but also through the wealthier middle or "merchant" classes of the Mediterranean world.[140] An obvious biblical example is Lydia, a seller of purple cloth, in Acts 16. Later the patriarch Lactantius would publicly criticize the emperor Diocletian's price-controlling Edict on Prices, arguing that interference in the process of price discovery would lead to "scarcity and...low grade articles."[141]

Concluding Comments

The economist sees well-defined property rights, voluntary exchange, and expanded opportunities for voluntary contracting as institutions for improving the lot of mankind in processes that avoid the zero-sum, winner-take-all outcomes of actions such as warfare, theft, plunder, and so forth.

Is such an easy evaluation forthcoming from a biblical perspective? Without difficulty we see in the Scriptures that there are human institutions that are almost uniformly condemned. Child sacrifice to pagan gods would be an obvious example. On the other hand, there other institutions of human society that form a tapestry of both good and evil. For example, sexual relations are not only a normal part of human existence but play a part in God's divine plan (Genesis 9:1). But from other parts of the Bible (in both the Old and New Testament) a believer will understand that certain manifestations of sex certainly exist (e.g. adultery) which are outside moral bounds. Similar arguments can be made about eating and drinking and even about the human desire to worship: the Bible clearly defines right and wrong ways to approach the Almighty. So it should come as no surprise that the same pattern follows the paradigms of property rights and voluntary contracting. On the other hand, gains in well-being from established property rights and mutually beneficial contracting are a part of the stories of everyday life that the Scriptures take as a given, but they are also prescribed to unfold within certain limits prescribed by God. The economist can see how much good these institutions can do and how much they can improve the lot of mankind. The discussion above shows that the Bible reflects this same dichotomy of usefulness and temptation to sin in markets as in many other human institutions.

After the Fall, man is told to "work the ground." After the Flood, God directs Noah and his sons to be fruitful and multiply—the same charge that he gave in the Garden of Eden before the Fall. The pillars of the market process, property rights, and voluntary action are institutions that have allowed mankind to fulfill God's wishes for humankind. Economics is a discipline that helps us to understand the evolution of property rights, markets, and voluntary institutions, how they work, and under what circumstances these institutions can assist us in the fulfilling the biblical mandates of "working the ground" and "helping the poor." The theologian can help to instruct us on the parallel types of boundaries for these human institutions, just as with regard to the biblical boundaries regarding sex, eating, drinking, and worship. Each is important, and these perspectives call for more cross-disciplinary interaction between economists and theologians.

Putting all of these things together, one sees that, to an economist, there are wonders in studying how markets and freedom of contracting can facilitate the path of human progress, increase material well-being, and reduce poverty. To the Christian, one is reminded that the direct restrictions of the Old Testament and the indirect re-ordering of values in both the Old and the New Testaments teach us that, although useful, markets are not themselves holy but can be fraught with sin. As the Lord told Cain, "Sin is crouching at the door. Its desire is for you, but you must rule over it." In the New Testament, there is a similar sentiment of the coexisting threat of sin and the possibility of goodness, and how we are expected to use our God-given faculties to achieve the latter. This is from Jesus as he sends out the twelve apostles: "Behold, I am sending you out as sheep in the midst of wolves, so be wise as serpents and innocent as doves" (Matthew 10:16).

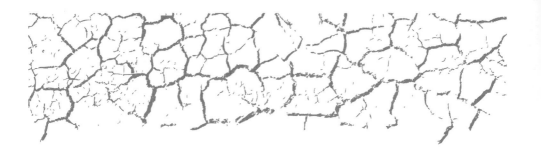

Fighting Poverty through Enterprise

**By Lord Brian Griffiths of Fforestfach,
Ph.D. & Dato Kim Tan, Ph.D.**

A great deal of Christian concern for the poor has involved charitable donations, foreign aid, and mission activity. Much of this has been motivated by the example and teaching of Jesus and has resulted in the relief of poverty. However, in this chapter we contend that there is one important dimension that has been given far too little attention in tackling poverty, namely the role of enterprise and wealth creation. This dimension has a clear biblical foundation, and empirical evidence shows that it works. It enables people to lift themselves out of poverty and lays a sustainable foundation for job creation and growth.

We believe the evidence suggests that foreign aid as the way of reducing global poverty has failed. If poverty is to be reduced in emerging market countries, they need to foster the creation of

Small-Medium-Size Enterprises (SMEs), which will offer opportunities for local entrepreneurs and will, unlike micro-finance enterprises, create permanent jobs for more people. Actively encouraging this offers great opportunities for Christians in business. Public policy should encourage impact investing, and Christians should take a lead in establishing networks of support to encourage local entrepreneurs.

The Nature of Biblical Concern for the Poor

All Christians should agree on one thing, namely that poverty is a scar on God's creation and an affront to human dignity. The first words of the book of Genesis are the ringing declaration, "In the beginning God created the heavens and the earth" (Genesis 1:1). The phrases used to describe creation—"let the water teem with living creatures," "let birds fly above the earth and the expanse of the sky," "let the land produce living creatures according to their kinds: livestock, creatures that move along the ground, and wild animals," "be fruitful and increase in number: fill the earth and subdue it,"—all suggest abundance, profusion, extravagance, even excess. After each stage of creation there is the recurring phrase "and God saw that it was good," and then, at its completion, the statement: "God saw all that he had made and it was very good" (Genesis 1:31). In a poetic comment the Psalmist writes that "the heavens declare the glory of God; the skies proclaim the work of his hands, day after day they pour fourth speech: night after night they display knowledge" (Psalm 19:1-2). Poverty was not what God intended for the world he created. Poverty is an affront to human dignity. Human beings are endowed with infinite dignity and entrusted with the power to exercise stewardship over the created world. Seen in this light, the scar on God's creation that is left by poverty is that much more painful. Poverty is the most extraordinary waste of human potential. People who are constantly hungry, are undernourished, lack clean water, suffer from HIV/AIDS and other diseases, are without work, and have no schooling, will forever struggle to realize their potential as human beings created in the image of God.

Given the huge disparities in the distribution of income and wealth in today's world, we need to remind ourselves that God's gift of creation is a gift to the whole of the human race. It is not just for those individuals and countries that have prospered. It is as much a gift for Africa, Asia, and Latin America as for the U.S. and Europe. Catholic Social Thought expresses this idea well when it speaks of "the universal destination of the earth's goods" or "the common purpose of goods." As the papal encyclical *Centesimus Annus* put it: "God gave the earth to the whole human race for the sustenance of all its members, without excluding or favouring anyone."[142]

The fact that 1% of the world's population earns as much as the bottom 57% combined is an uneasy statistic to live with.[143] This is not to create a guilt trip for first-world Christians. It would be much too simple to argue that the income of the 1% is the result of the exploitation of the bottom 57%. Neither is it to suggest that equality in the distribution of income between nations should be the overriding objective of the economic policies of G20 countries or institutions such as the World Bank. But the present disparity that exists between developing and developed countries in opportunities for education, treatment for disease, access to clean water, and life expectancy is something to which we as Christians can never be resigned. We cannot pray the Lord's Prayer, "thy kingdom come," and then sit back and do nothing about the plight of the poor.

One authentically Christian response is to help those in need. The God of the Bible is a God of infinite compassion who expects each one of his children to show personal compassion to those in need: "whoever is kind to the needy honours God" (Proverbs 14:30), "rescue the weak and the needy" (Psalm 82:4), "when you give a banquet invite the poor, the crippled, the lame, the blind and you will be blessed" (Luke 14:13). In Jesus's depiction of the final judgment, the criteria for separating the sheep from the goats was the response of individual persons to those in need. "For I was hungry and you gave me something to eat, I was thirsty and you gave me something to drink, I was a stranger and you invited me in, I needed clothes and you clothed me, I was sick and you looked after me, I was in prison and you came to visit me" (Matthew 25:35, 36).

The background to Jesus's example was the instruction of the Torah. As is mentioned more thoroughly in chapters one and two, there was an organized system of welfare based on kinship of the extended family, clan, and tribe.[144] The annual gleaning of harvests included provision for the poor to obtain food (Deuteronomy 24:18-22), as did the feast days and temple sacrifices. In the Sabbatical Year the poor were able to obtain food from the unplowed fields (Exodus 23:10, 11). Every three years there was a tithe from the harvest, which was stored as a food bank so that aliens, the fatherless, the widows, and the priests—none of whom had property—would have access to food in times of need.[145]

However, there was also another dimension. The various laws that related to economic life, such as the ban on the payment of interest on loans extended within the Jewish community, the cancelling of debts on the Sabbatical Year, and the restitution of property to their original owners in the Jubilee year, had as their objective that no family should be permanently excluded from having a stake in economic life.[146] The key capital asset in a simple agricultural society was land, and it is instructive that the various economic laws ensured that families, even if they suffered misfortune or mismanaged their affairs, would not be permanently excluded from the wealth creation process.

The Changing Landscape of Global Poverty

The biblical mandate is therefore crystal clear. What of the challenge of poverty today? In 1990, 12 million children across the globe died before the age of five, most from easily preventable diseases.[147] One quarter of the world did not have access to safe drinking water sources.[148] One billion people were illiterate.[149] Almost one quarter of children in developing countries were not even enrolled in primary school.[150] About two billion people lived on less than US$1.25 a day.[151]

Today, the number of people living on less than $1.25 a day has shrunk to about one-and-a-quarter billion.[152] However, the number of people living on just $2 a day has yet to improve, indicating that the development may not be as it seems.[153] Furthermore, the UN indicates that, in terms of the absolute number of people living in slums, the number has grown from 650 million in 1990 to an estimate of 863 million currently, though the share of people living in slums has decreased.[154] After more than fifty years of aid, racking up a bill of $2.3 trillion, there was, until recently, no significant change in Africa's poverty landscape.[155]

For the first time since records on poverty began, there has been a reduction in extreme poverty in all low-income regions of the world, including Sub-Saharan Africa. The U.N.'s Millennium Development Goals Report 2012 estimates that people in extreme poverty living on less than $1.25 per day fell to less than 500 million, half the 1990 rate.[156] During the same period over two billion people gained access to improved drinking water. Between 1981 and 2010, China alone lifted 680 million of its citizens out of extreme poverty.[157] While the overall reduction is encouraging, it is also uneven and has occurred largely because of the economic development in the BRIC's countries.

However, economic development in the BRIC countries has also led to increased inequality within those countries. The gap between rich and poor has widened noticeably in China and India, as have the gaps between urban-rural sectors and the provinces. As a testament to the increased inequality in these countries, tall, gleaming high-rise buildings sit alongside slum dwellings.

The Gini coefficient is a widely used and respected measure of income distribution.[158] A score of zero represents perfect equality, whereas a score of 1 would mean one individual controlled one hundred percent of income. According to World Bank data, South Africa, with a score of 0.631, and Colombia at 0.559, are among the most unequal societies in the world.[159] By contrast, Norway and Germany are two of the most equalitarian countries, with scores of 0.258 and 0.283 respectively.[160] The United States, again in the most recent data by the World Bank, had a Gini coefficient of 0.408.[161] China's Gini score is estimated to be 0.421, and India's is 0.339.[162] On the face of this data, it may appear that inequality in India is lower than in the United States, but the Gini coefficient in India is based on expenditure or consumption instead of income, which is the standard adopted by others.[163] Using comparative data, however, it has been shown that income disparity in India is in fact worse than in China and the USA, but income inequality will be discussed in more detail chapter eight.

So despite some progress in the last twenty years, the overall landscape of global poverty remains bleak, and serious inequality persists between developed and emerging countries and within emerging economies, as indicated by the Gini coefficient. The FAO (Food and Agriculture Organization) estimates that there are still 850 million living in poverty—15% of the world population.[164] About one third of children in Southern Asia were deemed malnourished and underweight in 2010.[165] Further strides in poverty reduction can be made only if economic development continues in all regions, especially in Africa. There have been signs of improvement on the poverty front in Africa, as the continent has seen average GDP growth of 6% per year in recent years.[166] Much of this growth has come from higher commodity prices; nevertheless Rwanda, Ghana, Kenya, Uganda, and South Africa have seen a reduction in poverty due to their economic development.

African countries are also making strides to improve their standing in terms of the ease of doing business. According to the World Bank report *Doing Business*, South Africa and Rwanda now rank higher than Luxembourg, Italy, the Czech Republic, and Greece.[167] Quite an achievement. Given the impressive GDP growth and improved politico-socio stability and corporate governance, a number of these African countries are positioning themselves as destinations for foreign direct investment. Western nations that have framed their relations with Africa in terms of aid and humanitarian assistance will have to change their stereotypical perception of the continent, however uncomfortable that may be. Almost 40% of the raw materials, agriculture, fresh water, and rainforest essential for global growth are in Africa.[168] Additionally, its one billion people are increasingly becoming important consumers.[169]

The emergence of China as a principal partner of many African nations has stimulated a new interest in engagement among Western governments. In the main, China's engagement with Africa has been viewed as a threat to Western interests. China has been labeled as the new colonial master of Africa, yet China's engagement and investment—imperfect as they are—have been largely welcomed by the African nations. Along with investments from South Korea, the Middle East, and Brazil, these emerging nations' engagement with Africa should force the West to think about the mutual benefits of investing in the continent's growing consumer and skills base in addition to its potential raw materials.

Africa has also been viewed as a potential food basket for the world given its land mass and rainfall. Asian and Middle Eastern countries have acquired vast tracts of land for agriculture as part of their food security strategy. These activities, while not without controversy with regard to environmental impact and economic colonialism, nevertheless demonstrate that the continent—famously labeled as the "Hopeless Continent" by *The Economist* a decade ago—is ready for investments and poised for more growth. Labor productivity is rising. Trade between Africa and the rest of the world has increased 200% since 2000. The IMF expects Sub-Saharan Africa's economies to expand by 5.75% in 2014, with some countries seeing 10% growth.[170] All these profound changes have led some to talk about the "Lion Economies," which is analogous to the "Asian Tigers."

The Limited and Marginal Role of Aid

Critics of foreign aid, ranging from Bauer, Easterly, Jenkins, Moyo have highlighted the failure and unintended consequences of aid. Economic data show that, as aid has increased over a ten-year period, the GDP of countries receiving aid has decreased.[171] While aid to Africa increased from 5% to 17% of GDP in the late 1990s, GDP growth actually decreased from 2% to 0%, and even negative growth.[172]

There is no demonstrable relationship between increased foreign aid and poverty reduction in the long run. Research indicates that giving aid does not benefit the individual, nor does it elevate their dignity. Poverty reduction should be relational, as we have seen in previous chapters; but aid is usually given to the government and used for corrupt purposes instead. For further research on the failure of aid in the past few decades, see Bauer and Easterly, two well-known development economics scholars. This research explores factors such as distortion of markets, dependency, inflationary effects of huge capital flows, misaligned incentives, no increase in the tax base, donors' need to be needed, lack of accountability between government and its citizens, and encouragement of the best and brightest in "recipient" countries to work for government or international NGOs.

Many factors contribute to poverty, including conflict, political instability, natural disaster, and diseases. Sierra Leone, Rwanda, Vietnam, and Cambodia have been able to develop economically only after the cessation of violent conflicts. Prolonged drought exacerbated by deforestation has rendered parts of Sub-Saharan Africa uninhabitable; if people of this region resist re-location, they will remain poor regardless of how much humanitarian aid is poured in. In Swaziland, where there are over 69,000 AIDS orphans (aged zero to seventeen years) and 180,000 infected out of a population of one million, poverty cannot be eliminated without tackling the AIDS epidemic.[173]

It is not the intention of this chapter to analyze in detail the failure of aid to alleviate global poverty; this subject has been well documented elsewhere by numerous authors. There will, however, always be a role for aid and philanthropy in meeting humanitarian, short-term crises such as tsunamis, earthquakes, floods, droughts, and violent conflicts. There may also be a role for grants in certain areas, such as public health—including vaccination and immunization—as long as such grants are subject to strict conditions in which the process is transparent and metrics can be easily constructed. But for long-term, sustainable transformation, aid is not the solution.

We have become convinced that business and enterprise is a better way—if not the only way—to achieve long-term, sustainable transformation and poverty reduction in the Low Income Countries

(LICs). As was mentioned in previous chapters, this type of development is also inherently biblical, given the cultural mandate. But from an economic perspective, the evidence that started us thinking this way was the experience of the Asian Tigers —South Korea, Singapore, Taiwan, Malaysia, and Hong Kong. These countries transformed their economies by supporting enterprise and foreign direct investment, not through aid or philanthropy. In recent years, China and India have reformed their economies and lifted millions of their citizens out of poverty—again, through enterprise, not aid. There are numerous examples from the HICs and Asian Tigers that locating a factory in an impoverished area of high unemployment can transform a region more effectively than providing humanitarian aid. Intentionally building a new factory close to a slum, creating jobs and contributing to the local economy through its monthly wage bill, is far more effective in tackling poverty than all the CSR activities that companies can ever do. In fact, according to author John Schneider, twenty-five countries in the last twenty years have virtually eliminated poverty within their borders through enterprise.[174]

SMEs as the Key to Development

We would now like to highlight several key issues that are not often discussed in the context of the causes of structural poverty. The first is the difference in the make-up of the GDP between HICs and LICs. In the HICs, the SME sector contributes more than 51% of the GDP of the country, with 13% coming from the informal sector, the sector of an economy that is not taxed or regulated and does not contribute to GNP. In LICs this is reversed, with the SMEs constituting only 16% of the GDP, while the informal economy is a massive 47%.[175] With such a large informal sector from which no taxes are collected, it is not surprising that governments have to depend on aid and philanthropy to run their essential services, such as healthcare and education. Activities that promote the informal sector in these countries, however well intentioned, will continue to condemn these nations to poverty.

Increasing the tax base is an important part of exiting structural poverty. The only way to enlarge the tax base is through enterprise, creating jobs and increasing corporate and employee tax revenues. Sadly, aid, philanthropy, and even micro-finance, however well intentioned, do not enlarge the tax base but actually propagate the informal sector. The current crisis in the Euro zone is salutary of what happens when governments cannot collect sufficient taxes because of a bloated informal sector, which, in Greece, Spain, and Italy, is greater than 20%.[176] In the Euro zone these countries need a "bail out." In Africa we call it "donor aid." A corollary to this is that, in many LICs, governments do not have a social contract with their citizens. These governments do not depend on tax revenues from their citizens to run their countries. They are outward facing and are more concerned with building relationships with foreign governmental and philanthropic donors than with the views of their own citizens.

Second, it follows from this that the poor will stay poor if they remain in the informal economy, where they have no property rights, no fixed abode with a postal address, no assets, no credit history, and no access to cheap financing. In many LICs, there are no land titles. The link between the lack of land titles, asset ownership, and poverty has been well documented by Hernando de Soto.[177] The poor do not own any assets. They have no capital. To end poverty, we need to transition the poor from the informal to the formal economy. The best way to do this is through businesses that create jobs so that the employee pays taxes and has a social security number. Businesses that can help the poor to build asset-based capital empower them through skills training (intellectual capital) and make them citizens of the formal economy, are what is needed for the LICs to lift their people out of poverty. People will remain poor if they are excluded from the networks within the formal economy that will connect them to trade, access to finance, technology, human capital development, and communications.

Third, while the backbone of the economy in the High Income Countries (HICs) is the SME sector—constituting 51% of GDP—it is only 16% in LICs.[178] This SME sector, the "missing middle," creates the most jobs and is where the entrepreneurial and innovative drive of the country is to be found. Again, activities that do not tackle the "missing middle" by building the SME backbone condemn the country to poverty. To address the "missing middle," various issues, such as energy and transport infrastructures, access to capital, and bank lending practices need to be tackled.

In Africa, businesses looking to expand consistently struggle to get access to capital. The angel and venture capital industry is nascent and under-developed. Bank loans, if available, have high interest rates. One extreme case was in 2009 when the Democratic Republic of the Congo's lending interest rate soared to 65%.[179] However, more typical examples over the last decade are Kenya, where the interest rate has been between 16% and 20%, and Botswana, where the interest rate has been between 11% and 17%.[180] Most businesses cannot afford to borrow at this rate, and in most instances, short-term debt is not the right kind of financing needed for growth. Patient equity capital is what is needed, but this is largely un-available. To really help these countries out of poverty, we need to build the ecosystem so that SMEs can develop and grow. There will be no growth of the middle class without this, and nations will continue to have unbalanced economies skewed towards the informal sector.

Fourth, rural and urban poverty are very different. Even with increasing urbanization, the majority of the global poor are still to be found in rural villages. The plight of the rural poor is different from that of the urban poor. The rural poor have access to land for subsistence farming and wood for fuel. The urban poor in the slums cannot carry out subsistence farming and have to use cash to buy wood or charcoal for fuel. Clearly, rural and urban poverty require different solutions.

Subsistence farming will not lift people out of poverty. Aid agencies and NGOs have actively supported rural villagers to stay on their land to continue with their subsistence farming. This is well-intentioned but flawed. An inefficient way of farming coupled with unpredictable weather changes means that their subsistence is precarious at best and disastrous at worst. In HICs, farming has been mechanized, using technology on consolidated farm land. This has been the only way to make farming viable. Why should it be any different in the LICs? Small-scale farming is simply not viable. This does not mean that the rural poor have to be displaced from their homes as large tracts of land "belonging" to them are consolidated by multinational corporations for agricultural purposes. It is disingenuous to accuse LICs of allowing this to happen because this kind of land consolidation in agriculture is precisely what has taken place in Western countries over the last century.

There is an alternative. Out-grower schemes, or "contract farming," allow the rural poor to stay on their land but binds producers, processors, and traders in a commercial arrangement involving technical and financial assistance, resulting in increased productivity and improved quality. African agriculture is dominated by small farms of less than 7.4 acres (three hectares). Subsistence farming is not the way out of poverty; commercial farming is. For the urban poor in slums and without land to carry out subsistence farming, the solution lies in enterprises that can create jobs.

But there are similarities between the urban and rural poor. Both require fuel for cooking and lighting. The urban poor spend 20-30% of their income on fuel, buying pre-chopped wood, charcoal, and briquettes. The rural poor, through deforestation, collect wood for cooking. Both need a clean-tech solution for their everyday cooking needs. Both urban and rural poor lack access to good education, healthcare, clean water, and sanitation.

Enterprise Priorities for Tackling Poverty

We believe that the focus of alleviation efforts must be shifted to factors that promote enterprise and wealth creation, which are more thoroughly discussed in the next chapter. Good governance, transparency, and political stability are prerequisites for attracting investments into the LICs. These, however, are the preserve of politicians. Progress has been made to improve the competitiveness of the African private sector; witness the improved ranking of Rwanda and Sierra Leone in the World Bank Competitiveness Index.

In our view there are three priorities for tackling poverty in the LICs:

First, the most pressing need of the poor is helping them find jobs that pay them in accordance with their productivity, thus incentivizing hard work. This gives them the dignity and independence they want in order to provide for their families. It is the same as what people in HICs also want. Africa and Asia's numerous SMEs offer the best opportunities for employment creation. They are the backbone of the high-income economies. Access to capital is the major constraint for many of these SMEs. In African countries, bank borrowing rates for SMEs are extremely high because they are perceived to be high-risk loans; for example, Ghana has rates of over 30%.[181] One way to assist this sector would be loan-guarantee schemes to encourage local banks to lend to SMEs, as well as the creation of SME Development Banks. Can part of the international aid budget be allocated to creating and supporting local SME development banks? Organizations like Opportunity International now have a number of such SME banks in Africa, and Fusion Fund provides revolving credit facilities to SMEs in the slums of Nairobi. If we believe that SMEs offer the best way to economic transformation, surely this sector should be targeted by all the donor agencies. Our inner cities have the same problems as the developing world. Grameen Banks, a key institution in community development using microfinance techniques in less developed countries, have opened up in inner-city New York!

A 2011 Gallup survey in twenty-seven African countries showed that one in five Africans between the ages of twenty-five and thirty-five would like to start their own businesses.[182] This is an extremely encouraging trend because, until recently, the dream job for many African MBA graduates has been to work for a large NGO, as they offer the best compensation packages and perks. An environment that encourages startups should include reducing bureaucracy to make it easier to register a business, carry out the import and export of goods, simplify accounting and reporting requirements, and make tax incentives available. In addition to this, an ecosystem to facilitate start-ups is needed.

Incubator and accelerator hubs, government business grants, angel networks, and venture capital providers are all components of this suggested ecosystem. Because start-ups do not usually have strong revenues, they cannot be funded through bank lending. They need patient risk capital, either through government grants or from angels and venture capital sources. Governments should facilitate and incentivize the setting up of this ecosystem so that risk capital can be made available to young entrepreneurs.

A second priority is access to energy. In LICs this is often unreliable and expensive (with the exception of Ethiopia, which boasts the cheapest source of electricity in Africa). This reduces competitiveness and has a negative impact on growth and job creation. Businesses need power. Technologies for small-scale solar, waste-to-energy, hydro, and wind are available and should be implemented. Promoting clean energy technologies can spur new businesses, creating jobs while providing power for new enterprises. Using small waste-to-energy power plants also has the side benefit of clearing up the rubbish that blights many cities and slums. LICs should take advantage of these technologies as an effective step forward.

Third, introduce more competition into the key infrastructure industries to reduce the cost of telecommunications, transportation, and energy. LICs need to be competitive in a globalized world dominated by a number of the Asian economies. Many LICs have government-linked companies that monopolize key industry sectors. These monopolies are not conducive for encouraging new entrants into the market, and this may make companies and countries less competitive. We say "may" because there are instances where government-linked companies can take a longer-term view than private companies and can keep costs low in order to stimulate the economy and give access to the poor. The Asian Tiger economies have done this successfully over several decades.

Impact Investing as a New Asset Class

Impact investments are investments made into companies, organizations, and funds with the objective of generating an economic

195

return that also has measurable social and environmental impacts. They are not philanthropy. They are commercial investments seeking a financial return like any other commercial organization, but without the dominant focus being on the financial pay-off. In emerging markets such investments have helped to create jobs, build affordable homes, provide clean drinking water, improve agricultural productivity, and provide access to better healthcare, education, and financial services.

The supply of capital for these investments comes from a number of different sources. One is private equity funds. Another is high net worth clients of banks—with private wealth management arms—who wish to invest a certain portion of their funds in this new asset class. Another source is family offices that wish to make a contribution to the reduction of poverty in developing countries and are prepared to allocate a certain percentage of their assets in this way. In addition, there are companies that have set up foundations and are looking to invest, in some cases in sectors and geographies with which they are familiar through business. In some countries, such as the UK and Norway, public sector institutions like the Commonwealth Development Corporation and Norfund have been established to provide development finance.

At present this market is relatively small—with around $50 billion of funds raised—and faces considerable inefficiencies.[183] Collaboration is difficult; there are barriers to information flow; there is a lack of businesses with records of successful investing; there is limited institutional infrastructure for the market; and many high net worth individuals and foundations still want to make a sharp distinction between for-profit and not-for-profit activities. For these reasons, impact investors tend to avoid this area. Although impact investments are small at present, some now predict that they will reach $500 billion by 2014, which is roughly 1% of all managed assets. One estimate suggests they could grow to $1 trillion over the next ten years.[184]

One priority in this market is to create innovations that can achieve depth and breadth in a short time. Despite the questions that have been raised recently regarding micro-finance, it has now reached 200 million people, but it took the best part of four decades to achieve this. By contrast, mobile telephony has enjoyed spectacular success. The first commercial mobile cellular services were established in 1979.[185]By 2012, the World Bank noted that the "number of mobile subscriptions... worldwide," had exceeded six billion, "of which nearly 5 billion (are) in developing countries."[186]

In some areas, such as the provision of clean water in slums and the supply of credit in remote villages, local gangs and cartels have prevented expansion. In other areas, however, such as the affordable private education sector, low-cost, environmentally-friendly lighting, and mobile payment systems, there are real success stories. Innovation can touch the lives of hundreds of million people for the better; but in order for it to do so, investors will need to move beyond cherry-picking investments in individual companies to take more risks within certain sectors.

But even if we believe that enterprise is the best way of tackling poverty, can it also address the social issues of human trafficking, HIV, literacy, conservation, global warming, and the environment? With some adjustments to the investment criteria, we believe it can. An experienced entrepreneur can look at social needs and design businesses that can address such needs while achieving a financial return. An enterprise approach to poverty alleviation is taken by building commercially sustainable SMEs that create jobs and empower the poor to improve their livelihoods and address their social and environmental issues.[187] The same principles and accountability as traditional venture capital are used, but they are adjusted for a triple bottom-line return—financial, social, and environmental. This is not an easy form of investment. It requires patient capital, local mentoring, and capacity building. Nevertheless, we believe this asset class resonates with Michael Porter's "shared value" investing and harkens back to the holistic businesses of the Quaker era in what has become known as Quaker Capitalism.[188]

A number of groups, foundations, and funds have been engaged in investing in this new asset class for a number of years, including the Shell Foundation, Omidyar Foundation, LGT, the Calvert Fund, Springhill, and the Transformational Business Network (TBN). An ecosystem for this asset class needs to be created, and tax incentives from Western governments to encourage private individuals to invest in this way could be a catalyst for releasing more private funds into it. Most governments allow tax deductions for donations to charities and transfers to philanthropic foundations and trusts, so why not apply the same tax incentives to impact investing that builds social enterprises among the poor? Club investing, through a circle of friends or through crowd-sourcing, is growing and shows an appetite for this kind of social investing. There are a growing number of social venture capital funds mirroring main stream venture capital and private equity funds in terms of their structure and incentives. Again, tax incentives from Western governments for investors to invest in these social venture capital funds would be a real stimulus.

Finally, there is a need for listed impact companies to demonstrate that exits are possible for impact investments, and to appeal to the ethical retail investors, moving them from a "do-no-harm" to a "do-positive-good" approach to their investments. For impact investing to become a recognized asset class, there needs to be an ecosystem that mirrors the mainstream.

Networks of Support

Businesses can grow only in environments that support entrepreneurial activities, which is important because we know that our individual work can be used together to help the common good. Businesses need lawyers, accountants, and access to various types of capital. But above all they need committed entrepreneurs and talented managers. Both kinds of human capital are lacking in many of the LICs, however. Local talents need to be supplemented with experienced advisors. In HICs, a company needing additional talents would hire the services of a consultancy firm. For a small business in a slum, such services are not usually available; or if they are, they are simply not affordable. This is where the value of outside networks can be invaluable. If a local business in the slum can tap into a network of experienced business people who can provide voluntary technical assistance as well as advice on their business and marketing plans and financing options, these businesses will stand a better chance of success. These business people can provide the advice either as investors or just because they are motivated.

A number of these networks exist. The Ashoka Network is one of the largest. Ashoka fellows are highly talented and motivated individuals who have built successful social enterprises and are engaged in assisting local, social entrepreneurs with building their businesses. Started by Bill Drayton, Ashoka Fellows and Ashoka-supported social entrepreneurs can now be found in over seventy countries. Another such network is the Transformational Business Network. TBN is a network of investors, entrepreneurs, and business people who are disillusioned with writing philanthropic checks, and who invest their time, talent, and money in building enterprises among the poor. Since 2004, the TBN network of 1500 members has invested in over sixty-five projects in fifteen countries, creating more than 20,000 jobs.[189] TBN networks are being formed in several more countries to mobilize local business people to engage in this form of investment. TBN members are also creating various forms of investment vehicles to attract more capital into this type of investment for social venture capital, revolving credit loan funds, fund of funds, and listed holding companies.

Such networks are challenging to build. They are often started by visionaries looking for innovative approaches to tackling poverty through enterprise. They tend to be funded by foundations or private individuals. Perhaps some international aid funding should be targeted at creating local entrepreneurial networks that are connected to global networks such as Ashoka and TBN. Such connections would help build local capacity, provide mentoring, and as is the experience of TBN members, lead to investment opportunities and long-term friendships.

Conclusions

1. Biblical concerns for the poor must include an emphasis on wealth creation led by indigenous entrepreneurs in the SME sectors of LICs.

2. A greater emphasis on free enterprise over the state as the catalyst for development is paying dividends in terms of growth and job creation in LICs.

3. Government-to-government aid will never be the engine driving prosperity in LICs, but still has a limited and marginal role to play.

4. The key to the relief of poverty in LICs is the development of the SME sector.

5. The SME sector needs to be strengthened through better access to capital markets and energy provision. Greater competition in various sectors of the economy is also important.

6. Impact investing, which is neither charity nor straightforward commercial activity, is a key asset class that must be developed and should be supported globally by Christians.

7. Entrepreneurs in LICs need networks of support that offer greater opportunities for entrepreneurs in HICs.

All Scripture quotations, in this chapter are from the HOLY BIBLE, NEW INTERNATIONAL VERSION® NIV® Copyright © 1973, 1978, 1984, 2011 by Biblica, Inc.®. Used by permission. All rights reserved worldwide.

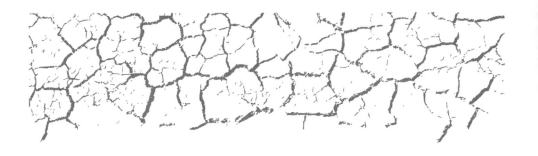

CHAPTER 8

Why Does Income Inequality Exist? An Economic and Biblical Explanation

By Anne Bradley, Ph.D.

Again, it will be like a man going on a journey, who called his servants and entrusted his wealth to them. To one he gave five bags of gold, to another two bags, and to another one bag, each according to his ability. (Matthew 25:14-15)

Each of you should use whatever gift you have received to serve others, as faithful stewards of God's grace in its various forms. If anyone speaks, they should do so as one who speaks the very words of God. If anyone serves, they should do so with the strength God provides, so that in all things God may be praised through Jesus Christ. To him be the glory and the power for ever and ever. Amen. (1 Peter 4:10-11)

There is a lot of talk in today's world about income inequality, and most of that talk casts it in a negative light. Many do not understand the true economic picture or some of the reasons why income inequality exists from a biblical or economic standpoint. This chapter will seek to better define what income inequality is, how it emerges in society, and its impact. Based on that understanding, we can better understand today's income inequality in light of biblical teachings and what our response should be as Christians, particularly in our own vocations.

It is important to note that this chapter does not seek to explore every factor of why income inequality may exist, nor does it seek to defend the status quo. We as Christians are called to seek justice and to care for the poor. We must be at the forefront of this discussion on income inequality—understanding where it is natural, and challenging the status quo where it is unjust. Corruption and injustices that cause poverty must be eradicated. Christians must also be leaders in cultivating and protecting an economic environment that creates opportunity for those in poverty to enjoy upward mobility through the dignity of work.

Part one of this chapter seeks to look at the reasons for income inequality from an economic perspective. Part two will look at some of the natural reasons for income inequality in Scripture.

Income Inequality from an Economic Perspective

Income inequality is a measurement of the distribution of wealth across households. It is a relative comparison of the gap in household incomes across a given region, country, or the world. Income inequality is measured using the "Gini coefficient" and calculates the extent to which the income distribution in a country deviates from perfect equity. A Gini coefficient of zero indicates perfect equality (everyone earns the same income), and a coefficient of one indicates perfect inequality (one person holds all the income and everyone else has zero).[190] Formally measuring income inequality is often used as a benchmark for the welfare of a society or country—the relative poverty or prosperity of a society—and is used as a justification for policy attempts at income redistribution.

Figure 1 presents a graphic representation of countries across the globe, categorized by their Gini coefficient.[191] Finland has relatively low levels of income inequality (in the .25 range) compared to the United States (in the .45 range), but solely based on those numbers it is not obvious which country is "better." Income inequality measurements are simply a way of measuring how income is held, and are not necessarily representative of overall prosperity or flourishing.

In the United States, the Gini coefficient has become slightly less equal, rather than more equal, over time. Figure 2 below highlights this. The United States Gini coefficient in 1967 was .399, and in 2001 it was recorded at .466. So we have become marginally less equal, but the question is: are we worse off? Do we have a lower level of flourishing, and how do the poor fare differently since 1967? We will examine these questions in greater detail as we articulate what goes into the numbers behind inequality.

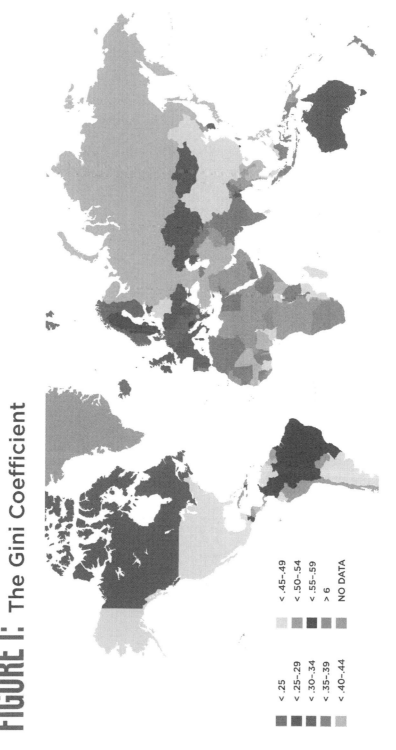

FIGURE I: The Gini Coefficient

Now that we understand what income inequality is, we need to examine why it occurs. Are there fundamental aspects to our economic condition—a world of choice under scarcity—that lead to an unequal distribution of income? Yes, there are, and understanding them is important for knowing what public policy is able or unable to accomplish, as well as what policy should attempt to accomplish from a biblical perspective. Author David Levy, in his paper on income distribution, details the four causes of income inequality listed below: family structure, technology, growing markets, and immigration.[192] To that list we add two more: property rights and income mobility.

Family Structure

The latter half of the twentieth century saw great changes in the labor force. The labor force participation rate rose from 59% in 1948 to 66% in 2005, and participation by women rose from 32% to 59%.[193] The family norm went from two-parent, one-earner families to either low-income, single-parent families or higher-income, two-parent, two-earner families. In the latter cases, the households were making a greater income because a family in the top quintile contains two to three times as many workers.

Technology

Rapid advancements in technology through the latter half of the twentieth century, and which continue today, have shifted labor demand from low-skilled labor toward high-skilled labor. Developments in computer technology have revolutionized cars, cell phones, and healthcare, and the ways we work, shop, read, and even worship. For example, you can follow along in worship using your Bible application on your smartphone.

FIGURE 2: Historical Income Tables - Income Equality

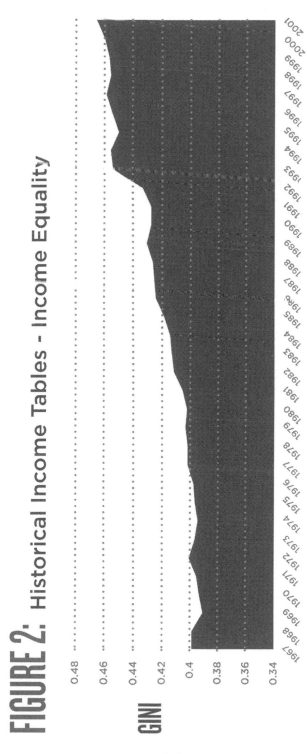

Source: U.S. Census Bureau, Current Population Survey, Annual Demographic Supplements

Technological progress has changed the type of labor needed to support the way we live and work, and it has created jobs where there were previously none. Technology creates the need for specialized workers who can fix cars, iPads, and hospital equipment, and it creates a need for higher-skilled labor. To this end, technological progress is correlated with increasing income inequality.[194] However, that same technology reduces the prices of consumption goods, and this has positive, real impacts on the well-being of the poor.[195]

Growing Markets

Globalized markets break down the boundaries of smaller, local markets and provide new platforms and new audiences for trade. They allow artisans, farmers, and manufacturers to open their products and services to the global economy. This means that these purveyors do not have to rely on small, local markets to make a living, and that others around the globe can have access to their goods. The International Monetary Fund (IMF) finds that the financial openness brought on by globalization increases the returns to human capital (puts a premium on higher skills) and increases income inequality.[196] Their research goes on to say:

> Real per capita incomes have risen across virtually all income and regional groups for even the poorest quintiles. Not only are the poor no worse off (with very few exceptions of post-crisis economies), in most cases the poor are significantly better off, during the most recent phase of globalization. Over the past two decades, income growth has been positive for all quintiles in virtually all regions and all income groups during the recent period of globalization. At the same time, however, income inequality has increased mainly in

middle- and high-income countries and less so in low income countries.[197]

Immigration

Immigration into a country changes the supply of labor, usually low-skilled labor, in that country. As the supply increases, there is a downward pressure put upon wages for low-skilled labor—more people competing for the same low-skilled jobs—and this can increase income inequality. The lowest quintile of income earners has more members. In 2009, 15.5% of the U.S. labor force (24 million workers) was foreign-born.[198] Remember, income inequality is a measure of the gap in income earnings across households. If everything else remained equal, and the lowest quintile got larger due to migrant workers in the U.S., income inequality would increase, although recent research suggests the impact is small (different studies put it between 10% and 5%). [199]

Is this immigration good or bad for the U.S. and for the migrant workers? Lerman, an economist who studies social policy, suggests that the wages of immigrants in the U.S. are much higher than they would have been in their home countries. To get the full picture, we must understand the changing dynamics in the U.S. labor force. In the U.S. there is a rising share of the workforce with some experience, and a declining share of the U.S. workforce without a high-school diploma or GED. Immigrant workers, however, have less education overall, especially those that emigrate from Mexico or Central America.[200] Rather than immigrant workers competing directly with U.S. low-skilled labor, they add less skilled labor to the overall workforce, which results in lower prices on goods and services. This is beneficial to the lowest quintile in that it makes goods and services more accessible than they otherwise would be.

Property Rights

Rights in property affect all of economic life. The security of those rights is crucial for economic growth. Property rights involve rights to maintain, sell, transfer, and modify that which you own. Property rights extend to both tangible objects (houses, cars) and intangible objects (ideas, air, spiritual gifts). Our accumulation of property tends to grow through our lifetime. When we are young we do not own much, aside from what our parents give us and what we are endowed with by God. As we get older, we acquire property through the fruits of our labor; we buy a home, start a business, and invest our capital in a variety of ways. By definition, we will all acquire different levels of income and capital based on how we invest our resources (talents, spiritual gifts, skills, and abilities), and some of those investments will have higher payoffs than others. Why is this? In a world of scarcity we must make choices about what to do with our time, what to consume, and what to save for later.

Because of this scarcity, the vast resources that God has put on this earth have multiple and competing ends. For example, when you choose a profession, you probably have a variety of options based on your comparative advantage. If you are interested in the medical field, you could be a nurse, doctor, or physician's assistant. Because your time is scarce, you cannot be all three or even two of these. You may have the ability to be a doctor but choose to be a nurse. Perhaps you do not want to spend ten years in training. There are many reasons you could choose to be a nurse instead. Because being a doctor is a much more specialized skill, it commands a higher payoff. Over his or her lifetime, the doctor may acquire greater property because doctors command a higher income.

This does not make doctors more or less valuable in God's eyes. It strictly means the nurse will likely earn a smaller income, but a measure of their overall wealth might show something much different. It is important to make the distinction between income and wealth; they are not the same. Income is compensation for work, investments, or government transfers. Wealth is the ownership of assets that produce income streams. Prosperity is related but different from either and has to do with the overall concept of flourishing, which extends beyond both income and wealth. Because we are all born with different gifts and created individually, we will all have different earthly income levels, which means income inequality will always exist on some level. Property rights are crucial for economic growth in a world of scarcity, and they are based on biblical truth. Theologian Walter Kaiser suggests that this comes first and foremost from the commandment "Thou shalt not steal" in Exodus 20:15. Kaiser goes on to say that, not only does this command recognize individual ownership, it regards as criminal all attempts to take that property from a person in a fraudulent way.[201]

Income Mobility

Another facet of economic life and market exchange that must be considered is dynamism. Markets for goods and services are not static; they are always moving and changing, ultimately based on the desires and preferences of those doing the purchasing. We greatly misunderstand the notion of income inequality if we do not understand income mobility.

In researching the topic over fifty years ago, Nobel laureate economist Simon Kuznets suggested that the distinction between "low" and "high" income classes loses its meaning if the people within those groupings have changed over time.[202] Remember that the Gini coefficient of one indicates that one person has all the income and everyone else has zero. While we do not observe this in reality, we hear talk about the rich getting more income at the expense of the poor. If that is true, it is also an undesirable situation. It assumes a zero-sum game. If I win, it's because you lose. Economies based on voluntary exchange are not zero-sum. If I trade some portion of my income for a winter coat, I benefit by freely giving up some of my income to gain extra warmth in the winter months.

If I work harder, become more innovative, and earn a greater income through hard work and discipline, I benefit without harming anyone. In fact, the opposite occurs; I benefit through a higher income if and only if I serve others. As a coat manufacturer I must serve my customers well if I expect them to purchase my product. If I succeed in this venture, I will earn a higher income, which means I have moved out of one income quintile and into another. This is called income mobility and is critical for getting a full picture of what income inequality truly implies.

Go back to our Gini-coefficient-of-one situation. If one person holds all the income and everyone else has zero, it's not just a bad situation because the needs of everyone else go unmet; it's a bad situation because there is no obvious way for those who have zero to gain income. In a market economy, most people start out at a lower income bracket. They enter the labor market with few skills and little experience. As they progress in their work, they gain both. As they gain skills, knowledge, experience, and awareness of what they are good at, they earn more income over time.

Solely looking at income inequality levels from one decade to the next does not tell us anything about who is in those income brackets. Those people who were in the lowest quintile in 1990 are probably not in the lowest quintile in 2000 or 2010 because, with the passage of time, those people who started at the bottom have theoretically gained skills, experience, and knowledge to be better at what they do. And there is evidence to support this theory. A 2008 report by the U.S. Treasury on income mobility found that between 1996 and 2005, more than half of all U.S. taxpayers moved into a higher income quintile. Roughly half who started in the lowest quintile in 1996 had moved into a higher quintile by 2005, in only nine years. For the highest income earners the results were not the same:

> Among those with the very highest incomes in 1996—the top 1/100 of 1 percent—only 25 percent remained in this group in 2005. Moreover, the median real income of these taxpayers declined over this period.

Additional research supports this data. A 2010 report by the St. Louis Federal Reserve economist Thomas Garrett suggests that it is much more likely for a person in the highest one, five, and ten income percentiles to move to a lower group than it is for a person in the lowest income brackets to remain where they are or move down.[203] The data is presented graphically in Figures 3 and 4 below.

FIGURE 3: Movement to Higher Income Quintiles, 1996-2005

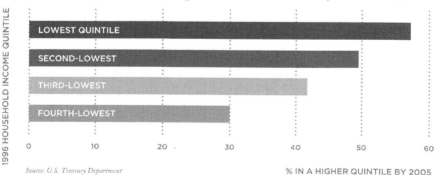

Source: U.S. Treasury Department

% IN A HIGHER QUINTILE BY 2005

FIGURE 4: Movement to Lower Income Group, 1996-2005

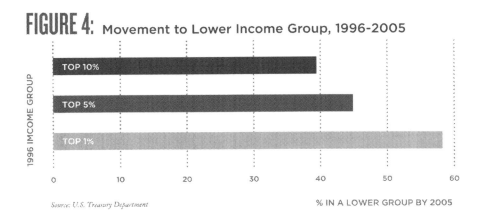

Source: U.S. Treasury Department

% IN A LOWER GROUP BY 2005

The report also found that the levels of income mobility described above were unchanged from the former decade (1987-1996),[204] meaning that income mobility is neither new nor particular to this time period.

The Problem of Measurement

Our attempts to understand the economic implications of income inequality and the basic facts of economic life reveal that some level of income inequality is inevitable. In other words, we will not all make the same income, and this is a fact of economic life. Efforts to lessen income inequality run counter to the way we are created—to the human condition itself.

To truly understand income inequality, we must understand the nuance in how it is measured. Measuring inequality is a complex task, and getting the measurement correct has important ramifications for policy responses. For if income inequality is shown to be on the rise, as has been reported in recent years, a common response is to legislate policy that will redistribute that income so as to lessen the inequality.

Estimates of rising inequality are often based on federal income tax returns. Those income tax returns appear to show that the share of U.S. income going to the top one percent has increased substantially since the 1970s.[205] This has received a great deal of press in the last few years and is a point of protest for the "Occupy Wall Street" movement. Before proceeding to the measurement problems that plague inequality data, however, it is important to note that, in a dynamic economy, "share of income" is a mental construct.

There is no preexisting pot of income that gets divided by some person or agency based on who did what. Income is created by the voluntary exchange of individuals through the buying and selling of goods and services. Profit is a reward for meeting consumer demand; loss is a penalty for not meeting consumer demand. Not even a government can create income, because it doesn't buy and sell its services through voluntary exchange. To raise "income," it must coercively tax or inflate (print money). Rather than say "income going to the top one percent," it is better to say "income earned by the top one percent." Anyone who seeks and gets preferential support from the government through subsidies, favors, or tariffs is not earning that income through voluntary exchange. Rather, they curry protection at the expense of some other business or a competitor.

There are significant issues that make understanding the real level of income inequality difficult. We mentioned that most claims about income inequality rely on data that suggests that it has increased substantially since the 1970s. Recent research by economist Alan Reynolds can provide a greater understanding as to why this is so.

Changes in U.S. Tax Rules

Since 1980, there have been several significant changes to the U.S. tax rules that change how income is reported. There were sharp reductions in individual income tax rates in both 1981 and 1986. As a result, corporate executives switched from accepting stock options taxed as capital gains to nonqualified stock options reported and taxed as salaries. Thus, the tax change caused a shift in the reporting of income from corporate to personal, making it appear as if income inequality increased. In those specific years, all that occurred was that income changed categories. The Tax Reform Act of 1986 caused the top marginal tax rate to go from 50% in 1986, to 37.5% in 1987, to 28% in 1988, which means that corporate executives reported more income on their tax returns. This shifting between corporate and individual tax reporting has accounted for more than half of the increase in the top 1% income share since 1986.[206]

Changes in Investment Income

Prior to 1980, most income from investments was reported on individual tax returns. Since then, an increasingly large share of middle-income investment returns have been sheltered inside 401(k)s, IRAs, and 529 college savings plans. These investments are not reported on tax returns and are largely used by the middle-income groups.[207] This trend makes it look like the middle-income earners have less, when in fact some portion of their income is protected from taxation, so they are actually better off.

How We Define Income

The data cited by Piketty and Saez in their 2003 study documents the most egregious increase in income inequality and is most often used in the rhetoric around income inequality. Their data suggest that the top 1% of Americans "receive" 15% of all income, and that this is up from 8% in the 1960s and 1970s. However, their data does not account for transfer payments. [208]

A transfer payment is a one-way exchange by the government to a favored class of persons and is a form of wealth redistribution. Examples include Social Security, welfare payments, and farm subsidies. In 2000, there were $1.07 trillion in federal transfers. About 29%, or $312 billion, was means tested (earmarked for the poor),[209] which represents an increase in income. If this is not reflected in the data, it exacerbates the level of income inequality. The other 71% of that money was given out without regard to need. Even if all of it was given to the poor, there would be no visible change in income inequality if those transfers were not reflected in their incomes. This raises the question of whether those transfer payments help meet the needs of the poor, a subject that will be taken up in another chapter.

U.S. Trends in Income Inequality

The Congressional Budget Office (CBO) reports that from 1979 to 2007, real (inflation-adjusted) average household income grew by 62 percent.[210] This means that the average household experienced economic growth; they benefitted from growing income that moved them into different income quintiles than they were before. During that time, the report suggests that different income quintiles experienced different rates of growth in income, as seen in Figure 5 below. Those in the highest 20% of the population, the highest quintile, experienced income growth of 65% over that period. For those in the middle income quintiles (21st through the 80th percentiles), the growth was around 40%. For the lowest quintile, the growth was 18%.[211] It is especially important to understand that these numbers are dynamic, not static.

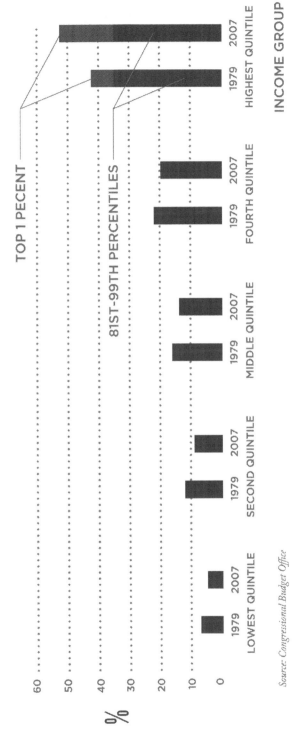

FIGURE 5: Shares of Income After Transfers and Federal Taxes, 1979 and 2007

Source: Congressional Budget Office

Remember the first data point cited: average income across all quintiles grew by 62%. Most people are quantitatively better off than they were in 1979. Secondly, even though the rate of growth across quintiles is not the same, all quintiles experienced growth. This has a critical implication: most of those who were in the bottom quintile in 1979 were in a higher income quintile by 2007. The 2007 numbers represent a new set of people. People who were born in 1979 and made no income were twenty-eight years old in 2007, and when they are forty-eight years old they will most likely be in a higher income quintile than they are now. If this data actually followed individuals from one year to another, then we would have a sense of the migration from one income quintile to the next. This would give us a more accurate measure of individual well-being.[212]

A society characterized by economic freedom and prosperity is one that provides opportunities for individuals to lift themselves into higher income quintiles. How is that accomplished? Value is created through exchange. That is what most of those in the highest income quintiles have done. Unless we all make an equal income, we will always be able to divide people into income quintiles. What matters is not so much how wide the gap is, but the ability to move from one quintile to the next, and the relative prosperity of those in the bottom quintiles.

Another way to measure this is consumption equality. What can the U.S. poor, those in the lowest income quintiles, afford to purchase? The poor in the U.S. are defined as those households with incomes below the official poverty thresholds. In 2011, the poverty threshold for a family of four was $22,350.[213] According to the Department of Energy RECS study in 2005, 99.6% of the poor have a refrigerator, 97.7% have one television, 32% have more than two televisions, 97.7% have a stove and oven, 81% have a microwave, 78% have air conditioning, 63.7% have cable or satellite television, and 70.6% have at least one VCR.[214]

This is not to say that there are none in the lowest quintile who aren't destitute, or that the poor don't have difficulty paying for these things. The issue is the relative prosperity of those among income quintiles and their ability to move out of that quintile, rather than the absolute earnings across quintiles.

The U.S. poor fare much better in terms of consumption equality than the poor in other countries. The World Bank reports that in 2005, 1.4 billion people in developing countries lived on less than $1.25 per day. Not coincidentally, this is down from 1.9 billion in 1981, and the developing world is on track to halve poverty from its 1990 levels by 2015. [215] Free-market exchange, supported by well-defined private property rights protected under the rule of law, is the only empirically-tested way to make this happen.

The relative prosperity and consumption ability among both the U.S. rich and poor is a new phenomenon. Most of human history has been an experience in mere survival. Now the poor and rich benefit from indoor plumbing and home refrigeration, among countless other innovations that make life easier across all income quintiles.

Income Inequality from a Biblical Perspective

Income inequality, as described above, is a fact of economic life. Different people are born with different gifts and choose to pursue them differently. Those gifts carry unequal earthly rewards, one of which is in the form of monetary income. The market is an earthly construct that can dole out only earthly rewards. In other words, the market will not reward you in the eternal realm for curing cancer. It will reward you monetarily for curing cancer, and the lure of that monetary reward is an important motivator to innovate.

The market rewards contributions to consumer demand through profit. The market punishes those who do not successfully satisfy consumer demand through losses. Profits and losses serve as signaling devices that are critical feedback mechanisms. They alter behavior. They serve as incentives for creativity and innovation.

The looming question is whether this economic reality is necessarily unbiblical or, instead, is biblical and pleasing to God. In the scope of this chapter, we will examine the biblical indicators that suggest that an existence of income inequality is not necessarily unjust or unnatural. To best understand this, we need to go to the Scriptures on two fundamental points: the distribution of gifts and abilities, and examples of God's earthly rewards for stewardship within the context of market exchange. Outside of market activity, God can and does reward the stewardship of our gifts and abilities in alternative ways. It is important to remember that income is derived from market activity; it is one way Christians are rewarded for use of their gifts, but not the only way. Dr. Kaiser highlights the Proverbs, which tell us that possessions or property can be gained by industriousness (Proverbs 13:4; 14:23), wisdom (Proverbs 3:16; 24:3), or the development of insight (Proverbs 14:15).[216]

There are two possible scenarios:

1. We are all equally loved by God and also created with the same gifts, and thus he will reward us equally on earth.
2. We are all equally loved by God and created with different gifts, and thus we should all be rewarded differently on earth.

Scripture is clear on the first part: we are all equally loved by God, we are all created in his image, and he wants fellowship with all of us, even though he knows some will not choose this. John 3:16 tells us that

"God so loved the *world*" that he sent his Son as a sacrifice. The term *world* is all-inclusive; he loves everyone equally and universally.

Diversity of Gifts

Understanding why income inequality exists requires an understanding of how we are created. Scripture tells us that we are created in God's image (Genesis 1:26-27), and that implies uniqueness. God is unique—there is only one God. Man, too, is unique both physically and spiritually. Each person on this earth has a unique genetic code, or DNA, that distinguishes us. From that code we each have a unique voice, fingerprint, personality, etc., all of which makes us matchless. In addition to our specific genetic proclivities, we are all created with unique sets of spiritual gifts. Tim Tebow was created uniquely as a quarterback, just as Billy Graham was created uniquely as a public evangelist. They both can, and arguably have, furthered the kingdom of God through their very different gifts and their different application of those gifts. It is not the gifts that matter as much as how we apply them to this life.

Economists refer to this uniqueness as the law of comparative advantage. If one individual or company can produce a good or service at a lower marginal and opportunity cost, then they are better off specializing in the production of that good/service and trading with others. This is a relative comparison of skills across individuals or companies.

There may be good reason why you choose to take your suit to the dry-cleaners rather than pressing it at home. It takes a specific skill and specialized machines to press a suit or shirt. You might be able to get something clean by doing it at home, but it would take time. That time may be better dedicated to making dinner or being with family or washing the floors. A similar calculation is made by the dry-cleaning business. They don't make their own hangers, even though hangers are a critical part of a successful dry-cleaning business.

Why? It takes specific skill and specialized machines to make wire hangers. The dry-cleaners could try, but they would spend all day doing it, and the hangers would not be nearly as good as the hangers they purchase from businesses who specialize in hangers.

Specialization frees up our time to focus in on using our gifts productively, and that freed time is an opportunity to further the kingdom of God. The wife who sends out her dry-cleaning rather than attempting to spend fruitless hours on it herself frees herself for kingdom-building work. That kingdom-building work could be more time spent with her children and her husband, volunteer work, personal devotion, and countless other things.

All of this comes down to the fact that each individual is born with unique skills and abilities. Our work on earth, pursued with a true understanding of how God has called us to use our gifts— our purpose—can further his kingdom. And that can occur through owning a dry-cleaning business, playing professional football, being a professional evangelist, and countless other vocations, even though those gifts can and do bring different earthly rewards. Tim Tebow has a net worth of $3 million, and Billy Graham's is recorded at $25 million.[217] Those dollars reflect the market return to their comparative advantage. The market rewards and punishes in dollars.

Heavenly rewards will be manifested much differently than in the market. One of the reasons for this is scarcity. Markets are an earthly construct—given to us by God—that allocate scarce resources most productively. Scarcity is a result of the Fall. All of our choices now represent tradeoffs. Those scarce resources have multiple and competing ends. Markets help resolve to what ends we allocate our scarce resources by bringing together the most willing demanders with the most willing suppliers. As a result, everyone is better off than they would be without this resource allocation mechanism.

Heaven will not be characterized by the scarcity we know today, the scarcity of a fallen world.

Returning to our two possible scenarios, Scripture supports the second: *We are all equally loved by God and created with different gifts, and thus we should all be rewarded differently on earth.*

If this is true, then income inequality is an economic reality manifested from the biblical principle of uniqueness. We are created differently, and some of us will earn higher incomes than others. Income is not the only earthly reward, either. It's just the only reward bestowed by the market. Scripture is clear that some will earn more earthly rewards for efficient stewardship over the resources with which we are endowed.

Diversity of Gifts Allows Specialization

It's not just what we are endowed with; it's how we use what we have been given. What we are given refers to abilities, gifts, and talents. As we are all created in God's image, we are all given different degrees, types, and combinations of talents. It is this specific combination that allows Tim Tebow to pursue professional football rather than some other vocation.

I Corinthians 12:4-11, in reference to spiritual gifts, says:

> There are different kinds of gifts, but the same Spirit distributes them. There are different kinds of service, but the same Lord. There are different kinds of working, but in all of them and in everyone it is the same God at work. Now to each one the

manifestation of the Spirit is given for the common good. To one there is given through the Spirit a message of wisdom, to another a message of knowledge by means of the same Spirit, to another faith by the same Spirit, to another gifts of healing by that one Spirit, to another miraculous powers, to another prophecy, to another distinguishing between spirits, to another speaking in different kinds of tongues, and to still another the interpretation of tongues. All these are the work of one and the same Spirit, and he distributes them to each one, just as he determines.

Verses 4-6 are of particular importance in the context of income inequality. Paul writes that the gifts are different, the service of those gifts is different, and there are different types of working (the gifts manifest themselves in entirely different ways), but in all of them God is at work for the common good. God bestows different gifts upon each of his unique children, and we have different propensities in how we apply those gifts (i.e., different levels of perseverance), but it is all for the common good. So we are unequal, and that inborn inequality serves to make us all better off. How so? Because it releases us from trying to become perfect in all things, thus we can focus on our gifts and make positive contributions to the world.

If I had to possess all of the gifts in a fallen world, I could never accomplish anything. The market is a God-given construct, a methodology for exercising our gifts; and through our unique contributions, whether they are through the church (Billy Graham), the business world, or motherhood, we can make a contribution to the common good.

Diversity in Abilities

There is empirical evidence that reveals that a diversity in abilities and effort leads to a diversity in income. Markets and private property have lifted millions out of abject poverty. Private enterprise is an effective way to contribute to the common good of mankind. There is more scriptural evidence for income disparity based on diverse abilities found in the parable of the talents from Matthew 25:14-30:

> Again, it will be like a man going on a journey, who called his servants and entrusted his wealth to them. To one he gave five bags of gold, to another two bags, and to another one bag, each according to his ability. Then he went on his journey. The man who had received five bags of gold went at once and put his money to work and gained five bags more. So also, the one with two bags of gold gained two more. But the man who had received one bag went off, dug a hole in the ground and hid his master's money.
>
> After a long time the master of those servants returned and settled accounts with them. The man who had received five bags of gold brought the other five. 'Master,' he said, 'you entrusted me with five bags of gold. See, I have gained five more.' His master replied, 'Well done, good and faithful servant! You have been faithful with a few things; I will put you in charge of many things. Come and share your master's happiness!' The man with two bags of gold also came. 'Master,' he said, 'you entrusted me with two bags of gold; see, I have gained two more.' His master replied, 'Well done, good and faithful servant! You have been faithful with a few things; I will put you in charge of many things. Come and share your

master's happiness!' Then the man who had received one bag of gold came. 'Master,' he said, 'I knew that you are a hard man, harvesting where you have not sown and gathering where you have not scattered seed. So I was afraid and went out and hid your gold in the ground. See, here is what belongs to you.' His master replied, 'You wicked, lazy servant! So you knew that I harvest where I have not sown and gather where I have not scattered seed? Well then, you should have put my money on deposit with the bankers, so that when I returned I would have received it back with interest. So take the bag of gold from him and give it to the one who has ten bags.' For whoever has will be given more, and they will have an abundance. Whoever does not have, even what they have will be taken from them. And throw that worthless servant outside, into the darkness, where there will be weeping and gnashing of teeth.

It is important to note that, although it's a parable, it is neither arbitrary nor capricious. The story and its components are intentional and convey a specific message that can further a biblical perspective on income inequality.

There are several key aspects of the parable that require further exploration. Verse 15 says that each servant was given a different amount, each *according to his ability*. The master, as an "employer" (it is not clear whether they are slave or free, but we can assume that he knew them well enough to understand their different abilities and talents), divided the bags of gold unequally because he knew that each man had a different level of ability to use that gold productively.

This is consistent with both how we are created by God (not all of us have the ability to become neurosurgeons, professional football players, or leaders of Fortune 500 companies) and how we are hired and rewarded in the workplace.

The scarcity we endure as a repercussion of the Fall results in our inability to be perfect in all things and sets in place a life bound by trade-offs. Trade-offs represent constraints. I am not unbound; if I invest my time going to school to be a neurosurgeon, I am, by definition, not doing something else. This means we cannot have absolute advantage in all things, but we can have comparative advantage across some things. The master understood this and awarded the talents according to his understanding of his servants' comparative advantage.

The two servants who attempted to use their gold productively, i.e., tried to invest it to gain a return on behalf of their master, both earned 100%. Verses 16-17 give us the details. The servant who received five bags "went at once and put his money to work," and he earned five more. The servant who received two bags earned two more. Interestingly, we are given no details on what *type* of work they did to invest the master's money. There is no reason to assume it was the same work, especially in light of our understanding of comparative advantage. If they each had the same skills, they may have been given the same amount and perhaps invested the money the same way. But the Scripture is clear that they did not have the same skills; so there is no reason to assume they engaged in the same work to invest the money. They each invested the money diligently according to their abilities and earned 100%. The dollar amounts they earned were different, but they both doubled what they were given.

This is the message of the parable: diligently apply the gifts God has given you, and you will be rewarded fully. Those earthly rewards will have different dollar amounts attached to them, but that is not what matters. Obediently applying the gifts you have been given is the call of Christ. In fact, obediently applying the gifts you have been given may carry no earthly financial reward. Motherhood is the best example of this. There is no pecuniary gain, but there are many non-pecuniary rewards that make it worth doing.

The servant who buried his bag of gold had a zero rate of return and was punished by the master. He was asked to give that bag to the one who had ten bags. The master started with eight talents. Had each servant put their allocation of gold to the best possible use given their abilities, the master would have doubled his gold and ended up with sixteen bags. Instead, he ended up with fifteen bags. We can surmise from this that the master was wise to give only one bag to the last servant. Had he given the last servant five bags, he would have had a net loss of five; instead he had a net loss of one. By giving each servant an unequal amount, the master was being obedient and faithful with the resources he owned. Had he given each man an equal amount, putting equality over ability, he would have squandered his resources. By putting servants in charge of his resources according to their skills and diligence, he created more than he would have had otherwise.

We might ask why the master didn't give all the bags of gold to the most productive servant. Why not give him all eight talents? Wouldn't he be guaranteed to earn sixteen bags of gold and double his money? Not necessarily. Diminishing returns to labor apply to everyone and occur at different rates, so we don't know when that might have happened had the first servant been given all the bags of gold. But perhaps this was done because by giving to each person in the manner that the master did, he was able to provide them all with the opportunity to earn more and still double his investment. This message applies to how we are created. Not one person has all the talents or bags of gold. God spreads out talent throughout the universe, uniquely.

Opportunity is an important lesson here. God gives us unequal talents, and we need the opportunity to put them to productive use.

The rest is up to us. We can choose how we will steward the gifts and resources with which we are gifted. There will be both earthly and eternal consequences for how we steward our gifts. The talents referred to in this parable are a metaphor for the skills and abilities that God has given us in addition to any earthly income we earn through our work. The rewards can be and often are financial, but they are more than that. These gifts, if pursued with excellence and purpose, allow us to further the kingdom of God by creating other opportunities for others through our work.

Markets force sellers to serve buyers. Not all the demands of buyers are free from sin, i.e. markets produce pornography. As Christians, we would argue that pornography is sinful and should be avoided. But the question to be asked is what resource allocation mechanism can unleash our creativity and relish the human dignity with which we were created? Markets are not perfect, but they embrace God's creation and provide better opportunities for human flourishing than any other resource allocation mechanism ever tested.

Implications for Work

If income inequality is a fact of economic life that derives from the uniqueness in which we are created by God, how then should we work? Do we pursue opportunities that have the highest salary attached? There is no scriptural support for pursuing the job that carries the highest salary. Rather, Scripture calls us to seek our true comparative advantage and pursue it with excellence. Some are called to be innovators who are top income earners, and some are called to pursue manufacturing or farming vocations that pay less. All of these professions allow us to further God's kingdom by putting our unique gifts toward productive work. Our gifts allow us to create something that did not previously exist.

Market economies reward value-creation. Markets are made up of millions of people who, through exchange, make each other better off. God has given us the market mechanism as an efficient allocator of resources precisely because we cannot be perfected in all things.

The farmer, who grows soybeans and sells to others, frees those of us who do not have the capabilities to grow soybeans to purchase them and devote our newly freed time to activities in which we have a greater propensity to create value. That is part of how the farmer serves his customers. The only people who are rewarded in markets are those who effectively and, at the lowest relative cost, serve the needs of others.

It is important to make the distinction between free-market exchange and rent-seeking (cronyism). The farmer who grows soybeans, innovates, and keeps costs down will be rewarded through profit by the market. The farmer who grows soybeans and lobbies the federal government for subsidies that protect him from more productive soybean farmers is not serving his customers. Rather, he is lobbying the government for money that he did not earn, and the "profit" he secures in this fashion is appropriated from taxpayers. The market result is that the farmer who benefits from a subsidy does not face the same incentive to innovate and serve his customers by competing to offer lower prices. Ultimately, in this example, these strategies disproportionately hurt those in the lowest income quintiles by raising the price of food.

This research suggests that there is some amount of income inequality that results from the uniqueness with which we are created. However, it is economically unwise to exacerbate any natural level of income inequality by not letting businesses fail when they deserve to fail (bailouts), protecting some businesses from competition (subsidies and tariffs), and letting some businesses succeed over others through protective legislations (licensing and other regulatory requirements). All of these policies choose certain groups of people to earn a higher income than they normally might through market competition. The only way to do this is through coercive taxation that favors certain industries over others, and there is no moral foundation for tax policies that support one industry at the expense of another through political favor.

Conclusion

We are fallen people who are created uniquely. Our gifts are different in nature, combination, and degree. We are called to use our gifts toward the common good, and that implies our work. From the basis of our research, we assert that you can use your God-given gifts for the common good by embracing your talents, focusing in on your comparative advantage, and creating value. This occurs not only in the church; in fact, most of our professions are outside the church. Markets are a space where we can unleash our creativity and serve the world through innovation. Markets bring us goods and services that make everyone better off, including the poorest among us. By bringing our creativity to the market through goods and services, we serve each other. We use our creativity to make others better off than they were before.

The market is capable of rewarding only through financial profit, and it punishes with monetary losses. These are in terms of dollars. Because the goods and services we bring to the market are valued subjectively by the purchaser, income inequality is a fact of economic life, and economics pervades all of our life choices.

The following are the primary findings of this research:

- Diversity is a biblical premise of creation. We are born with different gifts.
- By focusing on our gifts, we can unleash our comparative advantage and bring value to the marketplace by serving others.
- In a free society, absent cronyism, disparity of wages is not a sign of injustice.
- If we care about a society that reduces poverty and assists the poor, we should be concerned, not about income inequality, but about the relative prosperity of those at the bottom and their income mobility.
- An opportunity society is the best way to unleash the creativity and dignity with which we are created, and to serve others with our gifts.

We assert that income inequality is a natural part of the human condition. We are created uniquely, and that means that there is no universal biblical standard for income equality. The question that must be addressed biblically, and through public policy, is the relative prosperity of the poorest among us and their ability to gain income through the pursuit of their gifts. To that end, we need an opportunity society that embraces our uniqueness, unleashes our creativity and potential, and serves the common good. Markets have empirically demonstrated that they are better than any other system at lifting the poor out of destitution.

All Scripture quotations, in this chapter are from the HOLY BIBLE, NEW INTERNATIONAL VERSION® NIV® Copyright © 1973, 1978, 1984, 2011 by Biblica, Inc.®. Used by permission. All rights reserved worldwide.

CHAPTER 9

The Moral Potential of the Free Economy

By Robert A. Sirico, M.Div.

T he free market is not inherently moral; what it produces is not necessarily moral; and those operating in it are not necessarily virtuous. Something that is a potential is not guaranteed; it merely contains the capacity to do something. All the same, a free economy is better suited to promote human well-being and flourishing than are its various alternatives. Moreover, Christian business people need not suffer from a kind of moral schizophrenia between their identity as Christians and their identity as business people. Finally, a correct understanding of Christology and anthropology enables believers to bring a transcendent vision to the tasks of both working and assisting the poor. This biblical approach does not depend on manifestly ineffectual state interventions oriented around aggressive redistribution; instead, it encourages human flourishing through authentic class encounter.

We have all seen the various stereotypes of the Wall Street tycoon grinding the little guy under his thousand-dollar dress shoes on his way to the top. In the popular imagination it is almost inconceivable to think that someone could obtain economic success or wealth without exploiting the vulnerable. Morally sensitive people are confronted with a set of closely related questions in all this: Can entrepreneurs operate in an ethical manner within a capitalist economy, or does the economic success of one person by necessity require the exploitation of another? And does anything other than greed drive people to succeed in a market economy?

Let us be clear at the outset that greed is operative in the free market, in the same way that numerous other vices are to be found wherever human beings exist in this life. Is there lust among married people? Of course. Does that mean that marriage encourages lust? Of course not. Can one find pride among ministers? Sure. Does that mean that ministry leads to egoism as rain leads to mud? Hardly. You get the point. Greed is no more the core of economic liberty than lust or pride is the essence of marriage or ministry.

Far more crucial to a vibrant and free economy than greed is an overriding and energetic creativity that seeks to find new and innovative ways to get things done, to solve problems, and to meet un-met needs. Greed, lust, and pride are always options, of course; but so are generosity, chastity, and humility.

Let's dig a little deeper to see why this is the case.

What Is Greed?

When we think of greed in relation to market activity, several things come to mind. We tend to think of consumerism, materialism, envy, egoism, ruthlessness, and the like. All of this represents a *disordered* human appetite. The disordered appetite, not the appetite itself, presents the problem. In a moral understanding of the world, we say that something is disordered when it is imbalanced and disregards reason as well as the mandate of Scripture. We see how deeply unethical and disordered something is especially when it leads us to disregard the dignity of other people, to use them as objects or tools for our own pleasure rather than as persons who are ends within themselves. Naturally, this would apply as well to the way in which some people disregard their own dignity by "workaholism" and a sense of work solely animated by greed.

It should be easy to see how the sins of greed, avarice, and envy run much deeper than their mere reflection in material objects. These vices, like the roots of many moral failings, are first related to the internal disposition or direction of our hearts, which later leads to pronounced external manifestations. The reason this is important to grasp is that if we are going to identify or remedy a vice such as greed, it does little good to identify the external matter as if it were the root cause of the moral problem. This is too superficial. We need to keep in mind that the vice of avarice does not apply only to material things. It is about a general imbalance to living: certainly an unbalanced value placed on riches for their own sake, but also a person's desire for fulfillment in status, prestige, or living for the approval of others. The antidote to this vice is achieving and maintaining balance in our relation to things and people.

The reason that greed or avarice is one of the "deadly sins" is that it kills the soul to the extent that it substitutes things for God as the object of worship and inclines people to commit other moral violations along the way.

Profits

With this traditional Christian understanding of greed in mind, let us turn now to the charge that business is inherently greedy. "See," one often hears, "the businessman is not interested in the well-being of people. All he is interested in is earning profits—what he can make from the deal." For a moment, set aside the claim that profit is all the entrepreneur is interested in. Let's ask ourselves, should one invest one's time, energy, talent, and wealth into a business in order to obtain a loss on the balance sheets? For that you could have stayed home. Profit is simply an indicator to a business owner that he or she is accomplishing what he or she set out to do in a sustainable way. In a narrower sense, it tells us that income is outpacing costs.[218] Companies that earn profits bring in more money than they expend in costs. The opposite of this process is financial loss, and any business that consistently loses rather than makes money cannot survive very long. At some point, then, profits become necessary for the success and continuation of businesses, not to mention the prosperity of society as a whole, as well as its survival. No business or society can long function wherein more resources are wasted than created.

Public sector bailouts are increasingly seen as a way to resolve poor economic performance, but this approach only passes the buck to society as a whole in the form of taxes (either now or later) and utilizes profits earned by others to subsidize the unprofitability of the company being bailed out. This can go on for only so long before those whose profits are taken from them begin to wonder why they are working so hard to support failing companies. It should be obvious that earning a profit is an indication that things are going as planned in meeting the needs of clients, and conversely, that when a profit is not attained something is going wrong. When subsidies swoop down to rescue poorly executed plans or inefficient production methods and the like, what incentive is given for a company to become more efficient, to make the often hard choices necessary to get back on a profitable footing? History is replete with experiences bearing this out.[219]

The art and talent required for profitability is seen in those enterprises that discover creative ways to make products and services available at accessible and attractive prices, while covering their own costs and then some. These are the companies that serve their clients, the reward for which is built right into the process.

Of course the common stereotype of the profit-maker (frequently laden with vicious anti-Semitic images) is the person blinded by greed and avarice, and who employs others for his own ends as instruments of his enrichment. He is like the successful Monopoly player who grows rich through luck and cutthroat competition. Victory in Monopoly comes not when a player gets rich by creating new value in a business enterprise, but rather by successfully taking everybody else's money and driving them all into bankruptcy. Monopoly is literally a zero-sum *game;* and in the stereotype of the ruthless, parasitical profit-maker, some people confuse the real world with a game of Monopoly, and so fall into the fallacy of believing that one person gains in a market only if others lose. Thus, if there are poor people, clearly it must be because the rich have taken such a massive piece of the existing pie that there was little left for the poor folks. If that's the case, the obvious solution is to take the pie by force and divide it up equitably.

Those who fall prey to the zero-sum-game fallacy fail to consider that maybe the pie wasn't always just sitting there, the exact same size from all eternity. Maybe some of those who are rich didn't take more than their fair share; maybe they *made* more than their fair share. The zero-sum assumption prevents people from ever asking whether the solution to poverty might be to grow the pie.

This zero-sum mentality is especially prevalent among pastors, who often view profits with disdain. In conversations with fellow clergy who take this view, I ask: If profits are morally dubious, are losses morally praiseworthy? The point of the question is to stimulate thought. In logic, this is referred to as a *reductio ad absurdum*—taking an inherently illogical line of thought to its logical extreme in order to make the illogic obvious. Of course, profits aren't inherently immoral any more than losses are a badge of saintliness. Profits suggest that a business is using its resources wisely; losses indicate that it is not. This isn't to say that profits and losses are a business's be-all and end-all, but they do serve as first-level indicators of whether a business is serving customers in an effective, sustainable manner.

The Price System

Because human wants always outstrip available resources, all societies need some guide for allocating scarce resources. For instance, something or someone has to decide whether a given quantity of water is best used for drinking, bathing, or irrigation, or whether a given ton of steel will go toward making cars, bridges, or tractors. The same is true for all social resources. Even the resource of time, which is also scarce, requires some tool for sensible allocation.

One solution to the problem is to have one or more people centrally control these decisions. To varying degrees, this is the solution pursued by socialism in its different forms. As bitter experience has demonstrated, this strategy presents a couple of problems. For one, it concentrates power in a few hands, and excessive power tends to corrupt people. And two, the people in charge don't have enough information to orchestrate something as complex as a large market. Even if they were morally perfect, they still wouldn't have enough data to manage buyers and sellers and prices and products effectively. These twin problems have bedeviled every centrally-planned economy in history.

Fortunately, there is a better strategy for allocating scarce resources: the network of prices that arises organically from voluntary exchanges among buyers and sellers in the market. Here is how it works: A lower price for any particular good signals relative abundance; people can buy more of that good. A higher price signals relative scarcity, prodding consumers to economize their use of the good. Higher prices also encourage producers to make more of something.

For instance, when entrepreneurs discovered how to pump, store, refine, and use petroleum oil, its price dropped well below that of whale oil. Whale oil was priced out of the market, and there was less pressure to kill whales for their fat. More recently, oil prices have been higher than usual (even adjusted for inflation), and this has encouraged oil exploration, since people in the oil business have the hope of selling newly recovered oil at a handsome price and can afford to invest in more intensive types of exploration. The customers' willingness to pay the higher price tells producers, "Go and find more of this stuff. We're interested." All other things being equal, increased production will, in turn, lower prices somewhat in the long run. However, if the government stepped in and said, "No one can sell oil for more than half the current exorbitant price," then all kinds of intensive oil exploration and extraction would suddenly become unprofitable and thus unsustainable. Consumers who wanted more petroleum products would suddenly find severe shortages. This is why government attempts to control gasoline prices have consistently led to long lines and shortages.

One caveat: a business's social obligations reach beyond making a profit. Business owners and managers must deal honestly, keep their word, serve the community in a broad sense, and tend to the moral dimensions of the investment process. The price system does not magically guarantee moral behavior. To give a painful example, the price system in a depraved society may signal that the most valued use of teenage girls from poor families is for them to become prostitutes. Confusion arises when people witness this sort of thing and assume that dispensing with the free market will magically erase the problem. A bit of reflection should reveal the error. Moving to a purely socialist economy won't remove lust and selfishness from the human heart. They go right on thriving and indeed are now fed by the state— with the added problem that poor families have even fewer ways to earn a living because the socialist economy has placed various morally preferable enterprises beyond their reach. The price system in a free economy does not provide a moral foundation for a society. It does not remove opportunities for ill-gotten gain. What it does do is beat every form of socialism at generating moral and socially beneficent options for escaping poverty.

Excess Profits?

Now some may concede that profits play a legitimate economic and social role but then complain about "excess profits." The term conjures up images of Wall Street titans with wads of money falling out of their overstuffed pockets, but what precisely constitutes excess profit? Did Thomas Edison profit excessively from his fiendishly lucrative invention of the light bulb, an invention that has enriched the lives of billions around the world? What about a business that makes only a meager 2% profit but does it by misleading customers?

The charge of inordinate profit-making is usually lodged against some business or business sector, based not on some objective criteria but out of a vaguely defined aesthetic distaste or ideological disapproval. So, for instance, every time gas prices spike, people start complaining about "big oil" taking "excessive profits" without stopping to ask what caused the spike (a sudden drop in oil supply from the Middle East because of a civil war, for instance) and without realizing that the higher prices are signaling consumers to conserve a scarce resource while simultaneously encouraging and enabling producers to go out and increase the supply of gasoline. Instead, those complaining assume that rapidly rising prices mean "big oil" is gouging "the little guy."

All of this doesn't just overlook the price system's function of efficiently signaling gasoline producers and consumers. It also overlooks the fact that oil and gasoline profits are well in line with the profits of firms in other industries. For the first quarter of 2011—when the big oil companies were being bashed for sticking it to the consumer— their profit margin averaged 6.1 cents per dollar of revenue, ranking them 114th out of 215 industries.[220] Where was the outcry over outsized profits in software, publishing, railroads, or various other sectors more profitable than big oil?

Even unusually thick profit margins serve a useful signaling function. High profits announce that people want more of some good or service than is being produced, and draw entrepreneurs and resources into the market to meet the demand over the long term. Notice too that the competitive bidding for resources and customers means no one is automatically in a profitable position. A business will go on earning high profits only through a combination of hard work, creativity, and vision, which in turn allows it to deliver value much more effectively than its competitors. This market dynamic constantly fuels innovation, since companies are constantly looking for new ways to deliver value more effectively than their competitors in order to realize higher profits.

Where unusually thick profits persist for a long time, this is usually a symptom of something hindering market freedom. If new producers are not entering a field that is providing outsized profits, it is often the result of government restricting competition. The solution is to remove government from the business of picking winners and losers in the market, to move away from crony capitalism toward free and transparent capitalism.

Moral Profits

As the president of an educational organization focused on helping pastors and entrepreneurs understand that business is a legitimate calling and that God has uniquely equipped some people to pursue this calling, I recognize the legitimate role of profits in business and try to steer my fellow pastors away from a misguided and categorical denunciation of business profits. At the same time, I recognize that a businessman may be legitimately urged to give up some or all of his profits for the sake of his soul. Whether that is prudent advice hinges on the person's circumstances. Jesus called on the rich young man to sell everything he had, give it to the poor, and then follow Jesus. The gospels record other examples of Jesus interacting with wealthy people, and in none of these other cases does he tell them to sell everything they have and give it to the poor. We can only surmise that Jesus discerned in the rich young man's heart a need for extreme measures. The story seems to be less about the rich young man's economic status than about his spiritual needs. It is a call to go beyond the bare minimum contained in the Decalogue's negative commandments. In other words, it is about heroism, not economics, a call to a life of generosity and detachment even from the things we do possess, as we strive to be good stewards of the things within our care.

Sixteenth-century priest Francis de Sales, when called to give pastoral advice to Christians involved in trades and other occupations, gave a different answer from what some might expect from a saint: "Have greater care than worldly men do to make your property profitable and fruitful ... our possessions are not our own. God has given them to us to cultivate and he wants us to make them fruitful and profitable ... therefore let us exercise this gracious care of preserving and even of increasing our temporal goods whenever just occasions present themselves."[221]

The field of economics has been developing for some four hundred years since those words were written, and yet de Sales understood the price system and moral nature of business enterprise far better than many clergy today. His advice is that of one who understands that the system of profit and loss can orient our behavioral compass toward activities that serve others, make good use of resources, and prepare us for the future. Again, it doesn't block people from using their business for evil; but without price signals in a free economy, our economic activities would be without order.

Imagine for a moment how long moral behavior and order would endure in a world without prices. A crucial form of guidance—one that helps us manage our innumerable daily economic activities—would be stripped away, the division of labor would crumble, and the standard of living would be systematically reduced until we reached a primitive stage. A world without monetary calculation would be a world in disarray.

The Michelin Man

One way to discern the moral potential of business enterprise is to study the lives of successful entrepreneurs. Francois Michelin is the head of the Michelin Company, an international company that offers everything from tires and heavy machinery to travel and dining guides. The head of this dynasty is the epitome, in many people's minds, of the global industrial titan. So when people learn that I know him, they often ask me what he's like. One story in particular captures the Francois Michelin I know.

In 2000 I was traveling in Europe, and Mr. Michelin invited me to visit him in his home town of Clermont Ferrand in central France. When my plane arrived, I was on the lookout for a driver holding a placard with my name on it—thinking I would be chauffeured to the company's offices. Instead, once I retrieved my bags, I was greeted by the modest Michelin in his usual simple grey suit. The seventy-seven-year-old tycoon (clearly recognized by people in the airport) reached to assist me with my suitcases. I initially declined, but when he persisted, I handed him one of the lighter bags, and we walked to the parking lot, where he approached a nondescript automobile and opened the trunk. As I went to get in, I glanced down to see if the tires were Michelin. I did not see the signature brand markings. Once seated in the car I joked with Mr. Michelin, "I see that you are not driving on Michelin tires."

"Mon Père [as he usually addresses me], let me show you something."

He pointed to a contraption between the two front seats and began pressing various buttons on the device, and as he did so the readout changed each time, jumping from the front right to the front left location, then to the back right and the back left locations. Each time, different numbers would appear.

"You are correct to observe these are not Michelin tires—not yet. This is a test car, and this meter lets me know the relative stress and heat on each of the experimental tires."

"You mean you are not yet sure these tires are secure?" I asked.

"I hope you will not worry. Our scientists have worked hard on these tires. But you would not expect me to offer tires for sale to my customers to drive their families on, if I were not willing to ride on them first."

At the time, newspaper headlines were filled with details of a controversy over the alleged failure of Firestone tires on certain Ford vehicles, a controversy that would eventually end the century-old relationship between Ford and Firestone. In light of this, I asked Michelin how his business was doing.

He replied with a frown, "It is a terrible moment for those of us in the tire business, terrible."

The answer surprised me, since his company's market share was likely to benefit from Firestone's loss of prestige. But his instinctive reply was to lament the crisis. He went on to say that any time an industry fails to protect its customers, it injures trust in the entire industry.

This snapshot of Francois Michelin does not, of course, disprove the existence of predatory business people in high places. But there is nothing in business or the market economy that mandates a selfish dog-eat-dog ethic.

The Apostle of Greed

The poster boy for the evil capitalist in our age may be the Gordon Gekko character in the movie *Wall Street*, played with charismatic verve by Michael Douglas. At one point in the film, the titan of high finance makes a presentation to the shareholders of the fictional Teldar Paper Corporation, in which he insists that greed is good. As he goes on to say, "Greed clarifies, cuts through, and captures the essence of the evolutionary spirit. Greed, in all of its forms—greed for life, for money, for love, knowledge—has marked the upward surge of mankind. And greed—you mark my words—will not only save Teldar Paper, but that other malfunctioning corporation called the USA."

Some trace this way of thinking back to the teachings of the Russian-born novelist and philosopher Ayn Rand, considered by many to be the Apostle of Greed for her defense of capitalism. In fact, Rand did not actually defend "greed," but rather a notion of "radical individualism" or "rational self-interest," which she delineated in her 1963 collection of essays co-authored with Nathaniel Branden, *The Virtue of Selfishness*.

Rand liked to play with language and use words in idiosyncratic ways. She condemned altruism, sacrifice, and self-sacrifice, but what she meant by those terms is not what most people mean. For instance, she defined sacrificial behavior as "the surrender of a greater value for the sake of a lesser one or of a non-value."[222] That is hardly how most people would describe the term. Or take the word "selfishness." Rand defined it as "concern with one's own interest,"[223] but the primary definition most people would think of when they hear that word would be more along the lines of the Merriam-Webster's "concerned excessively or exclusively with oneself: seeking or concentrating on one's own advantage, pleasure, or well-being without regard for others."[224]

It is an interesting question whether Rand's idiosyncratic use of words points to rhetorical daring or just muddled thinking. I will not try to settle that here. What I will argue is that her understanding of the human person was flawed at a crucial point. Her idea of man is noble, and she was an able defender of freedom in the face of the totalitarian impulse, of which she was an eyewitness growing up in the Soviet Union. She limned with great verve humanity's creative capacity and entrepreneurial potential; she championed the social conditions that protect man's freedom to be creative; she attacked with unflagging energy the collectivist creep of regulation and taxes that tend to batten on and sap human creativity; and she ably condemned the socialist disdain for individual human rights.

Particularly in Rand's novels these themes can be riveting and inspiring, but her foundational commitment to radical individualism—an autonomy that precludes social obligation and responsibility—is mistaken. Indeed, the selfishness and radical individualism at the center of her defense of capitalism clash with the very institutions she sought to defend. The free enterprise system rests on the fact that people are not just individuals but also social beings. Contracts, markets, stock exchanges, competition under the rule of law—these and other hallmarks of the market economy are fundamentally social in nature.

When some of my friends from Europe try to describe a system that tempers the individualism they complain about in a free economy, they speak of a "social market." But the phrase is a pleonasm, since markets are inherently social. Think about it. Entrepreneurs in a free market—much more so than government bureaucrats or central planners under socialism—must submit themselves to the wants and needs of the consumer in order to profit.

The labor market in a free economy is equally social: business owners must compete with other potential employers and jobs in their efforts to attract and retain employees. Employer and employee voluntarily settle on a mutually agreeable arrangement, a social bond known as the employer-employee relationship. A free-labor market encourages employers to behave more sociably toward their employees, to treat them better, since they know their workers have other opportunities. At the same time, the workers know that excellence is rewarded by employers who are competing for the best workers, encouraging them to serve their employers energetically.

Of course, most of us have known a mean or greedy business owner or at least heard a friend tell about one. But this does not mean that one has to be greedy to succeed in business. Instead of being spurred by greed, the person may want to pursue excellence in a business field or provide better educational opportunities for his or her children. As for those avaricious business owners, what often goes unnoticed is that a free economy offers the greedy person many socially beneficial ways to try to sate his greed. Any legal and beneficial good or service, including the skills of an adept surgeon, the services of a cleaning company in muddy Northern California, or the services of a window-tinting business in sunny Southern Arizona that makes house calls, offers a self-interested person with a knack for business a means of obtaining wealth while serving society.

Contrast this to the sort of economy that existed under the Soviet Union. There the main way a greedy person could pursue wealth was either in organized crime or by working one's way up in the Communist Party, which amounted to organized criminal brutality and exploitation on an imperial scale.

The communist economies of the twentieth century generated great material deprivation, since such conditions apparently encourage neither generosity nor detachment from material possessions. Instead, acquiring the basic material necessities became the all-consuming focus of everyone not fortunate enough to occupy important positions in the Party. The situation encouraged people to look at others as a means of access to scarce items. "We pretend to work and you pretend to pay us," was the common joke, but it was no joke to people suffering under the broken system.[225] Dishonesty and cynicism reigned supreme, bringing devastating consequences to both the spiritual and material lives of those trapped within its boundaries. If we want to encourage the traits of generosity and concern for others, we would do well to promote positive culture-forming institutions within a free society, not to rush after a utopian mirage that ultimately suppresses the very impulses that encourage a flourishing human life.

The Personable Person and the Market

I hope by now the answer to radical individualism is clear. It isn't socialist collectivism. Nor is radical individualism the answer to socialist collectivism, since man is simultaneously social and individual, autonomous and relational. Building a society in which we can flourish first requires an understanding of this complex human nature. If we get the anthropology—the science of the human person—wrong, we get the whole thing wrong. Seeing human beings as radically autonomous attenuates our rich complexity; so too does viewing us as just so many cogs in a collectivist historical dialectic. We are autonomous beings, but we came from someone. We are the result of a communion of love, and we reach beyond ourselves for love and knowledge. Children result from and expand this social dimension of our nature. More than this, we have a destiny for communion, not only in but also beyond this world. Trying to construct a society on radical individualism, which ignores the reality of human solidarity and society itself, would be to construct a ruthless, cold, libertine environment unworthy of human persons—and one, moreover, in which liberty, prosperity, and virtue could not long endure.

To bring all of this full circle, the best entrepreneurs are not those consumed with their own egotistical desires, but instead are typically those with a finely tuned sense of other people's wants and needs. This capacity comes with pitfalls: the entrepreneur may discern and seek to fulfill destructive desires. The knack isn't itself virtuous. It is useful, but not always used for good ends. That is why it is so important that aspiring business people be formed in those moral habits that promote human flourishing rather than human degradation.

Vocation—Calling

Many today consider the phrase "the call of the entrepreneur" an oxymoron, like "the charity of the leech." From a historical perspective, this is paradoxical. The West is rooted in a Judeo-Christian worldview, with its positive view of the material creation and human creativity, and its positive vision of the moral potential of business. And yet many in the West are deeply suspicious of business, with even many business ethics courses presupposing that there is something inherently impious about business itself, such that an alien ethic must be imported to cage the Tasmanian devil of greed and exploitation. If business is by nature dishonest and destructive, then one could see the attraction of having government bureaucrats hyper-regulating its every move, much as one would put a tracking bracelet on a violent criminal out on bail and confine him to his neighborhood. The problem is two-pronged: Business is not inherently dishonest and destructive. And the political actors overseeing all of this hyper-regulation are not immaculately conceived nor untainted by the "original sin" of business, and so are not invulnerable to temptation.

We need a different paradigm of the economy to fully understand man in the marketplace. Mother Teresa, who was neither an economist nor a theologian, provided a glimpse of how we ought to see economic issues and demolished Marx's notion of class struggle all in a single comment. "We have no right to judge the rich," she said. "For our part, what we desire is not a class struggle but a class encounter, in which the rich save the poor and the poor save the rich."[226]

What Mother Teresa is pointing toward is nothing less than a path from the mirage of communism to the hope of true community. It is also a remedy for the radical individualism that poses as *the* solution to a socialist century. We are more than *homo economicus*, more than utility-maximizers. The radical individualism assumed by so many secular economists is, frankly, a truncated picture of humanity. (I don't mean *rugged individualism* in the sense of a John Wayne type stepping in to save the town before riding off into the sunset. We call those brave men heroes, not radical individualists.) Of course some people who have succeeded in capitalist economies do live self-serving and largely isolated lives of pleasure-seeking, using others primarily for their own selfish ends. But if one's political philosophy is fixated on protecting and promoting such a lifestyle—at the expense of the civil institutions and other cultural resources that strengthen, enrich, and connect people in community—then one's society will not long remain either free or virtuous.

It is tempting to view freedom as an end in itself. But freedom, despite the natural human yearning for it, is not a goal or a virtue in itself. We have freedom *for* something. Once the millions living under the Soviet Union's totalitarian yoke were freed, they had to use their newfound liberty for *something*. Freedom is an instrumental goal. Once it is achieved, we naturally ask, "Now what do I do with it?" If freedom is to lead to human flourishing, then the aim of freedom must be the truth, and the ground of all truth is him "in whom we live and move and have our being." Truth is freedom's proper end—and also, as a practical matter, its guarantor.

This is why the role of religious institutions in addressing our cultural and economic problems goes beyond their instrumental value as social service providers. Only an understanding of man that encompasses his transcendent destiny can serve as the proper foundation for a flourishing society. Such a faith reminds us of the limits of material existence, and of our final destination. This, in turn, serves as a crucial guide for individuals as we organize our life together. Recognizing that heaven on earth is impossible, we do not pursue utopian schemes.

But we also recognize that what we do in this life contains the seeds of eternity. Some lines from one of the documents that came out of the Catholic Church's Second Vatican Council in the 1960s convey it well: "While we are warned that it profits a man nothing if he gain the whole world and lose himself, the expectation of a new earth must not weaken but rather stimulate our concern for cultivating this one. For here grows the body of a new human family, a body which even now is able to give some kind of foreshadowing of the new age."[227]

German Lutheran theologian and World War II martyr Dietrich Bonhoeffer also spoke to this. "The Christian's field of activity is the world," he wrote at a time when Hitler was gathering strength, and not long before many German Christians would begin to accommodate rather than stand up against Nazi power. "It is here that Christians are to become engaged, are to work and be active, here that they are to do the will of God; and for that reason, Christians are not resigned pessimists, but are those who while admittedly not expecting much from the world are for that very reason already joyous and cheerful in the world, for that world is the seedbed of eternity."[228]

It isn't mere coincidence that Christian civilization created a broader middle class than ever before in history, a class that grew up out of the artisans and merchants and craftsmen that the aristocratic class tends to disdain, the kind of enterprising workers who, in all previous civilizations, were never allowed to thrive and flourish in any great number. It's more than coincidence because the doctrine of the Incarnation taught European men and women that their Creator had sent his Son to be born of a virgin, to work with his hands as a humble carpenter here on this earth. The pagan aristocratic disdain for the earthy and mundane could still get a foothold in the sinful human heart; but where Christianity interpenetrated a civilization, such a disdain no longer had a theological foothold. This is because the Judeo-Christian worldview teaches men and women that ordinary physical labor is dignified, and that it's also worthwhile to try to further dignify it. This view spread throughout society and transformed the way people approached all kinds of occupations.

This calls to mind the story of a young man who entered a monastery. When the fellow was finally allowed to do so, he wrote his parents and told them of his joy in discovering his vocation, telling how the monks would rise from their beds in the middle of the night to return to the chapel. There, "when the entire world is hushed," the young monk explained in the letter, they would pray for the world, the solemn voices of the monks chanting psalms that resonated through the chapel's stone walls. It was through this moving experience, he explained to his father, that he had discovered his vocation.

His father, a wise and devout man, wrote this back to his son: "Dear Son, your mother and I are overjoyed to hear how you are adjusting to your vocation and your new life inside the walls of the monastery, and please know that we will pray for you now as we always have prayed for you. There is only one thing I ask you to keep in mind, my son, as you grow in the knowledge of your vocation and that is this: many a night, 'when all the world was hushed,' your mother and I rose from our beds to change your dirty diapers. And in doing this we found our vocation."

To be able to find God's call in the mess of a baby's dirty diapers is, surprising as it may seem, a reiteration of the message of the Incarnation: The eternal, ineffable God was born into the world and laid in a manger—a feed trough for animals! He became flesh and dwelt among us because he desires for us to know him concretely, personally, intimately. He is Emmanuel, "God with us," in our work and play, on the floors of our stock exchanges and in our butcher shops. He is in even these places, or there is no Emmanuel. The Incarnation demonstrates God's love for us, but it also testifies to the truth that God's creation is "good" and has purpose beyond its physicality. The Jesuit poet Gerard Manley Hopkins put it memorably when he wrote that "The world is charged with the grandeur of God," and not merely when a shaft of sunlight pierces a bank of clouds over an ocean or mountaintop. "It will flame out," as the poem goes on to say, "like shining from shook foil." That is, the world is so charged with God's grandeur that, if we had but eyes for it, we would discover his glory—and his grace—breaking out in the most ordinary of situations.

The physical, then, is itself a kind of catechism of God's offer of love, pouring forth speech day and night, as King David repeatedly put it in the psalms. To creatively touch it anywhere, to seek to grasp its deep meaning and perceive its veiled glory, is to invite a discovery of the author as well. Thus I am convinced that the pursuit of excellence in even the humblest craft or profession affords the possibility of encountering the truth of the universe, is an inchoate search for God. "Sacred" and "temporal" do not describe things radically separate, but rather a relationship between two interpenetrating realities—the "dust of the ground" and "the breath of life" out of which God formed man (Genesis 2:7).

At the same time, in the midst of this glory, the Christian understanding of human sinfulness encourages an appropriate modesty in our plans. It encourages us to build, as James Madison put it, nations fit for men, not angels.[229] The doctrine of original sin leaves no room for a vision of pre-fallen mandarins safely entrusted with unchecked political power. The atheistic and neo-pagan political ideologies of the previous century (communism and Nazism, both branches of the tree of socialism) lacked this notion of fallenness and a concomitant modesty. Lacking a proper fear of unchecked political power, they quickly produced totalitarian regimes.

Finally, sound theology encourages a right understanding of human equality—which is not a call for class warfare or material leveling. Rather, it speaks of inherent human dignity and worth, of an equality of rights, and of that bond of solidarity we share by virtue of our common origin as creatures made in the image of God, all of which draws us to care for the vulnerable, even at personal risk and sacrifice.

The Role of Business

I say that sound theology encourages such an understanding— rather than causing it—for good reason. Since co-founding the Acton Institute I have had the occasion to travel around the world and speak with religious leaders in scores of countries from across the ecumenical spectrum. I find many of them, though well-meaning and motivated by a deep love for God and humanity, and guided by a robust understanding of both the Fall and of human transcendence, nevertheless lack the faintest notion of business enterprise as a potentially moral endeavor, much less of the importance of entrepreneurial creativity for a flourishing economy that lifts people out of poverty. This basic disconnect is the reason the Acton Institute was founded in the first place.

As a pastor myself, I understand how easy it is to map the fixed-pie realm of the offering plate onto the economy as a whole. The weekly offering is a transfer of wealth in which the pastor need never ask how the wealth was created in the first place. All the same, it's a mistake to view wealth as if there were a static quantity of it, and redistribution as the answer to poverty. It is an equal mistake to think that those who participate by their commitment, risk, and ingenuity in creating more wealth cannot do so with a deep sense of moral and ethical responsibility, or that their success is linked to the exploitation of others. Moreover, these are mistakes that need not persist. Mother

Teresa spoke of class encounter. We also need a vocational encounter between the entrepreneurial vocation—distinguished by its creativity, willingness to risk, and insight into the wants and needs of customers—and the pastoral-religious frame of reference, with its priority of tending to the needs of the most vulnerable out of the love with which God has first loved us. The approaches are complementary, not adversarial, for the societies that have freed the entrepreneur to create new wealth have generated greater reserves of wealth, both in the charitable realm and in the economy as a whole.

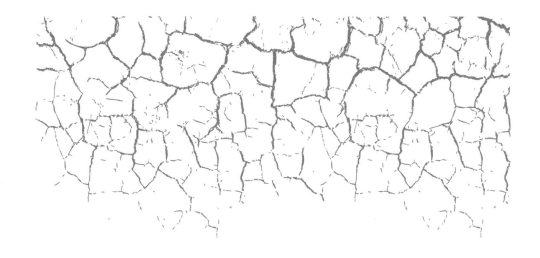

PART 3

POVERTY ALLEVIATION IN PRACTICE

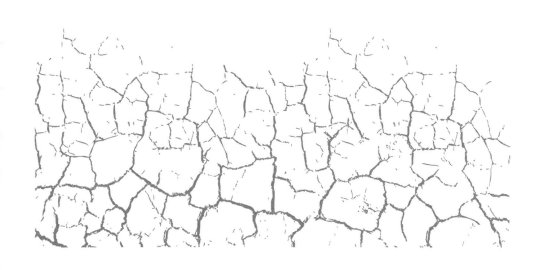

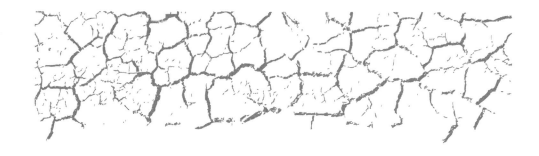

CHAPTER 10

A Poverty Program
That Worked

By Lawrence W. Reed, M.A.

The goal of this chapter is to make an effort to understand
the American experiment in poverty alleviation. The
United States has long held the position of being one of
the most prosperous and free societies in the world, with massive
wealth accumulation over the past two hundred years. Prior to the
mid-twentieth century there was no formal federal poverty alleviation
program; but since the founding, Americans were able to grow more
prosperous and wealthy with each generation. The chapter will examine
the American tradition of poverty alleviation and its results—both
prior to national welfare programs and after—and offer suggestions
for lessons we can learn from history—lessons that embrace a biblical
narrative of caring for the poor.

More than half of America's presidents held office before 1900, yet
few Americans could tell you much about any more than two or three

of them. That is an unfortunate commentary. Those chief executives helped mightily to shape and steer the country for a majority of our experience as a nation. They presided over the most successful progress against poverty in world history. Today's world could learn a great deal from this history, but so could most of today's Americans.

We've become accustomed to thinking of poverty-fighting as a twentieth-century undertaking, with the federal government leading the way. For that reason, this quotation from an American president might come as a surprise:

> The lessons of history, confirmed by the evidence immediately before me, show conclusively that continued dependence upon relief induces a spiritual and moral disintegration fundamentally destructive to the national fiber. To dole out relief in this way is to administer a narcotic, a subtle destroyer of the human spirit. It is inimical to the dictates of sound policy. It is in violation of the traditions of America.[230]

Those were *not* the words of a nineteenth-century politician. They came from the lips of our thirty-second chief executive, Franklin Delano Roosevelt, in his State of the Union Address on January 4, 1935. A moment later, he declared, "The Federal Government must and shall quit this business of relief."[231]

Of course, as we know all too painfully well, it didn't. Indeed, thirty years later Lyndon Johnson would take "this business of relief" to new and expensive heights in an official "War on Poverty." In 1996—another thirty years and more than $5 trillion in federal welfare later—a Democratic president signed a bill into law that replaced the federal entitlement to welfare with added flexibility, allowing states to implement work requirements, time limits, and other measures to encourage personal responsibility. As Ronald Reagan had observed before it dawned on Bill Clinton, "We fought a war on poverty, and poverty won."[232]

What Reagan instinctively knew, Bill Clinton finally admitted, and FDR preached but didn't practice was that government poverty programs are themselves poverty-stricken, especially in their fiscal and pathological effects. We have paid an awful price in lives and treasure to learn some things that the vast majority of Americans in the nineteenth century—and the chief executives they elected—could have plainly told us: Government welfare or "relief" programs encourage idleness, break up families, produce intergenerational dependency and hopelessness, cost taxpayers a fortune, and yield harmful cultural trends that may take generations to cure.

The failure of the dole was *so* complete that one journalist a decade ago posed a question to which just about everybody knows the answer and the lesson it implies. "Ask yourself," wrote John Fund of *The Wall Street Journal*, "if you had a financial windfall and wanted to help the poor, would you even *think* about giving time or a check to the government?"

The preeminent beneficiaries of the whole twentieth-century experiment in federal poverty-fighting were not those whom the programs were ostensibly intended to help; rather, those beneficiaries were primarily two other groups:

1. Politicians who got elected and reelected as champions of the needy and downtrodden. Some were sincere and well-meaning. Others were cynical, ill-informed, short-sighted, and opportunistic. *All* were deluded into traveling paths down which not a single administration of the nineteenth century ever ventured—the use of the public treasury for

widespread handouts to the needy. My good friend, the late Tennessee humorist Tom Anderson, put it well when he said so many times in public speeches that the welfare state got its name because "The politicians get *well*, while everybody else pays the *fare*."

2. The bureaucracies—the armies of professional poverty-fighters whose jobs and empires always seemed secure regardless of the actual effects of the programs they administered. I have heard economist Walter Williams describe this many times as "feeding the sparrows through the horses." Williams also famously observed, "A lot of people went to Washington [D.C.] to do good, and apparently have done very well."

An unabashed, unrepentant believer in the welfare state would probably survey the men who held the highest office in the land during the nineteenth century and dismiss them as heartless, uncaring, and hopelessly medieval. Even during the severe depressions of the 1830s and the 1890s, Presidents Martin Van Buren and Grover Cleveland never proposed that Washington, D.C. extend its reach to the relief of private distress, broadly speaking, and they opposed even the smallest suggestions of that kind.

Those critics make a crucial error, however, when they imply that it was left to presidents of a more enlightened twentieth century to finally care enough to help the poor. The fact is, our leaders in the 1800s *did* mount a war on poverty—the most comprehensive and effective ever mounted by any central government anywhere. It just didn't have a gimmicky name like "Great Society," nor did it have a public relations office and elitist poverty conferences at expensive seaside resorts. If you could have pressed them then for a name for it, most if not all of those early chief executives might well have said their anti-poverty program was, in a word, *liberty*. This word meant things like self-reliance, hard work, entrepreneurship, the institutions of civil society, a strong and free economy, and government confined to its constitutional role as protector of liberty by keeping the peace—concepts that have deep biblical roots.

In hindsight, it's a little amazing that the last president of the nineteenth century, William McKinley, was just about as faithful to that legacy of liberty as the first great one of that century, Thomas Jefferson. In 1900, the federal government was still many years away from any sort of national program for public payments to the indigent.

To be sure, in many other respects the Washington, D.C. establishment was bigger than Jefferson had left it—alarmingly so, in most cases. But it was not yet even remotely a welfare state. The presidents of that period did not read any of the modern welfare-state assumptions into the Constitution. They understood these essential verities: Government has nothing to give anybody except what it first takes from somebody, and a government big enough to give the people everything they want is big enough to take away everything they have. These chief executives had other things going for them, too—notably, a humbling faith in divine providence and a healthy confidence in what a free and compassionate people could do without federal help.

And what a poverty program *liberty* proved to be! In spite of a horrendous civil war, half a dozen economic downturns, and wave after wave of impoverished immigrants, America progressed from near universal poverty at the start of the century to within reach of the world's highest per-capita income at the end of the century. The poverty that remained stood out like the proverbial sore thumb because it was now the exception, no longer the rule. In the absence of stultifying government welfare programs, our free and self-reliant citizenry spawned so many private, distress-relieving initiatives that

American generosity became one of the marvels of the world. This essentially spontaneous, non-centrally-planned "war on poverty" stands in stark contrast to Lyndon Johnson's "Great Society" because *it actually worked.*

The U.S. population in 1900—76 million—was more than fourteen times its 1800 level, yet per capita GDP had quadrupled. That explosion in production and creativity translated into a gigantic leap for average personal income and a steep plunge in the portion of Americans living in abject poverty. Of economic progress in the nineteenth century, despite a civil war and other setbacks, Dr. Barry Asmus has written:

> On the eve of World War I, after a century of remarkable progress in the United States, economic growth and its benefits for raising the standard of living were evident for all to see. It was a time during which capitalism (cynics call it "Social Darwinism") was given a chance, the role of government in economic affairs, while substantial in some instances, was quite limited in scope. Living standards, longevity, and economic opportunity grew to levels unimaginable merely a hundred years earlier. Though progress was uneven, and some people grew fabulously rich, it was in part the poor who experienced the greatest improvements. By the end of the nineteenth century, America's poor enjoyed material living standards significantly higher than most of the world's population.[233]

For decades after the adoption of the Constitution in 1789, few Americans—and none of our presidents—pressed for direct government aid to the impoverished, even though the great majority of people were living in poverty by almost any standard. That was not because they were a cruel and heartless people, but rather because they saw the alleviation of poverty as a personal assignment, not a government duty.

Consider Jefferson—the author of the Declaration of Independence, America's third president, and a man who exerted enormous intellectual influence during this country's formative years. His were the first two presidential terms of America's first full century as a nation. His election in 1800 marked a turning point from twelve years of Federalist Party rule and set the tone for decades to follow. In his First Inaugural Address in 1801, Jefferson gave us a splendid summation of what government should do. He did not describe welfare programs, but rather, "A wise and frugal government, which shall restrain men from injuring one another, shall leave them otherwise free to regulate their own pursuits of industry and improvement, and shall not take from the mouth of labor the bread it has earned. This is the sum of good government."[234]

A similar view was held by James Madison, a key figure in the construction of the Constitution, a prime defender of it in the Federalist Papers, and our fourth president. Madison vetoed bills that called for so-called "internal improvements"—such as roads—to be made at federal expense, so it would have been inconceivable to him that it was constitutional to use the power of government to take from some people and give to others because the others were poor and needed aid. While there might be a reasonable, even constitutional, case for certain federal road-building projects for national defense purposes (or at least the benefit of everyone), Madison and Jefferson saw *no* constitutional case to be made for assistance to individuals in poverty.

In a speech in the U.S. House of Representatives years before he became president, Madison declared: "The government of the United States is a definite government, confined to specified objects. It is not like state governments, whose powers are more general. Charity is no part of the legislative duty of the government."[235]

Why didn't Jefferson, Madison, and other American presidents of the nineteenth century not simply stretch the Constitution until it included poverty assistance to individuals? Why does it seem to have hardly ever occurred to them? Many factors and reasons explain this, but one was paramount: *Such power was not to be found in the rule book.*

Let me elaborate. Imagine playing a game—baseball, gin rummy, Monopoly or whatever—in which there is only one rule: *anything goes.*

What kind of a game would this be? Chaotic, frustrating, unpredictable, impossible. Eventually the whole thing would degenerate into a free-for-all. While simple games would be intolerable if played this way, the consequences for the many deadly-serious things humans engage in—from driving on the highways to waging war—would be too frightful to imagine.

The most profound political and philosophical trend of our time is the lack of any general consensus about what government is supposed to do and what it is *not* supposed to do. This was not so in Jefferson's and Madison's day. The "instruction books" at that time were America's founding documents, namely the Declaration of Independence and the Constitution, including the Bill of Rights. In the spirit of those great works, most Americans shared a common view of "the sum of good government"—the protection of life and property.

Today, many people seem to think that government exists to do almost anything for anybody at any time they ask for it, from children's daycare to handouts for artists. Former Texas congressman and presidential candidate Ron Paul frequently blew the whistle whenever a bill was proposed that violated the spirit or the letter of the Constitution. Quite often he did so all by himself. Congress routinely dismissed such concerns.

Some years ago, I gave a series of lectures to high school seniors, and I asked the students what they thought the responsibilities of government were. I heard "provide jobs" or "take care of the poor" far more often than I heard anything like "safeguard our freedoms." (In fact, I think the only time I heard the latter was when I said it myself.)

A while back, an organization called the Communitarian Network made news when it called for the federal government to make organ donations mandatory, so that each citizen's body after death could be "harvested" for the benefit of sick people. Helping sick people is a good cause, but is it really a duty of government to take your kidneys?

In the era of Jefferson and Madison, Americans appreciated the concept of individual rights and entertained very little of this nonsense. But there is no consensus today on what even constitutes a right, let alone what rights free citizens possess.

Years ago, when the Reagan administration proposed abolishing subsidies to Amtrak, the nationalized passenger rail service, I was struck by a dissenter who phrased her objection on national television this way: "I don't know how those people in Washington expect us to get around out here. We have a right to this service."

Once, when Congress voted to stop funding the printing of *Playboy* magazine in Braille, the American Council of the Blind filed suit in federal court, charging that the congressional action constituted censorship and *denial of a basic right.*

Lest the reader mistakenly assume that I am skeptical of only these relatively small handouts from Washington, or only of public welfare for the poor, please know that the same objections apply at least as well to the hundreds of billions of dollars doled out every year in various forms of "corporate" welfare. What economists call "rent-seeking"— private benefits from one's use of political connections—is big in Washington these days and reeks of corruption and inequity.

The lofty notion that individuals possess certain rights—definable, inalienable and sacred rights—has been cheapened beyond anything our founders and early presidents would recognize. When those gifted thinkers asserted rights to "freedom of speech," "freedom of the press," or "freedom of assembly," they did not mean to say that one has a right to be given a microphone, a printing press, a lecture hall, or a *Playboy* magazine at someone else's expense.

Indeed, their concept of rights did not require the initiation of force against others or the elevation of any "want" to a lawful lien on the life or property of any other citizen. Each individual was deemed a unique and sovereign being, requiring only that other citizens deal with him honestly and voluntarily or not at all. It was this notion of rights that became an important theme of America's founding documents and early presidencies. It is the *only* notion of rights that does not produce an unruly mob in which each person has his hands in someone else's pocket.

This wisdom prompted early Americans to add a Bill of Rights to a Constitution that already contained a separation of government powers, checks and balances, and numerous "thou-shalt-nots" directed at government itself. They knew—unlike tens of millions of Americans today—that a government that lacks narrow rules and strict boundaries, that robs Peter to pay Paul, that confuses rights with wants, will yield financial ruin at best and political tyranny at worst.

Jefferson, Madison, and almost all of the succeeding twenty presidents of the nineteenth century were constrained by this view of the federal government, and most of them were happy to comply with it. When doing so, they were faithful to their charge. They were true poverty-fighters because they knew that if liberty were not preserved, poverty would be the least of our troubles. They had read the rule book, and they knew the importance of following the rules. Perhaps they also understood a cardinal rule of economics, namely, that real wealth (goods and services) springs from production, incentive, innovation, risk-taking, investment, and trade.

Andrew Jackson, whose tenure stretched from 1829 to 1837, was our seventh president and an exceedingly popular one. He, too, reminded Congress frequently in Jeffersonian terms what the federal role was. In his Fourth Annual Message on December 4, 1832, he wrote:

> Limited to a general superintending power to maintain peace at home and abroad, and to prescribe laws on a few subjects of general interest not calculated to restrict human liberty, but to enforce human rights, this government will find its strength and its glory in the faithful discharge of these plain and simple duties.[236]

In his Second Inaugural Address, three months later, Jackson again underscored the federal government's limited mission. He said:

> It will be my aim to inculcate by my official acts the necessity of exercising by the General Government those powers only that are clearly delegated; to encourage simplicity and economy in the expenditures of the Government; to raise no more money from the people than may be requisite for these objects, and in a manner that will best promote the interests of all classes of the community and of all portions of the Union.[237]

As if to head off any misunderstandings about the role of the federal government, Jackson went on to say, "To suppose that because our Government has been instituted for the benefit of the people it must therefore have the power to do whatever may seem to conduce to the public good is an error into which even honest minds are too apt to fall."[238]

Compared to giants like Jefferson, Madison, and Jackson, Franklin Pierce of New Hampshire is often thought of as a mere cipher. But he was another in a long string of nineteenth-century American presidents who greeted the idea of federal poverty assistance with great skepticism. Among his nine vetoes was one in 1854 that nixed a bill to help the mentally ill. Here's what Pierce said:

> It cannot be questioned that if Congress has power to make provision for the indigent insane ... it has the same power to provide for the indigent who are *not* insane, and thus to transfer to the Federal Government the charge of all the poor in all the States. It has the same power to provide hospitals and other local establishments for the care and cure of every species of human infirmity, and thus to assume all that duty of either public philanthropy, or public necessity to the dependent, the orphan, the sick, or the needy which is now discharged by the States themselves or by corporate institutions or private endowments existing under the legislation of the States. The whole field of public beneficence is thrown open to the care and culture of the Federal Government ... If Congress may and ought to provide for any one of these objects, it may and ought to provide for them all.[239]

It is a testament to the lack of federal welfare-style programs during more than sixty years under our first thirteen presidents that Pierce, our fourteenth, termed as "novel" the very idea of "providing for the care and support of all those among the people of the United States who by any form of calamity become fit objects of public philanthropy."[240]

Meanwhile, the poor of virtually every other nation on the planet were poor because of what governments were doing *to* them, often in the name of doing something *for* them: taxing and regulating them into penury, seizing their property and businesses, persecuting them for their faith, torturing and killing them because they held views different from those in power, and squandering their resources on official luxury, mindless warfare, and wasteful boondoggles. America was about government *not* doing such things to people; and that one fact was, all by itself, a powerfully effective anti-poverty program.

Americans of all colors pulled themselves out of poverty in the nineteenth century by creating wealth through invention and enterprise. As they did so, they generously gave much of their income—along with their time and personal attention—to the aid of their neighbors and communities. When the French social commentator Alexis de Tocqueville visited a young, bustling America during the Jackson administration in the 1830s, he cited the vibrancy of this "civil society" as one of our greatest assets.

Tocqueville was amazed that Americans were constantly forming "associations" to advance the arts, build libraries and hospitals, and meet social needs of every kind. If something good needed to be done, it didn't occur to Andrew Jackson or his fellow citizens to expect politicians and bureaucrats, who were distant in both space and spirit, to do it for them. "Among the laws that rule human societies," wrote Tocqueville in *Democracy in America,* "there is one which seems to be more precise and clear than all others. If men are to remain civilized or to become so, the art of associating together must grow and improve."

Indeed, this "art of associating together" in the nineteenth century produced the most remarkable flowering of private charitable assistance ever seen. This era saw the founding of many of America's most notable, lasting private associations—including the Red Cross and, "imported" from Britain, the Salvation Army.

For many reasons, such groups are generally far more effective in solving social problems—poverty, homelessness, and illiteracy, for instance—than are government programs. They are more likely to get to the root of problems that stem from spiritual, attitudinal, and behavioral deficiencies. They are also more inclined to demand accountability, which means they won't simply cut a check every two weeks without expecting the recipient to do something in return, such as changing destructive patterns of behavior. Ultimately, private associations also tend to promote self-reliance instead of dependency. The Bible calls us to closer, personal relationships with the poor, relationships that elevate their dignity and initiative. When private groups accomplish this from a faith-based mission, they are in keeping with biblical command.

And if these groups don't produce results, they usually wither; the parishioners or others who voluntarily support them will put their money elsewhere. In contrast, when a government program fails to perform, its lobbyists make a case for more funding. Worse, they usually get it.

From start to finish, what private charities do represents a manifestation of free will. No one is compelled to provide assistance. No one is coerced to pay for it. No one is required to accept it. All parties come together of their own volition.

And therein lies the magic of it all! The link between the giver, the provider, and the receiver is strong precisely because each knows he can walk away from it at the slightest hint of insincerity, broken promises, or poor performance. Because each party gives his own time or resources voluntarily, he tends to focus on the mission and doesn't get bogged down in secondary agendas like filling out the proper paperwork or currying favor with those in power. Management expert Peter Drucker summed it up well when he said that private charities, both faith-based and secular, "spend far less for results than governments spend for failure."[241]

Men and women of faith should be the first to argue that God does not need federal funds to do his work. When they get involved in charitable work, it's usually with the knowledge that a change of heart will often do more than a welfare check to conquer poverty. They focus on changing hearts, one heart at a time.

That's the way most Americans thought and behaved in the nineteenth century. They would have thought it a cop-out of the first order to pass these responsibilities on to politicians. Instead, Americans became the most generous people on earth. Christians specifically viewed personal, charitable involvement as "servanthood" commanded of them by Christ.

Consider a story that I first learned from a good friend and eminent Hillsdale College historian, Burton Folsom. It involves a huge natural calamity.

In 1881, a raging fire swept through the state of Michigan's "Thumb" area, killing nearly 200 people and destroying more than one million acres of timberland. "The flames ran faster than a horse could gallop," said one survivor of the devastating blaze. Its hurricane-like fury uprooted trees, blew away buildings, and destroyed millions of dollars of property across four counties.

This disaster produced an outpouring of generosity from Americans everywhere. In fact, the Michigan fire became the first disaster relief effort of Clara Barton and the newly formed American Red Cross. As the smoke billowed eastward across the nation, Barton's hometown of Dansville, New York, became a focal point of relief. According to the officers of the Dansville Red Cross, a call from Clara Barton "rallied us to our work."

"Instantly," they said, "we felt the help and strength of our organization (the Red Cross), young and untried as it was."[242] Men, women, and children throughout western New York brought food, clothing, and other gifts. Folsom points out that before the Red Cross would send them to Michigan, a committee of ladies inspected each item and re-stitched garments or replaced food when necessary.[243]

Speed was important, not only because many were hungry, but also because winter was approaching. Bedding and heavy clothing were in demand. Railroads provided the shipping. People left jobs and homes and trekked to Michigan to get personally involved in the rebuilding. Soon the Red Cross in New York and the local relief committees in Michigan were working together to distribute supplies until "no more were needed," according to the final report from the Red Cross.

According to Folsom, the Red Cross's assistance was much appreciated "and it made disaster relief faster, more efficient and national in scope."[244]

But even if such help had not come, Michiganians were prepared to organize relief voluntarily within the state. During an 1871 fire that left nearly 3,000 Michigan families homeless, Governor Henry Baldwin personally organized the relief efforts and gave about $150,000 out of his own pockets—a sum equivalent to more than $3 million today. Few, if any, thought it necessary to create a federal relief bureaucracy.

Baldwin and the Red Cross met the true definition of compassion. They suffered with the fire victims and worked personally to reduce their pain. Baldwin, the Red Cross, and the fire victims themselves might even have felt that aid from Washington, D.C., might have dampened the enthusiasm of the volunteers who gave their energy and resources out of a sense of duty and brotherly love. And this was in a year when the federal budget had a $100 million *surplus*, not the trillion-dollar annual red ink of today!

Government relief is in fact preemptive. There is little reason to believe that politicians are more compassionate or caring than the population that elects them. There is little reason to believe that politicians who are not on the scenes of either poverty or disaster and don't know the families affected will be more knowledgeable about how best to help them than those who *are* present and personally know the victims. There is even less reason to believe that politicians spend other people's money more effectively than those people to whom it belongs in the first place. Instead, when government gets involved, there is *good* reason to believe that much of its effort simply displaces what private people and groups would do better and more cost-effectively if government stayed home.

All of which leads me to a few words about a president whose character and record cry out for renewed attention today: Grover Cleveland—our twenty-second and twenty-fourth president (the only one to serve two nonconsecutive terms) and the humble son of a Presbyterian minister.

Cleveland said what he meant and meant what he said. He did not lust for political office, and he never felt he had to cut corners, equivocate, or connive in order to get elected. He was so forthright and plain-spoken that he makes Harry Truman seem indecisive by comparison.

This strong streak of honesty led him to the right policy conclusion again and again. H.L. Mencken, who was known for cutting politicians down to size, even wrote a nice little essay on Cleveland titled "A Good Man in a Bad Trade."

Cleveland thought it was an act of fundamental dishonesty for some to use government for their own benefit at everyone else's expense.

Accordingly, he took a firm stand against some early stirrings of an American welfare state.

In *The American Leadership Tradition: Moral Vision from Washington to Clinton,* Marvin Olasky noted that when Cleveland was mayor of Buffalo, New York, in the early 1880s, his "willingness to resist demands for government handouts made his name known throughout New York State," catapulting him to the governorship in 1882 and the presidency in 1884.[245]

Indeed, frequent warnings against using the government to redistribute income were characteristic of Cleveland's tenure. He regarded as a "serious danger" the notion that government should dispense favors and advantages to individuals or their businesses. This conviction led him to veto a wagonload of bills—414 in his first term and 170 in his second—far more than all the previous twenty-one presidents combined. "I ought to have a monument over me when I die," he once said, "not for anything I have ever done, but for the foolishness I have put a stop to."[246]

In vetoing a bill in 1887 that would have appropriated $10,000 in aid for Texas farmers struggling through a drought, Cleveland wrote:

> I can find no warrant for such an appropriation in the Constitution; and I do not believe that the power and duty of the General Government ought to be extended to the relief of individual suffering which is in no manner properly related to the public service or benefit. A prevalent tendency to disregard the limited mission of this power and duty should, I think, be steadfastly resisted, to the end that the lesson should be constantly enforced that, though the people support the Government, the Government should not support the people.[247]

Cleveland went on to point out that "The friendliness and charity of our countrymen can always be relied upon to relieve their fellow-citizens in misfortune."[248] Americans proved him right. Those Texas farmers eventually received more than ten times more in private aid than what the vetoed bill would have provided.[249]

As a devoted Christian, Cleveland saw the notion of taking from some to give to others as a violation of the Eighth and Tenth Commandments, which warn against theft and envy. He noticed what twentieth-century welfare statists did not, namely, that there was a *period* after the word "steal" in the Eighth Commandment, with no added qualifications. It does not say, "Thou shalt not steal unless the other guy has more than you do, or unless a government representative does it for you, or unless you can't find anyone who will give it to you freely, or unless you're totally convinced you can spend it better than the guy to whom it belongs."

Cleveland had been faithful to the founders and to what he believed were God's commandments, common sense, and historical experience. I can't say the same for certain of his successors who, in more recent times, cast wisdom to the winds and set America on a very different course.

For the first 150 years of American history, government at all levels played little role in social welfare. In a 1995 Heritage Foundation document titled "America's Failed $5.4 Trillion War on Poverty," Robert Rector and William Lauber pointed out, "As late as 1929, before the onset of the Great Depression, federal, state, and local welfare expenditures were only $90 million." In inflation-adjusted dollars, that would be under $1 billion today. By 1939, welfare spending was almost fifty times that amount, but at least the politicians of the day thought of it as a temporary bridge for its recipients. Welfare spending then fell and would not return to the 1939 levels until Lyndon Johnson's "War on Poverty" in the mid-1960s.[250]

And now we know, after $5.4 trillion and a series of catastrophic fiscal and social consequences, those old-fashioned virtues and principles generally embraced by America's nineteenth-century presidents were right on the mark.

More than 100 years ago, the great intellectual and crusader for liberty Auberon Herbert offered a cogent observation from his native Britain. His remarks neatly summarize the views of the men I've discussed here:

> No amount of state education will make a really intelligent nation; no amount of Poor Laws will place a nation above want; no amount of Factory Acts will make us better parents....To have our wants supplied from without by a huge state machinery, to be regulated and inspected by great armies of officials, who are themselves slaves of the system which they administer, will in the long run teach us nothing, will profit us nothing.[251]

The powerful wealth-creator known as a free economy certainly generated vast improvements in the general standard of living in the nineteenth century. The only thing socialism has done for poor people in the long run is give them lots of company. There is a missing but critical element in this story, however, to which I have only tangentially alluded up to this point. It was arguably just as important in reducing poverty as a free economy, and it explains the immense outpouring of private, charitable initiative in the 1800s. That element is *character.*

In America's first century, we possessed personal character in abundance; and even though it lacked think tanks, significant economic education, or policy research, it kept our liberties substantially intact.

People generally opposed the expansion of government power, not because they read policy studies or earned degrees in economics, but because they placed a high priority on character. Using government to get something at somebody else's expense, or mortgaging the future for near-term gain, seemed dishonest and cynical to them, if not downright sinful and immoral. Most Americans preferred to work on problems themselves instead of expecting a distant and expensive bureaucracy to butt in.

Within government, character is what differentiates a politician from a statesman. Statesmen don't seek public office for personal gain or attention. Often they are people who take time out from productive careers to temporarily serve the public. They don't have to work for government because that's all they know how to do. They stand for a principled vision, not for what they think citizens will fall for. When a statesman gets elected, he doesn't forget the public-spirited citizens who sent him to office, thereby becoming a mouthpiece for the permanent bureaucracy or some special interest that greased his campaign.

Because they seek the truth, statesmen are more likely to do what's right than what may be politically popular at the moment. You know where they stand because they say what they mean and they mean what they say. They do not engage in class warfare, race-baiting, or other divisive or partisan tactics that pull people apart. They do not buy votes with tax dollars, nor do they make promises they can't keep or intend to break. They take responsibility for their actions. A statesman doesn't try to pull himself up by dragging somebody else down, and he doesn't try to convince people they're victims just to posture as their savior.

When it comes to managing public finances, statesmen prioritize. They don't behave as though government deserves an endlessly larger share of other people's money. They exhibit the courage to cut less important expenses to make way for more pressing ones. They don't try to build empires. Instead, they keep government within its proper bounds and trust in what free and enterprising people can accomplish. Politicians think that they're smart enough to plan other people's lives; statesmen are wise enough to understand the utter folly of such an arrogant attitude. A statesman, in other words, possesses a level of character that an ordinary politician does not.

By almost any measure, the standards we as citizens keep and expect of those we elect have slipped badly in recent years. Though everybody complains about politicians who pander, perhaps they pander because we are increasingly a panderable people. Too many are willing to look the other way when politicians misbehave, as long as they are of the right party or deliver the goods we personally want.

Our celebrity-drenched culture focuses incessantly on the vapid and the irresponsible. Our role models would make our grandparents cringe. To many, sterling character seems too strait-laced and old-fashioned. We cut corners and sacrifice character all the time for power, money, attention, or other ephemeral gratifications.

Yet character is ultimately more important than all the college degrees, public offices, or even knowledge that one might accumulate in a lifetime. It puts both a concrete floor under one's future and an iron ceiling over it. Who in their right mind would want to live in a world without it? It decides the course of nations and whether or not nations can actually solve problems or just perpetuate them.

Chief among the elements that define strong character are these: honesty, humility, responsibility, self-discipline, self-reliance, optimism, a long-term focus, and a lust for learning. A free society is impossible without them. For example, without these virtues, dishonest people will lie and cheat and become even bigger liars and cheaters in elected office; people who lack humility become arrogant, condescending, know-it-all central-planners; irresponsible citizens blame others for the consequences of their own poor judgment; people who will not discipline themselves invite the intrusive control of others; those who eschew self-reliance are easily manipulated by those on whom they are dependent; pessimists dismiss what individuals can accomplish when given the freedom to try; myopic citizens will mortgage their future for the sake of a short-term "solution;" and closed-minded, politically correct or head-in-the-sand types will never learn from the lessons of history and human action.

Bad character earns reproof and censure endlessly in Scripture. We learn in Proverbs 12:22 that "Lying lips are an abomination to the Lord." Humility earns praise in Proverbs 11:2: "When pride comes, then comes disgrace, but with the humble is wisdom." We are cautioned to guard our hearts, practice virtue, and keep good company in numerous places, including Philippians 4:8; 2 Peter 1:5-6; Proverbs 4:23; Matthew 15:18-20; and 1 Corinthians 15:33.

Good character is commanded of us throughout the Bible. Courage is explicitly *encouraged* in 2 Timothy 1:7: "For God gave us a spirit not of fear but of power and love and self-control." Character helps us weather the storms of our daily lives, as indicated by Proverbs 10:9: "Whoever walks in integrity walks securely, but he who makes his ways crooked will be found out." Titus 2:7-8 tells us that godly behavior produces good effects: "In everything set them an example by doing what is good. In your teaching show integrity, seriousness and soundness of speech that cannot be condemned, so that those who oppose you may be ashamed because they have nothing bad to say about us." The "fruits of the Spirit" in Galatians 5:22 are among the character traits that result from the saving grace of Christ: "love, joy, peace, forbearance, kindness, goodness, faithfulness, gentleness and self-control."

So it should come as no surprise that bad character leads to bad economics and bad public policy, which is bad for liberty and bad for all people—especially the poor, who have fewer options and fewer political connections in a socialistic society. Ultimately, whether we live free and in harmony with the laws of economics or stumble into thralldom is a *character* issue.

Americans of the few generations after the Constitution were mindful of Jefferson's warning: "We must not let our rulers load us with perpetual debt. We must make our election between economy and liberty or profusion and servitude." Today the magnitude of the red ink should terrify us, and it is a consequence of the widespread idea that "safety nets" should be provided by politicians instead of by the citizens and their private institutions.

The deficit that matters most is not denominated in dollars at all. Its currency is of the heart and mind. The values with which we circumscribe our actions are manifested in our purposes and our values. I speak of a deficit of *character*, which arguably is the root of all of our major economic and social troubles today.

Your character is not defined by what you *say* you believe. It is defined by the choices you make. Time and again, history painfully records that when a people allow their personal character to dissipate, they become putty in the hands of tyrants and demagogues.

When a person spurns his conscience and fails to do what he knows is right, he subtracts from his character. When he evades his responsibilities, foists his problems and burdens on others, or fails to exert self-discipline, he subtracts from his character. Permitting or encouraging wrongdoing on any scale subtracts from his character. When he attempts to reform the world without reforming himself first, he subtracts from his character. Obligating the yet-unborn to pay his current bills for him further subtracts from his character. When he expects politicians to solve problems that are properly his business alone, he subtracts from his character—and drags the rest of us down with him.

Mountainous debts, unconscionable deficits, irresponsible bailouts, and reckless spending—these are all *economic* problems because they sprang first from *character* problems. More citizens would understand this if they contemplated the inherent immorality of burdening generations yet unborn with the costs of the current generation's immediate gratification.

It is wrong to take a dollar from the responsible and give it to the irresponsible. It is wrong to take a dollar from the innocent and give it to the guilty. It is wrong to take a dollar from a man today, squander it on current consumption, and expect the man's grandchildren to pay for it many years later. What is it about doing these things a trillion times over that somehow makes them right? Moral conscience suggests the error is simply made a trillion times worse. Americans of the supposedly "backward" and "antiquated" nineteenth century understood that better than their descendants of today.

With character as their backstop and liberty as their vision, Americans built a vibrant, self-reliant, entrepreneurial culture with strong families and solid values. People occasionally needed help, but rarely did their fellow citizens or churches or Red Cross chapters say "Get lost."

Somewhere along the way, we lost our moral compass—another way of saying that we succumbed to sin. Like the Roman republic that rose on integrity and collapsed in turpitude, we thought the "bread and circuses" the government could provide us would buy us comfort and security. These days, we often act like we really don't want to be free and responsible citizens, so we get less responsibility from our leaders and less freedom for us. Shame on us.

Americans who are serious about fixing the country's fiscal mess *and* caring for the poor must begin by fixing their character. We can begin by pledging ourselves to lives of self-improvement so we can each be a model of integrity that friends and family members will want to emulate. We can take responsibility for our actions and decisions and try our best to impose no burdens on others that stem from our own poor judgments. We can strive to pay the highest respect for the lives, property, and rights of our fellow citizens. We can avoid using our votes to loot our fellow citizens. We can stand on our own two feet as far as our abilities allow. We can resolve to help others who genuinely need it by involving ourselves directly or by supporting those who are providing assistance through charitable institutions. We should stop complaining about a problem and insisting that government tinker with it at twice the cost and half the effectiveness of such private institutions. In short, we can behave like adults of character in a free and civil society, and we can expect the same of our children.

In March 2005, an international commission called on wealthy countries like the United States to dramatically increase their foreign aid. Many of the governments of Europe were in full support. But what would American presidents of the nineteenth century have had to say about that? I can imagine Cleveland, Johnson, Pierce, Van Buren, Jackson, Madison, or Jefferson reacting in disbelief at the very suggestion. Cleveland might have said, "Aid to foreign countries? We don't even dispense aid to *Americans*." And he would have had a century of unprecedented progress against poverty to point to as his example.

For the benefit of welfare statists here and abroad, I think Cleveland and the other presidents I've quoted herein would be very comfortable echoing the sentiments of the nineteenth century French economist and statesman Frederic Bastiat:

And now that the legislators and do-gooders have so futilely inflicted so many systems upon society, may they finally end where they should have begun: May they reject all systems, and try liberty; for liberty is an acknowledgment of faith in God and His works.[252]

Alleviating Poverty in the Abstract

By Marvin Olasky, Ph.D.

Greeks bearing gifts: That's what proponents of welfare have been, and still are, in two ways: one is obvious, the other subtle.

"Greeks bearing gifts" is not an ethnic slur but a literary and historical reference: As the Roman poet Virgil wrote in *The Aeneid*, the original Greek gift was the enormous wooden horse that ended the Trojan War. For ten years Troy's walls frustrated Europe's finest, and for two centuries ocean barriers protected America from Old World conflicts. But the giant horse, with soldiers inside, brought invaders within the city gates; and long-term governmental welfare has smuggled into America a psychological and financial invader that saps individual initiative and community spirit. Additionally, trillions of dollars added to U.S. debt could turn this country into contemporary Greece writ large.

The subtler Grecian formula concerns the nature of Hellenic thought. Philosopher David Naugle has pointed out that Hellenic thought veers toward abstraction, while the Hebraic mindset emphasizes the concrete. Naugle contends that Christian scholarship should be "primarily Hebraic rather than Hellenic," and he rhetorically asks, "Wouldn't neglecting the influential principles and patterns of a Hebrew mind deposited in the Bible seriously weaken a proper Christian scholarly understanding of God, the world, and ourselves? Should we think and live, primarily, with Greek or Hebrew lenses and hearts?"[253]

Naugle answers those questions affirmatively and concludes, "Christianity is Jewish....Yet most Western philosophy is derived from 'Athens' rather than 'Jerusalem.'"[254] I could say the same about most of the histories of American poverty-fighting that I have read and most of the speeches in defense of welfare I have heard. They typically deliver glittering generalities, avoid specific detail, and report at suite level rather than street level. We need an unblinking gaze at reality, but books with titles like *The Philosophy of Compassion, The Veins of Compassion, The Power of Compassion, The Beauty of Compassion, Truth and Compassion, A Spirituality Named Compassion, and Tear-Catchers: Developing the Gift of Compassion* view poverty through gauze.[255]

Such books sit high up on what writers call "the ladder of abstraction," a term used by S.I. Hayakawa half a century ago in *Language in Action*.[256] Journalists should stand lower on the ladder, since specific detail is the coin of reporters' realms; but too many stories settle for big numbers and dollar amounts. Welfare caseworkers have the same problem. One in California said, "With 125 cases it's hard to remember that they're all human beings."[257] One scene in a television drama conveyed the recipients' view: A welfare mom tells a government caseworker, "I'm a real person. If you remember that next time we'll have a better conversation."[258]

I am hoping this essay can engender a better conversation by starting with the story of one real person, Elizabeth "Cookie" Jones. I will then provide historical detail about real persons in the nineteenth and twentieth centuries and conclude by looking at today's welfare conversations.

The Story of "Cookie" Jones

In 1996, at the height of that decade's welfare reform debate, journalist (and 2012 National Book Award recipient) Katherine Boo decided to move beyond hurling theoretical thunderbolts and waving statistics. She profiled Elizabeth "Cookie" Jones, a longtime welfare recipient whom Boo met in a Washington, D.C. public-housing project. A friend of Jones—also on welfare—suggested that Jones, twenty-seven years old and the mother of three elementary school children by three different men, was making a mistake by going to work. The reason: "Her kids are raising themselves"—and that would ruin them in the long run.[259]

Jones agreed to spend time with Boo so that legislators would come to understand "the stomach-turning choices implicit in that bumper sticker of a phrase 'welfare-to-work.'"

Boo documented how Jones found a job but then "faced a choice: Ice the job, reclaim the welfare check, walk the kids home from school. Or keep the job and risk the kids." Jones decided to work because her mother had gone on welfare after having a child at age seventeen, and Jones had done the same—but she now vowed to break that pattern, "or I'll die trying."[260]

Jones, in short, was a purpose-driven heroine facing huge obstacles, including the bad public schools in her poor part of the District. Boo's implied question: Would Jones's children die as their mom tried to break the generational pattern? Boo described the children muttering "scary" as they walked past old vodka bottles, up a stinkweed path, and past one long block "where a man will days later be found murdered in his car." Jones believed the risk was worthwhile because her children would see work as more desirable than welfare.[261]

Five years later, in 2001, Boo wrote a new profile of Elizabeth Jones for *The New Yorker.* By then Jones had become a police officer, even though her children didn't like it: "They think she'll get hurt. She fears they'll get hurt if she gives it up." Boo wondered whether Elizabeth Jones and her children would have been better off had she stayed on welfare. Five years later Jones was still working, and Boo was still following her. Boo said on NPR, "The positive benefits that a mother is going to get from work—self-esteem and exposures to mainstream culture, the benefits of higher education—those are real benefits. But family life in the short-term, I think, isn't very pretty."[262]

I respected those Boo stories and wanted to learn what happened, so I had a *World* Washington reporter track down Elizabeth Jones. We learned that she persevered in police work, and in January of 2013 had served fifteen years. She helped bring to justice a woman eventually sentenced to twelve years in prison for physically abusing her foster son, as well as two men who were eventually sentenced to more than thirty years in prison for their roles in a fatal shooting. Looking back over the years and thinking about her original decision to go from welfare to work, Jones said, "I knew I had to do something. It's always been hard—from day one."[263]

The hardships were psychological and financial. When Jones came off welfare, her insurance coverage for a short time applied only to herself and not her three children—and during that window one of her sons broke an arm, while another broke a leg. (Yes, leaving welfare cost her an arm and a leg.) Jones's first job off welfare left her with fewer dollars than the friend who remained on welfare received. But Jones persevered, garnered increases in responsibility and salary, and raised three children, who are all in their twenties and doing well. One is a college graduate. Another spent four years in the Navy, is married and has a son. Her youngest child went to college for two years and is now working.[264]

Jones says her move off welfare helped her children "tremendously. They're not in jail, they're productive members of society, and they're responsible.... I remember being on public assistance and I would have to go and re-certify. I never took them. Not that I was hiding it from them, but that's not the picture that I wanted them to have when they got older - that this is how things are supposed to be." Several months ago Jones saw her friend who had remained on welfare for her children's sake, but the two did not talk long because "the vibe wasn't really pleasant." Jones says one of her friend's sons was killed on the Washington streets.[265]

The Three Dimensions of Fighting Poverty

Could I find stories of single-mom families that did not fare well when the mother went off welfare? Undoubtedly. But Elizabeth Jones's upward mobility is not unusual now—and was typical up until the 1960s. Jones ran toward opportunity as soon as she saw daylight, and that has been the American way. Government anti-poverty programs looked good to those sitting high up on the ladder of abstraction; but our history confirms that change-oriented compassion has three dimensions: it needs to be personal, spiritual, and challenging. That is a central theme of *The Tragedy of American Compassion*. State-issued welfare failed on one count during the nineteenth century and on two during the first half of the twentieth century. It has failed on all three counts since then.

Even in colonial America, effective poverty-fighters stressed person-to-person help. Minutes from the Fairfield, Connecticut town council meeting of April 16, 1673, show that "Seriant Squire and Sam Moorhouse [agreed] to take care of Roger Knap's family in this time of their great weakness."[266] Groups such as the Scots' Charitable Society (organized in 1684) "open[ed] the bowells of our compassion" to widows such as a Mrs. Stewart who had "lost the use of her left arm" and whose husband was "Wash'd Overboard in a Storm."[267]

Poverty-fighters respected human dignity, so Benjamin Franklin in 1766 was appalled to see that Britain's governmental provision deprived the poor of "inducements to industry, frugality and sobriety." What seemed virtuous in the abstract was—an unintended consequence—horrible in practice: "There is no country in the world in which the poor are more idle, dissolute, drunken and insolent."[268]

A decade later, as the thirteen colonies became states, Americans avoided British welfare practices and offered personal, spiritual, and challenging help to the needy. In one example from the North, merchant Stephen Girard, born in France in 1750, lost sight in one eye at age eight, left home as a boy, settled in Philadelphia at the start of the Revolution, built a shipping business, and became one of America's richest men. What made him a national hero, though, was his work during the yellow fever epidemic of 1793. He paid hospital bills and supplied food and fuel to those suffering and their families. He later took many orphans into his own home and established a school for poor orphan boys, where they gained biblical teaching and received the challenge to work hard.[269]

In the South, the Ladies Benevolent Society of Charleston in 1825 included a Mrs. Cowie, who suffered from blindness and leprosy and whose body was "a perfect skeleton;" Clarissa and Mary, two crippled black women; and Mary McNeile, a free black with leprosy.[270] Specific details changed the ladies' thinking: One newspaper, the *Southern Evangelical Intelligencer*, reported that society members witnessed "scenes of distress, want, misery, and woe, scarcely to be conceived by those who have never entered the frail and unsheltered tenements of this city, where poverty, sickness and wretchedness dwell."[271]

Americans sometimes fell into European patterns but quickly saw their error. New York Secretary of State J.V.N. Yates told his legislature in 1824 that "outdoor relief"—government distribution to the poor outside of workhouses—"had come to encourage the sturdy beggar and profligate vagrant."[272] Yates argued that "overseers not infrequently granted relief without sufficient examination into the circumstances or the ability of the party claiming it." When Philadelphia's outdoor relief did not exclude women with illegitimate children, a citizens' committee worried that the City of Brotherly Love's policy was "an encouragement to vice, and offers a premium for prostitution."[273] The committee noted that in Baltimore, Boston, and Salem, where mothers with illegitimate children were ineligible, cases of illegitimacy were rare, but there were "in Philadelphia 269!!!"[274]

The *American Quarterly Review* argued in 1835 that government subsidies seemed kind in theory, but they enabled individuals to become "degraded, dissolute, wasteful, profligate, and idle, by promising them a support if they do so."[275] Children would learn that income came without work, and the end result would be "generation after generation of hereditary paupers."[276] In New York, relief officials offering a "certainty of public provision" were said to hand out "invitations to become beggars."[277]

Nineteenth-century Americans learned to emphasize individual initiative, both among rich and poor, rather than gauzy sentiment.

Children generally learned how to read via McGuffey's Readers, and the 1844 edition's dialogue about poverty-fighting—between a "Mr. Fantom," who stood high on the ladder of abstraction, and a "Mr. Goodman," who paid attention to the needs around him—provided a key lesson:

> Mr. Fantom: I despise a narrow field. O for the reign of universal benevolence! I want to make all mankind good and happy.
>
> Mr. Goodman: Dear me! Sure that must be a wholesale sort of a job: had you not better try your hand at a town or neighborhood first?
>
> Mr. Fantom: Sir, I have a plan in my head for relieving the miseries of the whole world....
>
> Mr. Goodman: The utmost extent of my ambition at present is, to redress the wrongs of a poor apprentice, who has been cruelly used by his master....
>
> Mr. Fantom: You must not apply to me for the redress of such petty grievances.... It is provinces, empires, continents, that the benevolence of the philosopher embraces; every one can do a little paltry good to his next neighbor.

McGuffey gave Mr. Goodman a good comeback: "Every one can, but I do not see that every one does.... [You] have such a noble zeal for the millions, [yet] feel so little compassion for the units."[278]

Governor Thomas Cooper of Delaware told his legislature: "If the door of public commiseration is thrown too widely open the great stimulus to exertion, which providence in his wisdom, has implanted in the bosom of the community, is too apt to be weakened." While the theory of redistributing material to help the poor conveyed abstract appeal, nineteenth-century Americans studied historical experience and concluded the results were poor. Many referred to ancient Rome, where "politicians of the time" used "doles to the poor" to obtain "positions which they were far from competent to hold." A monthly distribution of corn to all "was sufficient to pauperize and render dependent a fearfully large proportion of one of the most manly races which have ever lived." Nathaniel Ware, after summarizing in 1845 this interpretation of Rome's fall, sadly predicted that an American governmental welfare system would develop, sooner or later, because poor voters would give power to those who offered them money.[279]

In 1853, pastor and author William Ruffner reminded his flock that "idleness and improvidence" result whenever "there are large funds provided—and especially when provided by state taxation, and disbursed by state officers."[280] He said, "Charity is a work requiring great tenderness and sympathy, and agents, who do their work for a price rather than for love, should not be trusted to execute the wishes of donors. The keepers of poor-houses (like undertakers) fall into a business, unfeeling way of doing their duties; which is wounding and often partial and cruel to the objects of their attention."[281]

Ruffner also explained that contributions of cash were abstract, while contributions of time were concrete. He didn't minimize the difficulties: "To cast a contribution into the box brought to the hand, or to attend committees and anniversaries, are very trifling exercises of Christian self-denial and devotion, compared with what is demanded in the weary perambulations through the street, the contact with filth, and often with rude and repulsive people."

Others, though, climbed up the ladder of abstraction from the dirty streets. The *Providence Journal* argued that the city treasury was "the savings bank in which is deposited a part of the earnings of every laborer," so each worker had an "equitable and Christian right [to] a dividend of these profits."[282] The mayor of Boston said city government had "the obligation to meet whatever need exists."[283] Just west of Boston, the *Waltham Sentinel* argued that the poor generally should claim government provision "as their right."[284]

Sometimes abstraction countered abstraction. In 1854, Congress responded to impassioned pleading by passing legislation for federal construction and maintenance of mental hospitals—but President Franklin Pierce vetoed the bill, explaining that he wished to help the mentally ill but saw danger. "If Congress has the power to make provision for the indigent insane," Pierce pointed out, "it has the same power for the indigent who are not insane."[285] Pierce added, "I cannot find any authority in the Constitution for making the Federal Government the great almoner of public charity throughout the United States." He contended that the law would be "prejudicial rather than beneficial to the noble offices of charity," since federal funds would discourage local assistance: "[S]hould this bill become a law, that Congress is to make provision for such objects, the foundations of charity will be dried up at home."[286] Congress upheld Pierce's veto.

Abstraction versus Application

The Civil War brought America to ground level. The war in itself provided lessons about the ladder of abstraction. Those who had shed blood on the battlefield were less likely to shed tears when those proposing government growth used as their rationale the need to help the poor.

Some insisted that a governmental program would enable people to remain poor instead of challenging them to leave poverty. Governmental welfare was "the least desirable form of relief," according to Baltimore charity executive Mary Richmond, because it "comes from what is regarded as a practically inexhaustible source, and people who once receive it are likely to regard it as a right, as a permanent pension, implying no obligation on their part."[287] She wanted givers to know specific circumstances before jumping in: "Relief given without reference to friends and neighbors is accompanied by moral loss. Poor neighborhoods are doomed to grow poorer and more sordid, whenever the natural ties of neighborliness are weakened by our well-meant but unintelligent interference."[288]

Richmond wrote that her hardest task was teaching volunteers "whose kindly but condescending attitude has quite blinded them to the everyday facts of the neighborhood life."[289] To be effective, volunteers had to leave behind "a conventional attitude toward the poor, seeing them through the comfortable haze of our own excellent intentions, and content to know that we wish them well, without being at any great pains to know them as they really are."[290] Volunteers had to learn that "well-meant interference, unaccompanied by personal knowledge of all the circumstances, often does more harm than good and becomes a temptation rather than a help."[291]

Some writers still sat high up on the ladder of abstraction; but liberal reformer Jacob Riis, in his 1890 book *How the Other Half Lives*, showed what could be accomplished by a journalist willing to haul heavy cameras up dozens of flights of tenement stairs, day after day, to provide striking photographs of dull-eyed families in crowded flats. Looking close-up at the evidence, he wrote of all those willing to help "when it is known that help is worthily wanted."[292] He wrote of how one charity group over eight years raised "4,500 families out of the rut of pauperism into proud, if modest, independence, without alms."[293] He noted that another "handful of noble women... accomplished what no machinery of government availed to do. Sixty thousand children have been rescued by them from the streets."[294]

Associated Charities of Boston argued that its agencies pushed clients toward personal improvement, but "Statutory provisions, however, would disarm the private citizen and render him powerless to restrict the growth of pauperism in the community.[295] The demoralizing effect of relief administered by the hands of city officials can hardly be overestimated, no matter how excellent the officials themselves may be. It created a dependent feeling, a dry rot, which leads the recipient of city bounty to look upon it as something due as a reward for destitution."[296]

A typical case from the files of the Associated Charities of Boston showed the wages of specificity. When one elderly widower applied for help, "the agent's investigation showed that there were relatives upon whom he might have a claim," and a brother-in-law who had not seen the old man for twenty-five years "promised to send a regular pension."[297] He came through with a contribution that paid the old man's living expenses and reunited him with his late wife's family. "If there had been no careful investigation," the caseworker noted, the man would have received some bread, but would have remained "wretched in his filthy abode."[298]

Careful observers noted that governmental welfare theoretically seemed good, but as Amos G. Warner cautioned at the end of the nineteenth century in his mammoth study, *American Charities*, "It is necessarily more impersonal and mechanical than private charity or individual action."[299] Charles Brace, who created the "orphan trains" that placed children in families throughout the United States, also saw dehumanizing abstraction as the enemy: "The child, most of all, needs individual care and sympathy. In an Asylum, he is 'Letter B, of Class 3,' or 'No. 2, of Cell 426.'"[300] The charity magazine *Lend a Hand* regularly reminded readers to "beware of mere charity with the tongs."[301]

Warner further noted that if officials taxed those who had just come out of poverty in order to pay for government welfare, new problems could result: "It is possible to do so much relief-work that, while one set of persons is relieved, another will be taxed across the pauper line.... the burden of supporting the State tends to diffuse itself along the lines of the least resistance; consequently, money which is raised for the relief of the poor may come out of pockets that can ill spare it."[302] He suggested that prating politicians could gain favor by taxing the near-poor to help the poor. He may have been thinking of Yale professor William Graham Sumner's term "the Forgotten Man," defined by Sumner as "the simple, honest laborer, ready to earn his living by productive work. We pass him by because he is independent, self-supporting, and asks no favors."[303]

Progressives gained some victories during the first three decades of the twentieth century, but most Americans maintained the position that Washington should provide for the common defense and promote the general welfare, not the specific welfare of a defined class of individuals. (Lawrence Reed discusses this aspect in his chapter.) Most Americans also hated the idea of becoming dependent on government. Even in the 1930s, when E. W. Bakke interviewed 2000 heads of families in New Haven, an accountant turned ditch-digger voiced a typical sentiment: "I'd rather stay out in that ditch the rest of my life than take one cent of direct relief."[304]

Franklin Roosevelt skillfully turned Sumner's "Forgotten Man" upside down, recasting him not as the taxed worker but as the unemployed. Amity Shlaes has argued that Roosevelt's expansion of government and constant experimentation prolonged the Depression— and it certainly provided the opportunity for previously depressed social workers to turn the crisis into joyful transformation.[305] "The great depression of the 1930s revolutionized social work," Frank Bruno wrote. "Instead of being the Cinderella that must be satisfied with the leavings, social work was placed by the depression among the primary functions of government."[306]

Roosevelt administration officials spoke not of revolution but of temporary function and gave their agencies names such as the Federal Emergency Relief Administration. Some recalled the nineteenth-century admonitions against government involvement in poverty relief efforts. Bureau of the Budget Director Lewis Douglas was one of them. He warned that "thousands would settle into government-made jobs" if programs were long-lasting and said a program given time to sink roots "might become so great that it might be impossible to end it."[307]

Roosevelt himself acknowledged the danger of welfare programs becoming "a habit with the country." In November of 1933, he said, "When any man or woman goes on a dole something happens to them mentally and the quicker they are taken off the dole the better it is for them the rest of their lives."[308] Early in 1935 Roosevelt argued, "We must preserve not only the bodies of the unemployed from destitution but also their self-respect, their self-reliance and courage and determination."[309] Later that year Roosevelt noted, "In this business of relief we are dealing with properly self-respecting Americans to whom a mere dole outrages every instinct of individual independence. Most Americans want to give something for what they get. That something, in this case honest work, is the saving barrier between them and moral disintegration. We propose to build that barrier high."[310]

That was abstract talk, though, and social-work leaders had concrete proposals for a low barrier that would not let the economic crisis to go to waste. They knew then what current Chicago mayor Rahm Emanuel said repeatedly in 2008 as he was helping Barack Obama become president: "Rule one: Never allow a crisis to go to waste: They are opportunities to do big things," and "You never want a serious crisis to go to waste.... This crisis provides the opportunity for us to do things that you could not do before."[311]

The American Association of Social Workers (AASW) kicked off its campaign in 1932 by contending that the United States had a "faulty distribution of wealth." This meant that "the future of social work is bound up with the coming of a sounder social order" based on social and economic planning, through which all who desired it would be entitled to governmental support.[312] Dorothy C. Kahn of the Pennsylvania School of Social Work (and former AASW president) spoke of the need to fight "the widely held belief that those who work, with the exception of an increasing group of so-called natural dependents, are the only ones who have a right to maintenance."[313] Even worse, Kahn said, ideas about relief were "accompanied by a tendency to believe that any provision for able-bodied workers, which does not result directly from their own efforts, is bound to have a demoralizing effect on the individual and tends to increase the numbers of such persons in any community." She said, "Social workers must try to modify the social attitudes.... We must remove the organic connection between work and maintenance."[314]

Kahn also decried beliefs in individual responsibility "rooted in our culture, fostered by religious injunctions, nourished by education....a significant indication of the outmoded doctrines influencing our social structure."[315] Social work gurus such as Mary Van Kleeck proposed a better structure. Van Kleeck regularly praised Soviet planning and demanded a "collective, worker-controlled society."[316] The National Conference of Social Work (NCSW) in 1934 awarded Van Kleeck a prize for her work that proposed "a socialized, planned economy for the raising of standards of living."[317] Gertrude Springer of *The Survey*, a social workers' journal, described the reaction to one of her NCSW speeches: "Never in a long experience of conferences has this observer witnessed such a prolonged ovation as followed."[318]

NCSW handed another prize to Eduard Lindeman for his paper on "Basic Unities in Social Work." He argued that social workers should "build a new society" based on "redistribution of national wealth....nationalization of utilities, currency, credits and marginal land [and] elevation of a large proportion of housing to the status of public utility."[319] Lindeman said, "Our task is to project a conception of society which is sufficiently revolutionary on the one hand to eliminate accumulated evils, and at the same time sufficiently indigenous to our cultural tradition to insure workability."[320] In 1937, NCSW president Edith Abbott made that goal less abstract by making one specific proposal: Relief should not be "means tested," and the unemployed should receive extensions of aid for any reason or no reason.[321]

Such talk raised concern about a permanent class of initiative-lacking recipients; but happily a host of abstract, foundation-sponsored studies over the next two decades purported to show that welfare stipends did not undermine individual independence and self-respect. Russell Sage Foundation official Donald Howard put out an 835-page study proposing an expansion of federal programs and spotlighting advantages—where others had stressed hazards—in the federal government's "freedom from inflexible constitutional or debt limitations."[322] New York Mayor Fiorello La Guardia had made similar arguments in 1939; he wanted Washington to take a larger role because "the Federal Government has unlimited credit. It has no constitutional tax limitation. It has no constitutional borrowing limitation."[323] Howard, who eventually became AASW president and dean of the UCLA School of Social Welfare, wanted relief to be depersonalized and a structure of "rights" established, so that "no person would have the discretionary power to deny to any eligible applicant the aid to which he is entitled."[324]

Howard concluded his Sage study with the recognition that Americans still valued personal responsibility and opposed entitlement when providing welfare: regrettably, "established mores are undoubtedly too deeply embedded in the American spirit for the present to permit adequate relief to employable persons without requiring work in return. Thus, to make the giving of relief contingent upon recipients' willingness to perform some kind of work may be regarded as a price that—public opinion and attitudes being what they are—must be paid for adequate and decent relief to employable persons."[325] Howard, though, was optimistic: "Fortunately for those who need public assistance...mores do change." He observed that "traditional attitudes toward 'getting something for nothing' are already undergoing change, and in the future will be further modified....It may not forever be necessary to think of direct assistance as 'demoralizing.'"[326]

A Shift to the Entitlement Mentality

Over the next thirty years, "temporary" New Deal programs gradually became institutionalized. The challenging and personal elements of help decreased, but many religion-based elements of an older understanding remained. For example, welfare was not for able-bodied men who should be working; so in order to receive governmental aid, mothers could not have a "man in the house," and they could lose their aid if they cohabited. That rule, sometimes enforced by inspections, held down the number of applicants; but it had perverse consequences in reducing the number of marriages and even the permanent presence of unmarried fathers, providing one more example of unintended consequences.

The 1960s saw such rules struck down by an odd coalition of rising feminists and rationalistic materialists. Leaders of both groups often saw the strictures of Judaism or Christianity as irrelevant. For example, in 1963 Ford Foundation official Paul N. Ylvisaker explained that a city should be viewed as a "social production system" in the same way that "A.T.&T., for example, has long viewed it as a communications system." Ylvisaker argued that "certain parts of the urban social system can be perfected by rational means and specific devices."[327] He then headed President Lyndon Johnson's Task Force on Cities and brought over the Ford Foundation's Model Cities program.

Those who saw poverty as a material matter alone ignored the need for challenge. A University of Michigan Survey Research Center study, funded by the Ford Foundation, declared that poverty could be abolished "simply by a stroke of the pen. To raise every individual and family in the nation now below a subsistence income to the subsistence level would cost but $10 billion a year. That is less than two percent of the gross national product. It is less than ten percent of tax revenues." Foundation-funded utopian materialists sitting at the top of the ladder of abstraction opined: "the elimination of poverty is well within the means of federal, state, and local governments."[328]

People at street level who truly wanted change, though, were disappointed. One caseworker voiced what thousands apparently thought: "The paper work is just amazing. There are copies and copies of everything, dozens of forms to fill out....All we have time to do is move paper. I have yet to solve any social problems."[329] When journalist Nathaniel Dunford in 1990 "fulfilled a long-standing dream by quitting a job at *The New York Times* to take a position at half the pay as a caseworker with New York City's Child Welfare Administration, [he] lasted two months....Cases would usually arrive in the morning....They would eventually reach our supervisor, to sit for a few more hours....

Nothing was allowed to interfere with the lunch break. Meanwhile, in various parts of the city, the children and the sympathetic adults trying to help them were left to fume."[330] Dunford moaned that he "had a calling; it was that simple. I wanted to help."[331]

Occasionally reporters actually reported how bureaucratic rules caused problems for those welfare moms who wanted to do the right thing. In the 1980s, Grace Capetillo, a thirty-six-year-old single mother on welfare, had tried to save some money. She shopped at thrift stores and stocked up on sale items at grocery stores. She bought secondhand winter clothes during the summer and warm-weather outfits during the winter. When her five-year-old daughter Michelle's T-shirts grew tight, she snipped them below the underarm so they would last longer. When Michelle asked for "Lil' Miss Makeup" for Christmas, Mrs. Capetillo did not pay $19.99 for it at Toys"R"Us, but $1.89 at Goodwill; she cleaned it up and tied a pink ribbon in its hair before giving the doll to Michelle. At Goodwill she even found the pieces of another popular toy, Mr. Potato Head, and bought them for seventy-nine cents, saving $3.18.[332]

Penny by penny, dollar by dollar, Capetillo saved $3,000 over four years, but found herself in court because she was retaining rather than spending money she received under the federal Aid To Families with Dependent Children program. She was ineligible for assistance once her savings eclipsed $1,000. In 1990 a judge sentenced her to one year's probation and ordered her to repay $1,000. Capetillo needed to get rid of another $1,000 to get under the savings limit, so she bought some furniture. Circuit Court Judge Charles B. Schudson refused to fine Mrs. Capetillo the full amount due and implied that changes in welfare rules are in order; Schudson commented, "I don't know how much more powerfully we could say to the poor in our society, 'Don't try to save.'"[333]

Officials had once discouraged poor individuals from going "on the dole," but in the 1980s and early 1990s they tried to sign up as many as they could. The food stamp participation rate—the percentage of those eligible who enrolled—had jumped from thirty-one percent in 1976 to seventy-five percent in 1994. Then something astonishing happened. The food stamp participation rate fell from seventy-five percent to fifty-two percent by the end of the decade. The number of food stamp recipients fell from twenty-eight million to seventeen million. A Rockefeller Institute study of New Yorkers showed that two-thirds of the nearly 700,000 people who left welfare during the late 1990s found jobs, and only one in five went back on welfare.

The drop came because of state-level and then federal-level welfare reforms that returned "challenge" to the equation by requiring more recipients to work. By 2000 the results were clear, as the *Cleveland Plain Dealer* noted about changes in Ohio: "Many of the 111,000 families leaving welfare are doing so because family members have found work....A survey conducted for the state found that a year after leaving welfare, 66 percent of the people were employed, averaging 38 hours a week at $8.65 an hour."[334] In 2000 President Bill Clinton, who had fought welfare reform and signed welfare legislation only under political duress, bragged in a speech, "If I had said...we'll cut the welfare rolls in half, you wouldn't have believed that....We know now, because of the success our country has had, that if we work together and we set common goals we can achieve them."

In 2000 a *Los Angeles Daily News* writer asked the right question: "In terms of measuring compassion, which is better: encouraging the California woman to turn to welfare or empowering her to find the independence that she had forgotten she could achieve?" The answer to that question would determine the future of government poverty-fighting. In 2000, the trend was toward fostering independence.

But by 2005 The Brookings Institution was developing a new way to look at food stamps. Its report, "Leaving Money (and Food) on the Table," spoke of "unclaimed benefits" when eligible individuals did not sign up for food stamps. Brookings argued, "State and local leaders need to now get serious about boosting participation in the food stamp program."[335]

Later that year and in 2007, other activists and think tankers, such as the Food Research and Action Center and the National Priorities Project, offered similar messages. The message soon spread around the country. In Vermont, the *Burlington Free Press* opined, "The food stamp benefit is not a welfare program; it's an entitlement program. Those who qualify are entitled to receive these government benefits." In California, Food for People leader Deborah Waxman told the *Eureka Times Standard*, "This is something you've paid into just like Social Security or Medicare. Those who qualify are entitled to receive these government benefits."[336]

Meanwhile, states were doing away with "stamps" for food and issuing cards that look just like credit or debit cards. Poverty advocates—food bank employees in San Antonio and San Diego, AmeriCorps volunteers in New Jersey, students at California State University, and other institutions—raced to sign up food stamp users, interpreting guidelines as broadly as possible. H&R Block gave tax preparation clients SNAP (Supplemental Nutrition Assistance Program) applications and instructions on filing them. The New York City Central Labor Council—the umbrella organization for 400 member unions—made a big enrollment push as well.[337]

A journalistic reversal from the late 1990s also aided the SNAP surge. From 1996 to 2001, stories often stated that states with the lowest percentages of people on welfare were winning the competition to help people become independent. But newspapers began turning that thinking upside down by viewing the greatest dependency-creators as the winners. For example, a decade ago *The Star-Ledger* (Newark, N.J.) might have headlined one story, "New Jersey has 6th-best independence rate." Now it was, "New Jersey has 6th-worst participation rate."[338]

Similarly, the *Miami Herald* reported, "Florida ranked 12th worst in the United States, with 43 percent of the state's low-income residents receiving food stamps." An alternative report could have been, "Florida ranked 12th best in the United States, with 57 percent of the state's low-income residents working to put food on the table instead of becoming dependent on government." The 1990s message—"Don't get onto welfare, don't be dependent on government"—had flipped to "Welfare is your right, and if you have qualms, don't think of food stamps as welfare. Think of them as an entitlement like Social Security."[339]

SNAP promoters also argued that their program was an economic stimulus, so that if prideful people didn't sign up they were hurting their neighbors. The *Atlanta Journal-Constitution* declared, "The state's economy is harmed each time an eligible food stamp applicant is denied," since "money comes from the federal government, not out of state coffers." The *Fresno Bee* editorialized, "Though it may seem admirable not to seek help, it becomes problematic on many levels. Our local economy suffers directly because large amounts of federal funds are going unused."[340]

Despite such pressure and financial incentives, opposition to increasing dependency popped up in places. In 2006, former Maine state employee Shannon Leary wrote in the *Kennebec Journal*, "The state should not take more people accepting benefits as a victory....During a meeting of public assistance supervisors and administrators, the person running the meeting told us that 83 percent of those who met the eligibility criteria for food stamps were receiving the benefit. We were told that was good but the goal was to have 100 percent receiving the benefit. It struck me as odd then, and still does today. Should we not be striving for less usage of benefits?"[341]

Leary continued, "As a self-employed adult with a young family several years ago, I found myself eligible for food stamps. But I had the same determination as my parents not to use them….The state should not be in the business of pushing so hard to get people to take public assistance….We need to promote a culture that gives people the ability to be independent rather than maintain a culture where benefits are easily attainable."[342]

In 2006 the *Cleveland Plain Dealer* reported that the Ohio Department of Job & Family Services was ordering officials in two counties that "feature the state's largest Amish populations to lift dismal food-stamp participation rates." County official Tim Taylor said, "No matter how much we do, the Amish won't sign up," and Amish farmer Levi Miller said his poor neighbors would just say no: "We believe that we are our brother's keeper." After discussing putting up a billboard within an Amish enclave to promote food stamp use, state and county officials agreed that the attempt would have been fruitless.[343]

SNAP as an Example

Those who sit up high on the ladder of abstraction have not wasted our most recent economic crisis. The Obama administration has also tried to speed up new SNAP enrollment. On November 20, 2009, just before Thanksgiving, the Department of Agriculture sent a letter to state administrators complaining that some of them were running their SNAP programs in a way that was "problematic and resulted in a more complex and difficult enrollment process." Agencies also tried fast enrollment: "The Greater Chicago Food Depository equipped food stamp outreach coordinators with Sprint 4G-powered laptops. They crisscrossed Cook County, going from food pantries to city agencies to churches to community centers to...speed up the sign-up process."[344]

SNAP proponents tried to break the will of those among the elderly who, following American traditions of independence, were reluctant to sign up. The Boston Globe reported, "Advocates for the elderly are pushing hard to get area senior citizens in need of assistance to apply for the federal food stamp program, but pride and embarrassment stand in the way." The *Globe* quoted officials in Newton—one of Boston's affluent and liberal suburbs—emphasizing that SNAP is "like Social Security or Medicare—something that seniors have paid taxes into and have earned the benefits in return....We educate seniors that this is a program they are entitled to."[345]

Signing up more people for food stamps is important for those who want to expand welfare generally, since SNAP enrollment is the admission card to many other welfare programs. That's why, when mini-rebellions occurred, officials and their allies took a hard line. Many, like Kristin Kiesel, director of the Sudbury (Massachusetts) Council on Aging, insisted that "Food stamps are not welfare." Newspapers lambasted governors who held out against pressure to juice the SNAP rolls. For example, the *Fort Wayne Journal Gazette* criticized Indiana governor Mitch Daniels because the percentage of local food bank clients receiving food stamps had fallen.[346]

SSI as an Example

SSI—Supplemental Security Income—has also been a growth area because the Social Security Administration now deems eight million people unable to hold a job now or at some future time. Washington now typically gives each person so classified about $700 per month. In 1972, Congress made disabled children eligible for SSI payments.

The goal was to help poor parents who lost wages by taking time off from work to care for children with muscular dystrophy or cerebral palsy. Politicians spoke of families having additional expenses such as wheelchairs or taxi rides to hospitals.

That all made sense, but psychologists then argued that depression can be as disabling as a bad physical ailment. That's also true from a perspective high up on the ladder of abstraction; but while tests reveal physical cancers, psychological ones are often judgment calls—and this means that ground-level money-seekers can game the system when they want the money that a diagnosis can generate. Many of the one million children who garner SSI income for their parents are now on drugs that they do not need.[347]

Even the decidedly liberal *Boston Globe*, which usually cheerleads for more governmental welfare, has seen something wrong with diagnosing psychological issues as benefit-eligible disabilities. The *Globe* editorialized in May 2011 that "The damage done to children who are misclassified as mentally ill is incalculable: Some linger in special ed. classes when they are capable of accelerated work; others come to believe themselves to be impaired when no such impairment exists." Washington officials high on the ladder of abstraction decreed that at least ten percent of preschoolers in Head Start programs needed to be classified as disabled. That created an incentive to have more children so classified, so hospitals and health insurers eager to pay their bills hired "eligibility service providers" to get poor patients onto SSI.[348]

Some SSI recipients need help—sometimes much more help than they receive. But many do not, and their subsidies signify a new national development. In the past, Americans—both rich and poor—were known for having a can-do, never-give-up attitude. Now the poor benefit from saying cannot do and never-start-up. In the past, Americans were sometimes known for bragging; we tried to seem better than we were. Now we have incentives to seem worse than we are. Globe reporter Patricia Wen learned this in 2010 when she interviewed Geneva Fielding, age thirty-four, a single mom for eighteen years with three sons, who opposed putting a child on psychotropic drugs but concluded, "To get the check…you've got to medicate the child."[349]

Wen also tracked down a mother whose two-year-old is now on SSI after being diagnosed with speech delay and potential signs of autism: "It's an easier and better form of welfare. You get more money, and they don't check up on you." That same mom was receiving $600 per month from SSI because she had obtained a diagnosis of depression. The bankable diagnosis she received for her toddler meant $700 more and an apartment upgrade. "I can move out," she happily told Wen, even as she described the cost to her spirit: "SSI sucks you in. Most people get lazy."

Some who aren't lazy are sucked in as well. One fifteen-year-old told reporter Wen that she wanted to work, but if she did, "they'll take money away from my mom. She needs it. I don't want my mom's money to go down." A young man said he wanted to work but "I'm afraid to lose the check. It's attached to me."[350] (No wonder both of them are depressed.)

Wen met many who had thought of getting a job but then visualized being laid off. They compared that uncertainty to the eternal security they thought a government check would afford them. She also observed that unmarried fathers have learned news they can use: work wages can be garnished for child support, but SSI checks cannot be. Wen concluded, "The sense of dependence on SSI checks, for children and for their families, can creep up slowly." She quoted a psychologist's view that "children who grow up on SSI often cannot see themselves ever living outside the system.…They develop an identity as being disabled."[351] In the movie *Forrest Gump*, Forrest has below-average intelligence, but his mother is always telling him, "You're not stupid." Today many mothers who are dependent on government assistance are effectively telling children of average intelligence "You are stupid" because they offer no hope beyond perpetual dependence on the system.

Given the logic of Social Security, SSI is a natural supplement to it. Administrators looked at mental disabilities without asking how the disabilities had occurred and whether money would make the situation worse. But when Congress grandly created the program forty years ago, leaders did not recognize that it would become a moral hazard for the impoverished, as SSI might provide incentives to act worse than they otherwise would.

Changing the Definition of the Poor

While we should be looking at ground-level reality rather than reveling in high-minded abstraction, the Obama administration is moving in the direction of abstraction in terms of defining who is poor. For three centuries, American poverty-fighting has rested on a principle that no citizen should go without a basic level of food, shelter, and clothing. The question was always, "What are the basics?" It was not, "How much income does a poor person have relative to an affluent person?" Since 1964 officials have defined poverty in terms of insufficient cash to fulfill basic needs. On September 1, 2011, though, the Obama administration unveiled a Supplementary Poverty Measure (SPM) based on what Americans at the thirty-third percentile pay for food, clothing, shelter, and utilities, plus an additional one-fifth of that for other purchases.

This makes a radical conceptual leap by defining the enemy not as poverty but as inequality. Europeans had already made poverty relative: the European Union defines poverty as an income below sixty percent of the national median, whatever that median is. If rich and poor both double their income, the poverty rate does not change; everything is relative. Now, with almost no public attention or discussion outside policy wonk circles, the United States is taking one more step toward Europeanization. Using the thirty-third percentile, the typical "poverty threshold" will climb from the current $??,000—in round numbers—to $25,000 for a household with two adults and two children. Suddenly the poverty rate will jump from about fourteen percent to about sixteen percent.[352]

Of course, designating households with incomes under $25,000 as "poor" is likely to be only a temporary stopping point. Since median household income in the U.S. is about $50,000, by European Union standards any household with an income less than $30,000 should be classified as poor. If everyone's income doubles over the course of a decade, but the number of people considered poor does not change, we will have moved from "a rising tide lifts all boats" understanding to "Your boat is still bigger than mine."[353]

What social work leaders on the left yearned for in the 1930s is now reality in welfare stipends unconnected to work. At the beginning of 2012 only four of the eighty or so federal welfare requirements had work requirements, and in July the Obama administration suspended the major improvement of 1990s welfare reform legislation: a work requirement connected with the Temporary Aid to Needy Families program. States would now be authorized to set up "career pathways models for TANF recipients that combine learning and work" and "projects that test systematically extending the period in which vocational training or job search/readiness programs count toward participation rates." Translation: Instead of working, welfare recipients could take classes, exercise, go on errands, or keep a journal.[354]

How Can We Do Better?

I've written elsewhere, and at length, on ways to renew American compassion by restoring the idea and practice of offering challenging, personal, and spiritual help. Here, I'll conclude with a note on the importance of moving lower on the ladder of abstraction by understanding the real experience of food stamp recipients and replicating proven ways to move people off welfare to work.

Two Houston residents, Jean Solis and Scott Wesley, exemplify the uses and abuses of SNAP. Seven years ago, Solis, then forty-eight with a ten-year-old daughter, lived in a battered-women's shelter. Eventually she entered a training course at The WorkFaith Connection, a Christian program in Houston that motivates the poor to get jobs and persevere in their careers. Four years ago the only job she found right away was in a distant part of the city. With no car, it took three hours by bus each way to get there and back. She worked four hours per day.[355]

That was when Solis reluctantly joined the millions on welfare. She had grown up believing that dependence on government was a sign of failure, but "I needed food stamps to feed my daughter." She worried about her daughter's perceptions. "What are you teaching your children when you don't stand up for yourself?" she asked. When Solis finally garnered a full-time position, she kissed food stamps goodbye. "I stopped on April 1, 2008. That was a good day for me."[356]

For Solis, welfare worked the way it is supposed to work: by providing temporary help that saved her child from hunger and gave a work-seeking parent time to get on her feet. The experience of Scott Wesley was different, however. At age twenty, Wesley—who was heavily using cocaine and alcohol at the time—impregnated his girlfriend. Over the subsequent twelve years they had four children and lived off numerous welfare programs, including food stamps. He felt no pressure to work: "I knew the rent would be paid and the children wouldn't go hungry."[357]

Wesley and his girlfriend never married, in part because that would have reduced their welfare income. He stole goods they wanted and traded food stamps for drugs, a common tendency. "When the police raided drug dealers' houses they'd find caches of food stamps," he said. Later, Wesley started manufacturing and selling meth. Eventually he went to prison, "falling upwards" because God changed his thinking there. When Wesley was released three years later, he found a job and has been employed for four years now. He criticizes the use of food stamps by those capable of working because "They allow you to be irresponsible."[358]

It is hard to know how many of the forty-seven million Americans now enrolled in SNAP are, like Solis, using them for temporary help, and how many like Wesley are using them as an aid to irresponsibility. It's fun, in a policy wonk way, to play with numbers. For example, adding the cash value of food stamps reduces the number of officially-defined poor people by two million. Other changes increase the numbers. But it's a bit like the joke about the old person delighted to learn that, due to border changes, her town in Russia was now part of Poland: "Wonderful—I couldn't stand any more of those Russian winters."

It's no joke, though, if we play with numbers instead of concentrating on helping those who are truly tired, aching, and without hope. It's no joke if the federal government increases the clout of officials whose power depends on defining more people as poor. It's no joke if we head down a relativizing road that makes envy, rather than enterprise, our national pastime. In 2012, Athenian rioters forced the world to see that the Trojan Horse of reliance on government has led to national tragedy in the country that created both the original Horse and tragedy in drama. Will the rest of the Western world be far behind?

To summarize: Welfare expenditures become tragic rather than merely troubling when they hurt the people they are supposed to help. In the United States, the easy availability of governmental funds has sucked in millions of our citizens. It has created a dependency that is detrimental to them and their children. Given budget pressures, we are likely to end up with watery soup, with some desperately needy families not getting help.

America has weakened as more citizens—now half of them—rely on government programs. In 1868 the key sentence of a popular song was "He'd fly through the air with the greatest of ease, that daring young man on the flying trapeze." The message today is: Flop into the safety net. You're entitled to it.

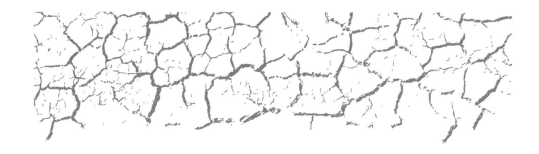

CHAPTER 12

"Stop Helping Us:" A Call to Compassionately Move beyond Charity

By Peter Greer, M.P.P.

This chapter introduces a new paradigm for an evangelical response to poverty alleviation. Being effective means recognizing that there is a difference between short-term aid, which is important and necessary, and the long-term elimination of poverty, which is the best defense against receding back into material poverty and the most effective method of elevating the dignity of all God's children. In this chapter we will see the stories of those who were transformed by effective, long-term aid that focused on the individuals rather than just numbers. Included are surveys of the poor and what they desire, showing that their goals have little to do with money and everything to do with using their skills, caring for their families, and embracing their God-given dignity.

The Story of Fadzai

Every time an employer discovered Fadzai Nhamo, a woman from Zimbabwe, was HIV positive, the door shut. "Life was difficult for me when I came to Harare," Fadzai later remarked. When Fadzai speaks, she covers her mouth to hide her missing front teeth, a daily reminder of the brutal way she contracted HIV. "I left my hometown after someone had beaten and raped me," she said. Following the assault, a friend took her to a clinic at the capital, Harare. There she discovered she was HIV positive. "When my husband found out I was sick [with HIV], he disappeared," Fadzai commented later. "I did not have a place to live." After her husband's abandonment, Fadzai was left a single mom, a stranger in a new city. With no place to call home, she moved from place to place with her children.

It is possible to debate many points of theology, but our faith clearly calls us to care for Fadzai, an individual who has been exploited and abused. She is the widow and foreigner so frequently mentioned throughout Scripture. When we hear the story of Fadzai's mistreatment and understand the message of grace in Scripture, we are compelled to respond.

John, one of Jesus's closest friends, asked the question, "If anyone has material possessions and sees a brother or sister in need but has no pity on them, how can the love of God be in that person?"[359] James, the brother of Jesus, questioned, "If one of you says to him, 'Go, I wish you well; keep warm and well fed,' but does nothing about his physical needs, what good is it?"[360] This concept was discussed in great detail in chapter three, but the takeaway is worth repeating here. Followers of Jesus have a rich history of responding to a gospel message of compassion. From New York City to New Delhi, the homeless find shelter and a compassionate response in Christian missions. In rural areas lacking access to healthcare, medical clinics have been built. Through prison ministry, thousands of prisoners are visited each year. Soup kitchens run by churches are a fixture in many cities.

Fadzai was one recipient of such care. After arriving in Harare, she found a charity that provided aid. But as with most charities, the support eventually ended. "I had a big problem when the charity that I was getting my food from stopped," Fadzai lamented. It is unclear whether Fadzai was better off as a result of the church's support, despite its good intentions. Although charity helped Fadzai for a time, it did not change her situation or address the underlying issues of her poverty. She was still in tremendous need. Having learned no additional skills, Fadzai was in no better position to provide for her children. Worse— as handouts often do over the long term—charity may have actually deepened her poverty.

What is Poverty?

In the 1990s, World Bank surveyed over sixty thousand of the financially poor throughout the developing world and how they described poverty. The poor did not focus on their material need; rather, they alluded to social and psychological aspects of poverty. Analyzing the study, Brian Fikkert and Steve Corbett of the Chalmers Center for Economic Development said, "Poor people typically talk in terms of shame, inferiority, powerlessness, humiliation, fear, hopelessness, depression, social isolation, and voicelessness."[361]

The study highlights that, by nature, poverty is innately social and psychological. In an informal survey, our clients at HOPE International in Rwanda affirmed that poverty is more than a lack of material possessions. In 2011, a lead trainer of a savings program in Rwanda posed a question to a group of twenty individuals within a savings group, most of whom lived on less than $2 a day. "How do you define poverty?" he asked.[362] Listed below are their answers in the order provided:

1. Poverty is an empty heart.
2. Not knowing your abilities and strengths.
3. Not being able to make progress.
4. Isolation.
5. No hope or belief in yourself. Knowing you can't take care of your family.
6. Broken relationships.
7. Not knowing God.
8. Not having basic things to eat. Not having money.
9. Poverty is a consequence of not sharing.
10. Lack of good thoughts.

As can be seen from the above, money was mentioned only once.

If poverty is not only a material deficit, but also not knowing one's potential, abilities, and strengths—as well as having an empty heart—then traditional charity neglects to address the root causes of poverty. In Fadzai's situation, receiving handouts did not enable her to recognize her abilities, maximize her potential, or believe her situation would ever change. When aid stopped, Fadzai said she hit the nadir of her life. Aid—a short-term solution—left her hopeless, despairing, and powerless in the long term. Suicidal, Fadzai felt unable to take care of her basic needs, while charity deepened her hopelessness.

The downward spiral of charity has been experienced by countless people eager to do good and serve the poor, but it is best described in *Toxic Charity* by author Bob Lupton. In this book, he details the negative cycle of giving related to traditional charity.

- "Give once and you elicit appreciation;
- Give twice and you create anticipation;
- Give three times and you create expectation;
- Give four times and it becomes entitlement;
- Give five times and you establish dependency."[363]

Even when offered with compassion, traditional charity, which should be only a temporary fix, can often enslave individuals—becoming a poverty trap—if extended into the long term. Instead of focusing on the potential of those like Fadzai, charity cheats them of using their God-given abilities and talents. The church is beginning to recognize the pitfalls of traditional charity and rediscover an alternative way of helping.

Your Help Isn't Helping

When the Soviet Union disintegrated in 1991, the newly independent nation of Ukraine faced numerous challenges. Between 1991 and 1997, Ukraine lost sixty percent of its GDP, inflation increased to five digits, and there were riots in the streets.[364]

Members of Calvary Monument Bible Church (CMBC) in Lancaster, Pennsylvania, asked, "How can we help?" Eager to put their faith in action, they partnered with a church in Zaporozhye, Ukraine, a city of a million people in the country's southeast. Leaders at CMBC had recently read Matthew 25 and desired to put this well-known passage about caring for the poor and needy into practice:

> When the Son of Man comes in his glory, and all the angels with him, he will sit on his glorious throne. All the nations will be gathered before him, and he will separate the people one

323

from another as a shepherd separates the sheep from the goats. He will put the sheep on his right and the goats on his left. Then the King will say to those on his right, 'Come, you who are blessed by my Father; take your inheritance, the kingdom prepared for you since the creation of the world. For I was hungry and you gave me something to eat, I was thirsty and you gave me something to drink, I was a stranger and you invited me in, I needed clothes and you clothed me, I was sick and you looked after me, I was in prison and you came to visit me.[365]

Matthew 25 is clear in its message, and is not an abstract allegory. The members of CMBC took the words seriously, knowing that "… whatever you did for one of the least of these brothers and sisters of mine, you did for me."[366] Considering it a privilege to respond in God's grace, they sought to care for the poor and needy as if they were directly serving Jesus.

I was hungry and you gave me something to eat.[367] Recognizing that years of Soviet rule had decimated local food production and distribution, they shipped flour, rice, and other staples of nutrition.

I needed clothes and you clothed me.[368] The Ukrainians wore old clothes often insufficient to face harsh winters. CMBC members shared warm clothes with their Ukrainian friends.

I was sick and you looked after me.[369] Hospitals and infirmaries in Zaporozhye had few or no supplies, so CMBC arranged for shipments of medicine and medical supplies donated by area doctors and hospitals.

Noticing Ukrainian believers only had a dilapidated, crowded building in which to worship, CMBC members helped purchase land and provide funds to build additional educational space.

This pattern continued for several years, marked annually by a special Thanksgiving offering. Afterward, the church would ship a container with food, clothing, and church supplies to Zaporozhye. But something was wrong. After three years, leaders from both sides of the Atlantic began to question whether the shipments were helpful. Both churches felt like they were entering the black hole of charity. Neither church had an exit strategy, nor did they believe this partnership was making a positive impact. The Ukrainian church would always have needs the American church could respond to, but it had stopped providing for its own needs in the process. This worried the Ukrainian pastor. Though grateful for the generous support, he recognized his congregation had less desire to serve one another. *Why sacrifice anything to feed or clothe a neighbor when an international shipment and team would soon arrive?*

As aid continued, the Ukrainian pastor had more questions: What would happen if the generous people in Pennsylvania suddenly stopped providing? Would this kind of assistance produce a stronger community long after the donations stopped?

Additionally, American aid impacted the Ukrainian economy. The generosity of the American church was hurting local businesses competing with free American goods and services entering their marketplace. The gifts from America, however well-intentioned, caused more problems than they solved. The American church knew its call to feed the hungry, clothe the needy, and invite the stranger in; but the way it was going about this was causing harm. The Ukrainian church, though grateful for the partnership, saw itself becoming increasingly dependent on charity. Both churches were learning a difficult lesson: compassionate responses to practical needs work well in the short term but cause many unintended consequences in the long term.

Effective versus Easy

Obedience to the biblical command to clothe the naked and to give food to the hungry is not easy. Requiring us to go beyond surface needs—the symptoms of poverty—an effective response demands a longer-term commitment. The starting point is to distinguish between aid and development. After a disaster, images of need flood airwaves. Donors rally together to provide an outpouring of support. Relief, a rapid provision of temporary resources to reduce immediate suffering, is required. Earthquakes, tsunamis, war, and natural disasters call for a full force and timely response.

On January 12, 2010, Haiti was struck by an earthquake more forceful than any it had seen in two centuries. Its magnitude: 7.0 on the Richter scale. The earthquake killed more than 200,000 people and left more than 300,000 injured.[370] In this case, short-term relief was entirely appropriate. People needed immediate access to medical care, food, and shelter. However, the earthquake in Haiti also offers insight into Haiti's need for development, as illustrated by another earthquake: one that struck in 1989, during the warm-up of the third game of the World Series between the Oakland Athletics and the San Francisco Giants. The world stopped to rally around San Francisco—the city at its epicenter—as it watched the disaster on television. The tragedy killed sixty-three people and collapsed viaducts and bridges. Its magnitude: 7.1.

Though it was terrible tragedy, why did only sixty-three people die in the 1989 earthquake, while over 200,000 people were killed in the 2010 earthquake? A major part of the difference is poverty. San Francisco was prepared, its infrastructure ready to deal with disasters. Haiti was not prepared. With over eighty percent of Haitians living in poverty, the country's population already suffered from poor sanitation, disease, inadequate healthcare, and malnutrition. As demonstrated by the 7.0-magnitude earthquakes in Haiti and San Francisco, while relief offers immediate return, it may take months, years, or even generations to see the full results of development.

Giles Bolton, a veteran African diplomat, described the difference between relief and development in *Africa Doesn't Matter*: "In consumer language, [development] is a bit like making an investment rather than an immediate purchase . . . [It's a] much better value if it works because it gives poor people control over their own lives and enables them better to withstand future humanitarian disasters without outside help."[371] Development is a long-term investment; it's not flashy. Unless development is part of the recovery plan for countries like Haiti, individuals will be just as vulnerable to earthquakes and other natural disasters as before.

The case study of the Lancaster and Ukrainian church partnership illustrates another reason why it is important to transition from aid to development. After the downfall of the Soviet Union, the initial response by the American church was warranted; food, clothing, and supplies were sent, and individuals had their immediate needs met. Three years later, the appropriate time for aid had passed. Toxic, ill-timed aid was crippling the Ukrainian church. The Ukrainian pastor had the courage to stop the inappropriate relationship between the two churches. He called the leaders of the American church aside and told them, "We need a hand-up, not a hand out."

The churches realized that the best way to help would be to equip local Ukrainians to create jobs or be better equipped to find a job. They discovered how a job would be far superior to any form of handouts. The churches stumbled on microfinance, a relatively new concept in Ukraine. At the time, only one microfinance institution—which offers training, savings, and small loans—was operating there.[372]

In 1997, individuals from Calvary Monument Bible Church offered twelve small loans to individuals in Ukraine. All were repaid, and the financially poor had the opportunity to provide for their families in a dignified way. This model emphasized enterprise instead of aid. While one concept crippled initiative, this approach to poverty alleviation created opportunity—and promoted work as a calling.

Work as Vocation

Throughout history, the church has underappreciated the role of work; however, in Genesis the Creator gave the initial mandate to work. From the beginning of creation, God elevated the role of work. Before sin entered the world, "God took the Man and set him down in the Garden of Eden to *work* the ground and keep it in order."[373] Work is a gift and a calling from God. Both the Old and New Testaments promote employment. One example is the emphasis on gleaning. At harvest, farmers were commanded not to "reap to the very edges of your field" so that the poor could gather the remainder (Leviticus 19:9-10; Deuteronomy 24:19-21; Ruth 2).[374] God provided for the poor in a manner in which they were active participants—not passive recipients—of charity.

In the New Testament, Paul wrote in his letter to the Thessalonians, "If a man will not work, he shall not eat."[375] Paul recognized that everyone capable of working should provide for themselves and their families. Likewise, in his letter to the Ephesians, Paul wrote, "Let those who are stealing, steal no longer, but rather let him work, doing honest work with his own hands, so that he may have something to share with anyone in need."[376] In this situation, employment was the tool that helped turn even thieves into generous givers. Elevating the role of work is not only part of the church's mandate, but dramatically transforms the global landscape from poverty to empowerment.

A New Model

According to the Brookings Institution, seventy million people— approximately the population of Turkey—are lifted out of poverty every year.[377] Between 1981 and 2005, the World Bank reported the number of people living in extreme poverty (or living on $1.25 or less per day) decreased from fifty-two percent to twenty-six percent.[378] *In one generation, poverty has been cut in half, not through charity but through job creation.* Economic heavyweights like China, India, and Brazil have fueled the reduction of poverty. For example, in 1981, eighty-four percent of China's population lived below the poverty line, and only four other countries in the world had a greater percentage of people living on less than $1.25 a day. By 2005, the percentage of China's population living beneath the poverty line dropped to twenty-five percent, according to World Bank. During this timeframe, China's GDP increased tenfold. Brazil and India followed the same path, as their poverty rates were cut from seventeen percent to eight percent, and sixty percent to forty percent, respectively, between 1981 and 2005, the changes being powered by economic growth.[379]

For too long, capitalism was treated as a bystander in poverty alleviation and human development. Rock stars and aid activists were calling for more charity and a greater response from the global community, but few were calling for investment in entrepreneurship and policies that promote economic development. "Our wrong, careless, romantic vision of the poor is that they're being so exploited that they should just be left to retreat into self-sufficiency, you know, the organic, holistic peasant, uncontaminated by the dirty business of a market economy," said Paul Collier, an author and economist at Oxford. "And of course that is just romantic nonsense."[380] A "romantic vision" of the poor has often led to a broken system of aid.

Recent history has exposed the underside of aid. On a macro scale, economist Dambisa Moyo reported in *Dead Aid* that Africa has received over $1 trillion in aid in the past fifty years, and in many countries, growth has stagnated—even plummeted. Countries in Sub-Saharan Africa still rank at the bottom of poverty indexes, such as World Bank's *Doing Business* report and the United Nations' *Human Development Index* (HDI).[381] Aid doesn't transform poverty to prosperity; it has actually hindered economic growth worldwide. Desmond Tutu, human rights leader and former Anglican bishop, has commented that, "[Aid] becomes a way of colonizing the economies of the poor countries—a system of economic slavery."[382]

In economist Bill Easterly's book *The White Man's Burden*, he writes about the ongoing "tragedy" of aid: "… the West spent $2.3 trillion on foreign aid over the last five decades and still had not managed to get twelve-cent medicines to children to prevent half of all malaria deaths. The West spent $2.3 trillion and still had not managed to get four-dollar bed nets to poor families. The West spent $2.3 trillion and still had not managed to get three dollars to each new mother to prevent five million child deaths."[383] One reason aid is ineffective is that the individuals benefiting from aid often do not decide how to address the problem of poverty.

"White Savior Industrial Complex"[384]

In 2005, Bob Geldoff, organizer of Live Aid, defined the global aid community's response to poverty when he said, "Something must be done; anything must be done, whether it works or not."[385] From G-8

Summits to Live Aid, the West has sought solutions to help the poor. Solutions from the West are often innovative but impractical, owing to a failure to listen to the poor themselves.

Consider this example. Philanthropists saw the need to provide clean water for communities in Africa and designed PlayPump. The concept appears straightforward. Promising to "harness the energy of children at play," PlayPump is a children's merry go-round that operates a water pump. PlayPump was the darling of the world's most powerful people: Laura Bush, Bill Clinton, and organizations like Save the Children all supported it. Many, such as Clinton, were overwhelmingly generous. During its campaign to provide clean water in 2006, the Clinton Global Initiative gave $16.4 million to PlayPump. Unfortunately, PBS investigations several years later exposed the fact that PlayPump was not highly effective. Many PlayPumps broke. Often a PlayPump was placed over the only existing water supply in a village. When the water pump broke, few in the community chose to fix it, and the entire community lost access to water. In one village in Mozambique, Amy Costello, a PBS correspondent, reported on what happened after the PlayPump broke. "They had to walk 40 minutes to the next village in order to get their water now, which was putting additional pressure on that community," Costello said. "They resented the 150 families that they were now having to share their water source with." PlayPump seemed like a good idea, but its effectiveness is judged by local communities, not the international aid community. The local community did not have ownership and was not as impressed with this solution. While the intention was to help, those supporting PlayPump sometimes knew they did not make a lasting impact. In a short amount of time, communities were once again without a water source. An outside solution, PlayPump was not widely successful because those receiving its services were not involved in its ideation and implementation.

Thankfully, there has been a rediscovery of the danger of outside solutions—which sometimes results in what Nigerian-American writer Teju Cole calls the "White Savior Industrial Complex"—to an approach focusing on individuals helping themselves.

Even the global aid community has begun to change its rhetoric. Consider Bob Geldof, the ringleader of Live Aid, who said that "Something must be done; anything must be done, whether it works or not." Today he's singing a different tune. Investing in Africa's economy, the former aid advocate has established a $200 million private equity firm. "The next part of [Africa's development] is jobs," says Geldof.[386] From Geldof and Bono to Paul Kagame, president of Rwanda, and economists like Paul Collier, there is a new model to alleviate global poverty: job creation. And the change already has influenced economies on a macro scale. According to World Bank, nations in Africa are on the verge of the same remarkable path toward wealth creation as China was thirty years ago.[387] From 2000-2011, trade between African nations and other countries grew 200 percent.[388] Through increased investment, African countries are being revitalized. According to the International Monetary Fund, on average the GDP of countries in Sub-Saharan Africa grew from five to seven percent in 2012.[389]

Investments have a huge role to play in the progress of Africa. According to *The New Africa: Emerging Opportunities for Business and Africa,* the impact of investments has already bypassed the effect of aid, generating 1.7 million jobs from 2003 to 2010.[390] Beyond investments, on a micro scale, financial tools, such as business training, savings, and small loans are empowering those like Fadzai to have a voice.

The Rest of the Story

Providentially, Fadzai was told to go to Central Baptist Church, Harare, for a very different form of assistance. Embracing its mission to care for the widow, the orphan, and the vulnerable, this church recognized that there are ways to help those in need beyond starting a soup kitchen. The members discovered a new approach to assisting Fadzai through the seemingly audacious belief that even impoverished people are capable of contributing to their own development. This approach was based on the belief that the greater gift they could give would be to equip Fadzai to provide for herself. Fadzai was open to a new opportunity and gathered with a group each week to participate in a training and savings program.

When she first heard about the program and the requirement that every week each member save some amount of money, she thought, "How do these people think I am going to get money for this?" Fadzai received business and biblical training as she gathered with eighteen other members. She understood grace and forgiveness through the gospel message. She was coached and mentored as she learned basic accounting. If she could not contribute the necessary savings for one particular week, another member covered for her. As this group started accumulating a greater amount of savings, they started making investments in each other's businesses. Eventually, Fadzai was able to receive a small loan to purchase farming supplies, seeds, and equipment and to begin farming a small plot of land with other members. Believing she had skills and abilities, she began to dream about the future—seeing a pathway out of poverty. But Fadzai also realized that change is more than economic. "I was also taught to pray about everything," she explained. In her case, God answered these prayers in ways she never thought possible. Miraculously, even Fadzai's husband came back. Fadzai's life is spiritually and materially different because a local church stopped simply pitying her. Willing to invest in her, the church saw what she had—and who she was in Christ—rather than what she lacked. Fadzai learned to forgive in relationships and now attends church regularly with her family. In her words, "For me, that's a very big deal." This hardworking mother, who used to be dependent on handouts, is now weekly earning a far greater amount of money than she ever received from charity. And this all occurred in less than a year's time. Despite the pain of the past, the future looks bright for her. Thankfully, more and more organizations are working to create an alternative to the charity trap.

Around the World

These principles apply not only in Zimbabwe. As needs are addressed overseas or in downtown Chicago, providing a job is more beneficial than offering a handout. Recognition is growing in post-industrial nations that the welfare mentality has handicapped the poor. Instead of being a ladder out of poverty, charity puts the most vulnerable in bondage. Churches and faith communities increasingly aim to provide essential tools to equip a family to work its way out of poverty, which include business training and job preparedness, financial literacy, business mentoring, and access to capital. These tools are efficient not only globally through the microenterprise development movement, but also throughout the U.S. Consider the following example of how the faith community is helping the financially poor.

Business Training and Job Preparedness

A survey presented by David Spickard, president of Jobs for Life (JfL), illustrates the need for a new paradigm in the church's approach to addressing poverty in the U.S. It lists the ten most prevalent ways organizations and churches help the poor. First on the list is providing food; second is housing; third, clothes. Last on the list is to help individuals find a job. However, what if we turned the list on its head?

Instead of first seeking to provide handouts, what if the church became a vehicle to foster entrepreneurship? Individuals in poverty could then buy their own food and clothes and invest in their own homes. JfL is just one of several organizations seeking to upend the paradigm of charity. Tapping into one of the most overlooked resources to provide job training—the church—JfL is coming alongside the church to equip individuals with skills to interview, to network, and to find and to retain a job. One graduate is Don Turner of Hendersonville, North Carolina. "I really shouldn't be here, I probably should be dead," he has said.[391]

Don was brought up by an alcoholic, abusive father. He became so angry and alienated from others in his adulthood that he took a bag of clothes and literally headed to the woods. Homeless, he was so cold one day that he left the woods and found himself at the front door of a church. Don learned about the love of Christ in the church and was taken care of by a mission. He also met David Spickard. Introduced to JfL, today Turner is a different man, married and self-employed. "I've gone from being homeless and hateful to finding a way to forgive my parents and have a relationship with them…to being an entrepreneur and self-employed," Turner says. Another organization that is riding the new wave of poverty alleviation is the Chalmers Center for Economic Development. The Chalmers Center is a world-class authority in creating business and savings curriculum in the developing world. Seeing its success abroad, as well as the overwhelming needs within the U.S., the Chalmers Center created a financial training curriculum to provide a hand up in the United States, a program director Brian Fikkert calls "Dave Ramsey for the poor."[392] The course, *Faith & Finances*, empowers churches and organizations to teach foundational principles of finance.

Mentoring

Catherine Rohr had a hypothesis. The twenty-seven-year-old Wall Street venture capitalist believed that some of the best entrepreneurs were behind bars. After visiting a state prison in Texas, she saw the brokenness of some the world's most dangerous criminals. But she also saw talent. Many used to manage networks—albeit illegal—and possessed ingenuity and the ability to think on their feet. Rohr left her six-figure salary to drive a van with all of her belongings from New York City to Texas. Prison Entrepreneurship Program (PEP) was born. Rohr saw criminals' potential rather than their past and invested everything in her vision to empower those forgotten by society.[393] "We don't make entrepreneurs," Rohr said, "We just take proven entrepreneurs who…understand execution and profitability, and we help transfer their interest to legitimate business so they can impact society."[394]

Rohr's philosophy is cultivating entrepreneurs through mentoring. Bringing in change agents to teach classes—business executives from Ivy League universities—PEP gives world-class training as well as access to the executives' professional networks so that prisoners can receive a job upon leaving prison. Rohr recently founded a similar program in New York City: Defy Ventures, an MBA boot camp for ex-convicts. At Defy, former prisoners receive executive training and the chance to win $150,000 in seed capital as they put together a business plan. Most importantly, Rohr connects prisoners with mentors who guide them through the business process and who open their lives to their mentees.

Programs like PEP and Defy use mentoring to challenge a broken system. While the U.S. makes up only five percent of the world's population, it contains twenty-five percent of the world's prison population.[395] The U.S. places more people behind bars than any other country, including China, although China has four times as many citizens.[396] Programs like PEP and Defy give prisoners hope. PEP's results have been remarkable. Within ninety days of getting out of prison, 100 percent of individuals at PEP find jobs. The recidivism rate of PEP's graduates is five percent, compared to sixty percent nationwide.[397] Beyond the overwhelming numbers of people in prison, the prison system reflects a nation bound by poverty. Eighty-nine percent of criminals who return to prison are unemployed when arrested. In sum: A job keeps people from going behind bars again.

Financial Services

Beyond tools and training, access to capital is key to poverty alleviation, as the developing world shows. Nobel Peace Prize winner Muhammad Yunus made microfinance a household name. He decided to take his pioneering Grameen Bank, which has served the poor globally, to New York City.

While New York is the world's capital of commerce, its poor are often marginalized. Across the United States, banks have little incentive to provide small loans when the same amount of paperwork and time is required for larger loans with higher dividends. Grameen is providing a niche service, enabling people to take out loans that they wouldn't receive from the formal banking sector in order to start a taxi business or a retail stand.

Microfinance has spread throughout the U.S. Grameen, Accion, and Prosper.com are just three organizations giving financial services, such as savings and small loans, and often business training, to get people on their feet again. When the poor experience an emergency, whether their car breaks down or a family member needs medical care, often their only options are loan sharks and "payday" lenders. Offering interest rates as steep as 400 percent, payday lenders keep the poor in a cycle of debt. In a study of 11,000 payday borrowers, most received a $300 loan and eventually had to pay $466 due to accumulating interest.[398] Almost fifty percent failed to pay their loans on time, and, on average, had their loan for over six months;[399] some had them for as many as twenty-four months.[400]

Grace Period offers an alternative to loan sharks. A nonprofit organization partnered with the church, Grace Period gives loans with reasonable interest rates immediately; free loans are given to the poor if the loans are repaid within thirteen days. Clients of Grace Period are also required to start saving, which helps them prepare in case of another emergency. Tony Wiles, president of the board, said of the work, "We have people who are actually saving money for the first time in their lives."[401] These are just some organizations giving people a hand up rather than a handout in the U.S.

Conclusion

Though the West's efforts through international aid have been well-intentioned, they have often done more harm than good. By focusing on what the poor lack, instead of what they have, the underlying message sent to the poor is this: you are incapable. When Fadzai walked through the door of Central Baptist Church in 2011, her head was hung low. She was skeptical when asked to save. Her dependency on aid, coupled with the injustice committed against her, rendered her feeling helpless. As she questioned her existence, her capacity, and her potential, she wondered—*Do I have anything to give?*

Today Fadzai stands tall. Under a tree outside Harare, a group of women gather. They sit huddled on blankets strewn across red-dirt ground as Fadzai walks among them, teaching. She leads the savings and loan process and also communicates through a curriculum how each one is made in the image of God. Like her, they have purpose. Fadzai's story reflects a changing philosophy on poverty alleviation. From handouts to enterprise, the new paradigm focuses more on the dignity, creativity, and capacity of the poor, rather than their material deficit.

It is also a paradigm that is changing the economic landscape. Between 1981 and 2005, global poverty rates were cut in half, primarily through job creation. Even Africa, which *The Economist* called "the hopeless continent" ten years ago, is now seeing signs of economic growth through job creation and investment.[402] Sustainable development through business is on the rise not only internationally but also domestically. Business training and mentoring, as well as access to capital, are universal principles empowering individuals through a hand up. It's a paradigm giving opportunity, responsibility, and dignity to the poor. No longer do we look to presidents, nonprofit organizations, the World Bank, and the U.N. to address poverty. Rather, the leaders of this new movement are individuals like Fadzai—those who are creating jobs, providing for their families, and bringing hope to their communities.

Conclusion

By Jay W. Richards, Th.M., M.Div., Ph.D.

On May 29, 1953, at 11:00 in the morning, beekeeper Edmund Hillary and his Sherpa guide, Tenzing Norgay, reached the summit of Mount Everest, the highest point on earth. Hillary was a native of mountain and-glacier-draped New Zealand and was part of a much larger British expedition led by John Hunt. He was one of ten elite climbers picked for their mountaineering prowess. "Our climbers were all chosen as potential summiteers," remembered George Band, who was one of the ten. "The basic plan was for two summit attempts, each by a pair of climbers, with a possible third assault if necessary."[403]

Their success depended on massive preparation beforehand. The expedition was obsessively outfitted, making it more like a military operation than any ordinary gentlemen's jaunt up a mountain. It included over 350 porters, 20 Sherpas—natives of the region who are accustomed to the extreme altitudes—and five tons of food. It also made use of cutting-edge technology, including oxygen tanks and radio transmitters.[404] "The enormous skill of Sir Edmund Hillary and Tensing Norgay was as expert mountaineers...but also combining that with the expertise that came with the technologies of the day," Alasdair McLeod of the Royal Geographical Society later explained.

The British had tried, and failed, in a 1921 expedition. There had been ten other major expeditions before 1953, nine of them British. All had failed, although a Swiss team, which had also included Norgay, had almost made it a year earlier.

The 1953 expedition established its first base camp in March, eventually reaching its final base at South Col in Nepal, 25,900 feet up. (The Chinese government had closed the North Col route in Tibet.) While on the mountain, the team had slowly adapted to the frigid and rarefied air, while waiting for the relative warmth of late spring.

But they still had over 3,000 feet to go, and unlike a walk along a level beach, every step up a towering mountain tends to grow more challenging than the one before. Even today, a shot at Everest's summit involves years of preparation, hundreds of thousands of dollars, and many weeks on and around Everest. But no future attempt was as bold as that one in the spring of 1953 for the simple reason that, in 1953, it hadn't been done before. Hillary and Norgay were the first to get to the top and live to tell about it. During the last, most treacherous legs of the climb, they had no detailed guide from climbers who had gone before. They had to cast themselves into the wide open and deadly cold blue of the Himalayan sky and hope for the best.

They were almost thwarted as they approached the summit when the edge of a large glacier met a vertical rock face, separated by a vertiginous void. "I was a bit worried about it at first but fortunately there was a crack between the ice and the rock," Hillary humbly told his brother Rex. "I got into this and I was able to wiggle my way up it."[405] That crack is now called the Hillary Step.

There are other ways up Everest, but none were known in 1953, and probably none are as conducive to success as Hillary's basic route. Indeed, in the intervening years, thousands of mountaineers have retraced Hillary and Norgay's steps in their own efforts to reach the top.

Along the way, they have established and outfitted many base camps that were not there before, making the route more accommodating for future expeditions. We now know, in detail, as Hillary and Norgay did not, the most accommodating way up the mountain.

The cultural path from widespread poverty to widespread prosperity is like that route up Mt. Everest. For centuries, most people lived in subsistence poverty, near sea level on the upward path to wealth. But in the last two centuries, more and more cultures have climbed the path of wealth creation from the low-lying flatlands and hills, to the base camps, and up to the summit, making the climb using a combination of innate capacity, hard work, and the accumulated insights of cultures that have made the climb before. And each culture that does it leaves new base camps and new insights and tools from which other cultures can learn in their efforts to rise out of poverty.

What this means is that when we encounter a "bottom billion" country mired in absolute poverty, an attitude of hopelessness is simply out of keeping with the evidence of the past century. We *know* how poverty is alleviated and wealth is created. We know the path to the summit of culture-wide wealth creation, and it is now well traveled by climbers from diverse places of origin. What is so perplexing, and so maddening, is how many Christian thinkers seek to eradicate the remaining poverty while largely ignoring the known and well-trod path. Instead, they persist in commending short cuts that have not simply been untraveled, but worse, are known to lead only to shifting and unstable ground, precipitous falls, and dead ends without easy return. This is neither prudent nor humane. Prudence is the virtue of discovering what the world is like and acting accordingly, not acting according to the world as we prefer it to be.

Whether we like it or not, no culture has emerged from absolute poverty through government-to-government aid or even private relief efforts that did not enable recipients to create wealth for themselves and others. Private charitable giving and even some government actions have an important role to play in our response to poverty—particularly as thoughtfully crafted, carefully modulated responses to large, unexpected disasters (e.g., the U.S. Navy's rapid response after the deadly 2004 tsunami in the Indian Ocean) and in church partnerships where the transforming power of the gospel isn't crowded out by a secular, redistributive humanitarianism masquerading as "the Social Gospel." An aid culture of redistribution and neocolonial dependency does not, and never has, worked to lift whole cultures out of extreme poverty. Haiti, for example, has more aid workers per capita than any other nation on earth, and yet it remains the poorest nation in the Western Hemisphere. If you are still holding out hope for this failed form of "help," reread Peter Greer's concluding chapter of this volume.

Why are so many well-intentioned Christians drawn to dead-end strategies? Perhaps it is because the right path seems counterintuitive. To untutored intuition, it seems obvious that if there are some rich people and some poor people, we can cure poverty by taking some of the wealth of the rich and giving it to the poor. It just doesn't happen to be true.

Sometimes Christians also wed misguided economic ideas with bad biblical interpretation. In these matters, our economic intuitions and understanding of Scripture must be tutored. I say "must" because getting the issue right is a matter of life or death for many around the world.

The Book of Scripture

As Christians, we have two interpenetrating and mutually reinforcing sources of knowledge that we need to properly interpret and integrate—the Book of Scripture and the Book of Nature. God is the ultimate author of both, and since in him there is no contradiction, these two books agree when properly interpreted.

In the Book of Scripture—God's "special revelation"—God has revealed his personal name, his great and salvific acts in history, the way of salvation, and at least a glimpse of his complete will for human beings and the entire creation. As Glenn Sunshine, Walter Kaiser, and David Kotter make clear in their chapters, this book of special revelation makes abundantly clear what our attitude toward the poor should be: every human being is made in God's image and should be accorded the rights and dignity appropriate to that status. This is as true of the investment banker in Lower Manhattan as it is for the African Bushman, the child in Guangzhou with no parents or prospects, and the elderly widow in Detroit who can no longer feed herself. We do not have the power to establish God's kingdom in its fullness, but our work on earth should be a precursor to the kingdom to come. Absolute poverty degrades and prevents people from fulfilling God's command to be fruitful and multiply. We should do whatever we can to help restore them.

To see this accurately, however, we have to separate solid exegesis from sloppy misreadings of Scripture. Art Lindsley focuses on two prominent examples: the misuse of the Old Testament "Jubilee Year" and the policy of sharing among early Christians in Jerusalem, both of which have been used to justify the forcible government redistribution of income. Quite apart from the negative economic effects of such a policy, it rests on serious interpretive myths far removed from careful interpretation.

This double error of bad exegesis and bad economics is doubly tragic because of the historical role that Christians and evangelicals have played in addressing oppression and poverty effectively, as Richard

Turnbull reminds us. For Christians, then, the answer to the "ought" question should be obvious, especially for those who have read this volume from the beginning. We know that we will be judged by how we treat those whom Jesus called "the least of these." We who enjoy the fruits of our labor should help those who cannot.

Scripture does far more than merely affirm our concern for the poor, however. It teaches us, for instance, how to love the poor without romanticizing poverty. It teaches us how to identify the poor and understand the nature and texture of poverty, and how to identify its diverse sources.

Any solution to economic poverty will require political and economic reforms and policies. And since politics and economics are, ultimately, about human beings in relation to each other, we can't have complete economic wisdom if we are ignorant of the truth about man. We are not merely apes in the trees, following the twin dictates of blind chance and physical necessity. We are not merely rational calculators or consumers and despoilers. We are creatures made in the image of the creative God, fallen but still bearing that image. "We make still," J.R.R. Tolkien once said, "by the law in which we're made."[406]

The Fall suggests that we need government to execute justice and punish evildoers (Romans 13), while at the same time avoiding "solutions" that involve giving unchecked or overweening power to anyone, including and especially the state. We should seek a government strong enough to enforce the rule of law but not so powerful that it can distort and violate the rule of law with impunity.

Our capacity for creativity suggests that we should seek cultural mores that make it possible for individuals to exercise their creative freedom, to discover and pursue their unique calling, and to work to create value for themselves and others.

At the same time, none of us is an isolated individual. We are born naked and dependent, and ideally we are educated and raised properly in a home with our mother and father. Many of us, in turn, bear and raise children; we interact with, help, and are helped, by our family, our neighbors, our co-workers, and many others. The pre-political institution of the family is inscribed in the creation, in the opening chapters of Scripture. A just society must respect it, as well as other spheres of civil society, such as the church and private voluntary organizations. A society hostile to these other institutions will be unlikely to provide the nourishment for true economic flourishing over the long term.

To understand our relational nature is to come to terms with the fact that we are finite, physical beings who must be situated in a specific time and place. This suggests that our responsibilities are, by necessity, particular. It doesn't follow that you have no responsibility for those far removed from you. (Indeed, you do.) It's just that you are more responsible for your child than for someone else's child—of whom you know nothing—on the other side of the planet. For one thing, you know and can provide far more effectively for your child than you can for an unknown child seven thousand miles away.

In his chapter, Glenn Sunshine distills this truth into the twin principles of moral proximity and subsidiarity. Although these are important governing principles throughout human relationships, including economic ones, these twin principles are especially pertinent to our understanding of charitable giving, teaching us that giving is most likely to succeed when it takes place within our realm of knowledge and responsibility. While there are certainly successful instances of distant giving, the Old Testament requirement that the Jews leave the "gleanings" of their crops after a harvest suggests an instructive norm. The giving happens locally, with the potential for relationship (see, for instance, the book of Ruth). The charity is modest—the poor are not being given artery-clogging feasts or three-bedroom apartments with flat screen TVs. Notice also that the poor have a dignified and functional role in the acquisition of the food, with their gleaning work making it a particularly cost-effective way to provide the food. And finally, notice that even the gleanings are the result of a prior abundance. In a land stricken with drought, or devastated by bad economic policies, such as Lenin's collectivization of Russian farms and Mao's Cultural Revolution, there is little or no harvest, and so little or no gleanings.

The Old Testament's gleaning policy isn't, of course, a practical strategy for an increasingly urbanized human population far removed from field or orchard; but the underlying principles of the gleaning strategy remain as applicable as ever.

There is much more to be said about the Bible and charity; but in light of the biblical truths expounded in these pages, it should now be clear that the Bible and Christian theological reflection are an abundant and indispensable source of moral and economic wisdom.

The Book of Nature

That leads to our second important source of knowledge on the question of poverty: economics. I do not quite mean the academic discipline of economics itself, which is filled with many things—some good, some bad, some indifferent—but rather the *theoretical insights and empirical discoveries* that economists and others have made in the economic realm. That realm is one sphere of God's creation—a part of his Book of Nature or "general revelation." Like his book of special revelation, God's Book of Nature is not beyond our ken. While it contains great mysteries, much as the Bible does, we nevertheless can investigate and interpret it, can *discover* what it is like, through the dialectical process of theorizing and testing those theories against the evidence. Both parts of this process—theory and testing—are essential for acquiring economic knowledge.

For instance, economists can predict that if the federal government caps the price of a gallon of gasoline well below the market price, then gas shortages will result. But they could confirm such predictions over and over and we might still not *know* whether the policy merely correlates with the shortages or causes them. That is where theoretical insight comes in. We can make the causal connection by understanding how prices communicate information about supply and demand and how price ceilings scramble those signals. This is of course a simple example, but many well-meaning Christians fail to accommodate it in their thinking.

If we step back and take in the big picture, what do we find? We have a wealth of biblical wisdom, empirical evidence, and theoretical insights about the factors that lead to widespread prosperity and wealth creation. We have identified the route up the mountain, the base stations, and the routes that have been tried to no avail. So, for instance, our charitable giving, as Turnbull notes, must be voluntary rather than coerced if it is to be an expression of virtue. Virtue can't be compelled from without. And Lawrence Reed and Marvin Olasky show that the twentieth century taught us the bitter truth that when the state attempts to take over these functions from civil society, it doesn't merely fail but actually weakens the spirit of voluntarism in the private sector and harms the dignity of its recipients. The so-called War on Poverty in the United States, which officially got started in the mid-1960s, could just as well be called the War on the Poor if we focus on its effects rather than its objectives.

Or to take a more obviously theological insight, human sinfulness means we should avoid political experiments that give unchecked power to one or a few. This has been confirmed by history, which also teaches us the economic truth that despotic cultures, in which the political sphere absorbs the spheres of the economy and civil society, invariably lack the conditions for widespread wealth creation.

Scripture also teaches that we should respect the property of others. Indeed, two of the Ten Commandments presuppose a right to private property. And we now know empirically that societies with well-enforced property laws and procedures for gaining title are much more broadly prosperous than societies that lack such provisions.

Respect for the property of others is not merely a matter of law, but is also a matter of individual and cultural morality. Morally sound families and communities are indispensable ingredients in wealth creation. To put the point in the argot of economics, societies with generally respectful and law-abiding citizens have much lower "transaction costs" than societies rife with corruption, fraud, and theft. For this and other reasons, we should not be surprised that there is a correlation between the "Christianization" of a culture and its increasing economic prosperity. That's not an endorsement of the prosperity gospel. It simply means that cultural virtue has economic effects.

As we noted above, we know theologically that man is made in the image of the Creator, and so Christians should expect that under certain conditions, we should be able to create value that was not there before, taking what God has already given us. And that is exactly what we have found. Under the right conditions, we can transform manure into fertilizer, mud and straw into bricks, oil into gasoline and kerosene, math into a wealth-creating financial instrument, sand into fiber optics and computer chips—and have their value shared widely rather than for just a few. Kim Tan and Lord Brian Griffiths argue strongly that enterprise is the way the developed world grew prosperous, and it is also the right path for the developing world.

It is only a slight simplification to sum up in a single phrase the pathway to widespread wealth creation: *economic freedom*. I do not mean freedom in the sense of getting to do whatever you want to do, but in the sense of "ordered liberty"—the conditions under which we can pursue our proper, God-given ends, and can engage in win-win exchanges with our fellow human beings. We now know that these conditions correlate with a reduction in poverty. In general, the more economic freedom a country enjoys, the more it prospers economically. We now have decades of research demonstrating this.

Again, Christians should expect that such an arrangement would hold. God created us free, and he values our freedom. It is more than fitting that ordered liberty should give rise to the creation of wealth. As Robert Sirico argues, a free and competitive market, with the rule of law, is by far the most moral and humane society that we have within our power to bring about—this side of glory.

God also created us diverse, and so, as Anne Bradley argues, we should neither expect nor attempt to equalize economic outcomes. The problem is not that some are prosperous and some live in extreme poverty. The problem is that some live in extreme poverty. And as it happens, countries that avoid draconian attempts to level economic results tend to be the countries in which the poor do the best.

If we are to help "the least of these," Christians can no longer ignore or misunderstand either the Book of Scripture or the Book of Nature. Our task, then, is to integrate our knowledge in order to determine how best to help those peoples languishing in poverty to find and follow the long and arduous but well-marked path up the mountain. In doing so, however, we must never forget that it is they, and not we, who will still have to make the climb.

There is a final symbolic lesson in that first historic ascent of Mount Everest, one particularly apropos for Christians tempted to come to the table of international development as if we were late comers rather than as members of the very religion whose members have done more than any other to fashion the tools of effective charity and widespread wealth creation. In their joint quest to climb Mt. Everest, Edmund Hillary and Tenzing Norgay spent fifteen minutes at the top of the world. They had no tracks to follow on their ascent, and—as they discovered on their descent—the snowfall had erased even the comfort of their own tracks. Still, Hillary and Norgay found their way down to other members of their team, back to base camp, and into history. Before they left the summit, Norgay left a small offering of chocolates. Hillary left behind an item given to him by expedition leader John Hunt: a cross.

Glossary

A

Absolute advantage – An economics concept in which an entity (e.g. a country, person, or company) produces all goods or services at a lower cost than another entity. (refer to comparative advantage)

B

Bailout – The act of saving an entity from bankruptcy by providing further loans or other forms of compensation. Usually corresponds to a government bailout in which the government provides funds to a failing, large corporation with the intention of preventing mass unemployment.

Bankruptcy – A legal status that indicates an entity cannot repay its debts.

Book of the Covenant – The Torah, which corresponds to the first five books of the Bible: Genesis, Exodus, Leviticus, Numbers, and Deuteronomy.

BRIC countries – Brazil, Russia, India, China.

C

Calvinism – A branch of Western Protestantism (also known as Reformed) that is loosely based on five major points: total depravity, unconditional election, limited atonement, irresistible grace, and perseverance of the saints. Total depravity indicates Calvinists' belief in original sin and, thus, that all people are subject to sinful nature and separated from God. Unconditional election claims that God has a chosen people based on his mercy alone, not based on people's works. Limited atonement asserts that when Jesus died on the cross, he atoned for the sins of God's elect, or chosen people. Irresistible grace indicates that all of God's elect will come to faith; they cannot resist God's grace. Finally, the perseverance of the saints is a statement of God's sovereignty and indicates that people of faith will not fall away from the faith irrespective of their circumstances.

Capitalism – An economic system characterized by limited government intervention, private property rights, and undistorted price, profit, and loss signals. It is marked by consumers and sellers operating for their own self-interest, bringing about benefits for the common good.

Civil law – The type of law passed through the legislative branch of government.

Common law – The type of law developed through the judicial branch of government by case rulings of judges.

Communism – In theory, a political system in which there exists no class, money, or government. In practice, a government system that consolidates power in the hands of a few and creates widespread poverty.

Comparative advantage – An economics concept in which an entity (e.g. a person, country, or company) can produce a good or service at a lower opportunity cost than the other entity. This concept is essential to the concept of trade, for entities who produce and trade according to their comparative advantage make gains from trade and are thus more profitable.

Corporatist fascism – This occurs when corporate companies have become so large they are able to control politicians and thus can control and shape society.

Covenant community – A group of people bound by a sound agreement, or covenant, usually for religious purposes.

Credit market – The market in which entities seek to increase their funds through issuance of debt, done in a number of different ways including bonds, mutual funds, mortgages, etc.

Revolving credit – An agreement in which a person can borrow up to a certain limit and, once repaying the amount borrowed, can continue to borrow up to that limit without reapplying for the loan. An example is a credit card in which you have a limit of debt, but as soon as the amount borrowed is paid, you can continue to borrow up to the initial level of debt.

Corporate social responsibility (CSR) – A business approach in which the company specifically takes into account ethics and their impact in their community, going above and beyond what is required of them by law.

Cultural mandate – also known as the Creation mandate – The idea comes from Genesis 1:28: "God blessed them and said to them, 'Be fruitful and increase in number, fill the earth and subdue it. Rule over the fish of the sea and the birds of the air and over every living creature that moves on the ground.'" Thus, the cultural mandate calls all God's people to cultivate the earth and engage in work that utilizes their God-given gifts and talents in order to give glory to God promote a flourishing society.

D

Day of Atonement – An annual day of repentance for the Old Testament people of Israel, the rites for which are set forth in Leviticus 16 (also see Exodus 30:10; Leviticus 23:27-31, 25:9; Numbers 29:7-11). It is described as the holiest day of the year, a Sabbath on which no food or drink could be consumed, and on which all work was forbidden. The high priest entered the Holy of Holies in the Temple to make sacrifices as an atonement for himself and for the people before God.

Decentralized knowledge – An important Hayekian concept that states that no one person or group of people knows all the information needed to set prices. Through the system of supply and demand, each person's information can together be utilized to set a price.

(financial) Derivative – A financial entity that has no intrinsic value in and of itself, but instead derives its value from other entities.

Diminishing returns (to labor) – This economics concept is comparable to the phrase "too many cooks in the kitchen." Diminishing returns to labor indicate that the first person a company hires will provide a high marginal benefit to the company. As more people are hired, the marginal benefit added to the company decreases because of a scarcity of resources.

Divine Providence – The means by and through which God governs all things in the universe.

Dominion mandate (see Cultural mandate)

Double coincidence of wants – The idea that when two people trade in a barter economy, each party needs to provide the other party with exactly what they want, which is a rarity. For example, a farmer would trade with a carpenter if the carpenter wanted some fresh vegetables and the farmer wanted a new barn. This concept indicates the difficulties of a barter economy and displays the necessity of money in an economy as an object with commonly accepted value.

E

Ecological rationality – As defined by Vernon Smith, "Ecological rationality uses reason— rational reconstruction—to examine the behavior of individuals based on their experience and folk knowledge, who are 'naive' in their ability to apply constructivist tools to the decisions they make; to understand the emergent order in human cultures; to discover the possible intelligence embodied in the rules, norms, and institutions of our cultural and biological heritage that are created from human interactions but not by deliberate human design." (Source: Vernon Smith, "Constructivist and Ecological Rationality in Economics, *The American Economic Review* [June 2003]: 470.)

Egalitarianism – The idea that equality should be for all persons in terms of political, economic, and civil rights.

Enlightenment – In the seventeenth and eighteenth centuries, the Enlightenment or the Age of Reason was a movement by intellectuals starting in England and later spreading to America. The movement focused on highlighting reason and science and diminishing the significance of faith in society.

Enterprise – This term can be used as another word for business; also could be used as a term to describe someone as entrepreneurial, innovative, and productive.

Eschatology – Refers to a theology's beliefs about the end times, specifically death, judgment, and the afterlife.

Evangelism – The action of Christians sharing the gospel with nonbelievers in order to spread God's word.

Expropriation – A person's private property being taken away. This often occurs when the government takes a citizen's land and uses it for government purposes.

Externalities – When two people make an agreement, an externality is a consequence of this agreement which affects a third party who was not a part of the original agreement. Externalities can be good or bad, meaning they can help or hurt the unaffiliated third party.

F

Fall – The rebellion of Adam and Eve against God in the Garden of Eden by eating the forbidden fruit. This action introduced sin into the world and separated human beings from God.

Feudalism – A societal setup in which people traded their work for a piece of land on which to live. It promoted deep inequality among classes of society and tended to prohibit movement among classes.

Free exchange – An aspect of capitalism in which the government does not intervene and allows self-interest of consumers and sellers to govern their choices due to undistorted prices, profit, and loss signals.

Fruits of the Spirit – A biblical concept coming from Galatians 5:22-23. This passage names the traits which should characterize a Christian's life after pursuing the Lord and meditating in his Word. Specifically the fruits include love, joy, peace, forbearance, kindness, goodness, faithfulness, gentleness, and self-control.

Fund of funds – An investment strategy in which the investor diversifies their financial assets by holding a fund made up of other investment funds instead of directly investing in specific investments such as stocks or bonds.

G

Ghetto poverty – A type of poverty in which many poor people live in one centralized location called a ghetto.

Gini coefficient – An economic index that measures the income inequality within a country. A Gini coefficient of 0 indicates that the country has perfect income equality, in which all people earn the same amount of income; a Gini coefficient of 1 indicates that the country has perfect income inequality, thus one person owns all the wealth in the economy.

Great Society – This refers to the laws passed by Lyndon B. Johnson's presidency that aimed to end poverty and racial injustice by increasing government intervention into education, medical care, and urban problems.

H

High Income Countries (HICs) -- According to the World Bank, HICs are the countries that have a 2011 per capita gross national income of $12,476 or more. There are 70 countries classified as HICs, such as France, the United States, and the United Kingdom.

Human Development Index (HDI) – Developed by the United Nations Development Programme, the HDI is a measure of overall development that ranges from 0 to 1 (0 being undeveloped and 1 being developed) that serves to rank countries into different categories of development. The main factors used to develop a country's rank are education, life expectancy, and income.

I

International Monetary Fund (IMF) – An international corporation who states their purpose "is to ensure the stability of the international monetary system—the system of exchange rates and international payments that enables countries (and their citizens) to transact with one other. This system is essential for promoting sustainable economic growth, increasing living standards, and reducing poverty." (Source: Factsheet, "IMF at a Glance," http://www.imf.org/external/np/exr/facts/glance.htm)

Income inequality – An unequal distribution of income among the peoples of an economy.

Informal economy/sector – The part of the economy that does not abide by any government business laws or tax laws. The informal sector of an economy can be very large; it includes everything from barter to paying a babysitter to having a vegetable stand on the side of the road. Usually the informal sector is larger in developing countries.

Institution – In economic terms, an institution is taken to mean any culturally accepted norm that contributes to how society works. Institutions can range from concepts such as marriage to private property rights. Many economists look to minimizing and maximizing certain institutions in order to promote economic growth and development.

Investment, foreign direct – Investment in an entity in one country by an entity in a different country.

Investment, impact – As defined by the Global Impact Investing Network, "Impact investments aim to solve social or environmental challenges while generating financial profit…Impact investors actively seek to place capital in businesses and funds that can harness the positive power of enterprise." (Source: Global Impact Investment Network, "What is Impact Investing?" http://giirs.org/about-giirs/what-is-impact-investing)

Investment, "shared value" – Investment into businesses with the shared value business model, in which a company's mission is not only to seek profit but also to develop the local community in some way. An example is Nestle, which no longer seeks to just produce food and beverages that consumers will buy, but also promotes nutrition and helps provide water access. The idea of "shared value" investment was developed my Michael Porter and Mark Kramer.

(*see:* http://investmentinnovation.wordpress.com/2013/06/12/global-shared-value-a-view-from-down-under/)

Invisible hand – A phrase coined by Adam Smith in his book *The Wealth of Nations* that highlights how market forces act like an invisible hand, leading sellers and consumers to make rational and beneficial decisions using price, profit, and loss signals.

J

Jubilee – In Leviticus 25, the Jubilee year occurred every 50 years and was a time in which debts were forgiven. All land was returned to its original owners and slaves were set free (see chapter 4 for more information).

L

Labor force – The sum of all unemployed and employed workers in the economy. Note that to be considered an unemployed worker, the person must be actively searching for a job. For example, someone who chooses to be a stay-at-home mom is not considered a part of the labor force.

Labor force participation rate – This number of people in the labor force divided by the total population of working-age adults in the economy.

Law of Gleaning – A law from Deuteronomy 24:19-21 that instructs the rich to leave excess crops for the poor to harvest. The passage reads: "When you are harvesting in your field and you overlook a sheaf, do not go back to get it. Leave it for the foreigner, the fatherless and the widow, so that the Lord your God may bless you in all the work of your hands. When you beat the olives from your trees, do not go over the branches a second time. Leave what remains for the foreigner, the fatherless and the widow. When you harvest the grapes in your vineyard, do not go over the vines again. Leave what remains for the foreigner, the fatherless and the widow."

Law of self-preservation – Known as the first law of nature, which states that a person's natural instinct, above all, is to protect himself or herself.

Lion Economies – This phrase is used to compare the African countries that are now currently experiencing significantly high economic growth rates to the Asian countries that developed very quickly starting in the 1960s, which were called the Asian Tigers.

Liturgy – This term describes publicly accepted ways of worship among different religious groups.

Low Income Countries (LICs) – According to the World Bank, LICs are the countries that have a 2011 gross national income per capita of $1,025 or less. These are 36 countries classified as LICs including Afghanistan, Uganda, and Haiti.

M

Marginal – Marginal changes hold all else equal and analyze the total change of the dependent variable as the independent variable changes by one. Economists make decisions at the margin to maximize efficiency.

Market – Any place where consumers and sellers can meet to exchange goods and services. The market can be a tangible place of business or intangible exchange, such as online markets.

Meta-Market – A broader market that includes multiple specific markets that all must come together in order to show the complete market of a given good or service. For example, the market for household furniture includes the market for furniture as well as the market for homes.

Microfinance – This term refers to financial arrangements to small businesses or micro-entrepreneurs that lack access to adequate banking systems.

Moral hazard – A situation in which an agreement has been made among two parties, such that the agreement gives incentive to one party to take risks given that the consequences of such risk will fall on the other party. An example is car insurance; a person who is insured may take more risks when driving a car than if they were not insured. However, if an insured driver is in an accident, the insurance company is responsible for the damage.

Moral proximity – A biblical idea that a Christian's responsibility is to serve the people closest to them first. A typical order of responsibility would be to the family first, then Christians in the local church, and finally the broader community.

N

Natural law – The type of law that is determined by nature and, thus, is considered to be universal.

New Deal – Occurring during Franklin D. Roosevelt's presidency, the New Deal was a series of economic policies passed with the intention of assisting the U.S. in rising from the Great Depression. The focus of these policies was the three Rs (Relief, Recovery, and

Reform). The New Deal was to provide relief for those in poverty in the U.S., recovery for the U.S. economy in terms of the Great Depression, and reform so the U.S. would never experience such economic downturn again.

New Institutional Economics – An economic theory that combines institutional and neoclassical economics. Institutional economics considers how institutions affect the economic system of a given country; neoclassical economics describes how prices, outputs, income, and other various economic factors are determined through markets of supply and demand. This economic theory is largely based in Ronald Coase's works about transaction costs and internalizing externalities. (See Institution, Transaction Cost, and Externalities for further information.)

NGOs – non-governmental organizations. These organizations are different than the typical for-profit business, tending to have a broader social mission, but remaining separate from politics. In the U.S., NGOs are often nonprofit organizations.

Nonqualified stock options – A stock option in which the employee must pay the regular income tax on the difference between the price at which the employee received the option and the price at which the employee sells the option. This is in contrast to an incentive stock option, in which the holder does not have to pay income tax on the stock; instead it is taxed at a capital gains rate.

O

Opportunity cost – When making a decision among many options, the opportunity cost of making a choice is the cost of the next best option.

In economics, opportunity cost is the basis of comparative advantage and trade (refer to Comparative Advantage for more information).

P

Pentecost – The day in which the Holy Spirit descended on the apostles, celebrated the seventh Sunday after Easter.

Predestination – In its broadest conception, the doctrine that because God is all-powerful, all-knowing, and completely sovereign, he "from all eternity did by the most wise and holy counsel of His own will, freely and unchangeably ordain whatsoever comes to pass."

Prosperity gospel – A religious belief that indicates followers of Christ will be successful and rich on earth. Furthermore, as a Christian donates money and increases in faith, he or she will be blessed in return and will receive health, wealth, and success. This gospel is not accepted by most theologians as a true version of the Christian gospel.

Protestant work ethic – The Protestants believed that working hard and exercising self-control were pleasing to the Lord and, thus, were known for their work ethic. In Max Weber's book *The Protestant Ethic and the Spirit of Capitalism,* Weber claims that the values of Christians, especially this work ethic, provided for an environment in which capitalism could be successful.

Q

Quaker capitalism – In Max Weber's book *The Protestant Ethic and the Spirit of Capitalism,* Weber claims that the values of the Christians at the time, including the Quakers, provided for an environment in which capitalism could be successful. Because Christians were characteristically hardworking and frugal combined with high moral integrity, the social structure of society would yield positive results from capitalism.

R

Real – Economists use this term to refer to numbers that are adjusted to today's dollars to account for inflation. Thus any data in real terms is better for comparing across different periods of time.

Redistribution tradition – The idea that income inequality is unjust and that government should intervene, taking from the rich and giving to the poor through taxes and transfers.

Relief – A general term for transfers from the rich to the poor by the government in order to provide "relief" for those who are in need.

Rent-seeking – An action in which a firm uses resources to lobby the government to pass policy that benefits their business instead of putting time, effort, and funds towards innovation and efficiency.

Resource allocation mechanism – (see Market)

"Rules of the game" – In economics, this phrase refers to the underlying assumptions of a culture in regard to the economic system. (see Institution)

S

Sabbatical Year – In the Old Testament, every 7th year was a year of rest. In this year the land was not to be worked, and debts were to be forgiven.

Sanctification – The process of becoming more holy; it can refer to growing in one's faith as a Christian by abiding in Jesus' principles and following his example.

Social gospel – A social movement by Protestant leaders that applied biblical morals to common social justice issues.

Socialism – An economic system in which the government owns the means of production and, thus, prices and outputs are determined by a central planner rather than market forces. This system is intended to provide equality among all people.

Social safety net – The combination of policies by the government such as welfare, Medicare, Medicaid, etc. that provide support for any citizen who is below a certain standard of living; these benefits are handouts, so they do not require individuals to help themselves get out of their situation.

Specialization of labor – A term defined by Adam Smith in *The Wealth of Nations*. Labor is divided among tasks, and each worker specializes in one area, providing focus and efficiency that is otherwise unattainable. Specialization of labor allows for businesses to be more efficient and, therefore, more profitable.

Statutory law – The broadest category of law, for all laws are statutes. It includes both criminal and civil law.

Stewardship – Stewardship expresses our obedience regarding the administration of everything God has placed under our control, which is all-encompassing. It is the commitment of one's self and possessions to God's service under the guidance of his law.

Stock options – A financial asset in which the buyer of the option has the right, but is not obligated, to buy or sell the option at a certain price given a specific period of time or date.

Stockholders – Entities that hold shares of stock in a given business, and thus are part owners.

Subsidiarity – The principle that situations should be handled by the lowest or least powerful person who is capable of handling the situation. It is supported by many Catholics and promotes the argument that family and community should step in to help the poor before the government should. (see Moral proximity)

Subsidies – Government handouts to businesses who lobby for them. These transfers tend to cause perverse incentives such as rent-seeking and are not efficient, nor profitable, for the economy.

T
Tariff – A tax on trade; it can be a tax on either import or export, and thus could be called an import tariff or export tariff.

Torah – The central book of the Jewish faith. It is generally considered as the first five books of the Old Testament: Genesis, Exodus, Leviticus, Numbers, and Deuteronomy.

Tory – A member of the Tory political party in England. From the 1600s to 1800s the Tories were recognized by their support for the monarchy; currently, Tory denotes a traditional and conservative view of politics.

Total depravity – The doctrine that, as a consequence of the Fall of man, every person born into the world is morally corrupt, enslaved to sin, and, apart from the grace of God, utterly unable to choose to follow God or choose to turn to Christ in faith for salvation.

Transaction cost – A cost incurred in participating in a market exchange. There are three types of transaction costs: searching cost, bargaining cost, and enforcement costs. In detail, the costs it takes to find the right good or service, decide on a price with the other party, and enforce the contract, respectively.

Transfer payment – A tool for redistributing income; the government taxes the rich and makes transfer payments to the poor in order to fight misconceived income inequality.

U

Millennium Development Goals – The United Nations' goals to eradicate poverty by 2015. The main categories are hunger, primary education, gender equality, child mortality, maternal health, HIV/AIDS and other diseases, environmental sustainability, and global partnerships.

Utility maximizers – In economics, utility is synonymous with happiness. Thus economists assume all people are naturally utility maximizers, meaning they attempt to maximize their own happiness.

V

VC funds – Venture capital funds, a form of investing that focuses on new firms that are characterized by high risk, but also high potential for success.

Voluntary exchange – see Market.

Voluntary principle – This idea highlights the importance of having aid be a voluntary action rather than state-mandated.

W

War on Poverty – Legislation passed during President Lyndon B. Johnson's presidency that focused on fighting poverty by expanding government intervention into the education and healthcare sectors.

"Welfare-to-work" – A government program that assists those who are on welfare in preparing for and finding employment.

World Bank – An international corporation whose mission is to reduce poverty by giving loans to developing countries in order to promote foreign investment, utilization of capital, and international trade.

Z

Zero-sum – A view of the economy in which, as one person earns more money, everyone else must be losing money. A helpful image is to view the economy as a pie. In order for one person to have a bigger slice of pie, everyone else has to have smaller pieces of the pie. Due to innovation, this is not, in fact, how economies work; but it is a view that supports the rationale of income redistribution.

Index

Catholic · 253

circumstances · 43, 70, 89, 100, 154, 243, 294, 298, 354

citizen · 15, 17, 45, 53, 55, 57, 145, 184, 188, 189, 190, 265, 269, 270, 273, 279, 281, 282, 283, 284, 285, 314, 318, 350, 358, 360, 368

class · 6, 16, 40, 45, 46, 50, 217, 251, 257, 271, 281, 303, 359
    middle · 126, 191, 253

Cleveland, Grover · 264, 277, 279, 286

Clinton, Bill · 307, 331

Clinton Global Initiative · 331

coerce · 84, 109, 110, 113, 170, 172, 173, 274, 349

collectivism
    socialist · 250

colonialism · 187

Colossians 3:23-24 · 80, 87

commandment · 5, 31, 52, 158, 164, 174, 176, 211, 243, 279, 350

commerce · 120, 123, 337

common good · xxviii, 121, 123, 199, 225, 226, 232, 233, 354

Commonwealth Development Corporation · 196

communism · 106, 109, 111, 151, 164, 251, 255, 354
    Comunist Party · 249

Communist Manifesto · 109

Communitarian Network · 269

community · 10, 11, 18, 20, 22, 30, 32, 33, 41, 44, 57, 92, 109, 110, 140, 141, 143, 172, 174, 194, 241, 251, 252, 288, 325, 331, 334, 364, 369
    covenant · 41
    coventant · 355
    early Christian · 106, 155
    Jewish · 183
    of goods · 22, 25

company · 199, 222, 237, 244, 246, 355, 356, 361
    limited liability · 172

compassion · xxiv, 14, 50, 55, 60, 62, 64, 84, 119, 121, 123, 125, 144, 145, 182, 276, 277, 289, 292, 316, 320, 323, 325

Compassion International · 30

competition · 118, 119, 123, 195, 201, 232, 238, 243, 248, 308

conflict · 188, 288

Congress · 17, 268, 269, 271, 272, 297, 311, 314

Congressional Budget Office · 217

Constitution · 265, 266, 267, 268, 270, 278, 284, 297, 303

consumer · 167, 186, 240, 242, 248, 327, 346, 354, 359, 361, 362, 363
    demand · 215, 221

consumerism · 235

consumption · 141, 167, 185, 208, 220, 285
    conspicuous · 10, 26
    equality · 219, 220

context · xxiv, 22, 107, 123, 129, 170, 189, 221, 225
    historical · 103
    moral · xxi

contracts · 160, 174, 176, 177, 248
    voluntary · 172

control · 283, 302, 327, 355, 368
    central · 239
    government · 240
    self · 283, 359, 366

Cooper, Lord Ashley · 117, 128

Cooper, Thomas · 295

Copleston, Edward · 123, 125

Cornelius · 111

corporation · 154, 170, 171, 246, 353, 360, 371
    multinational · 192

corruption · xxv, 16, 76, 82, 84, 87, 203, 269, 350

cost · 17, 120, 137, 152, 158, 162, 195, 238, 286, 348, 353
    oppurtunity · 222, 355, 365
    relative · 231
    transaction · 350, 365, 370
    welfare · 292

Costello, Amy · 331

H

I

illiterate · xxiii, 184
image of God · xxvii, 8, 22, 27, 29, 30,
     65, 182, 221, 222, 224, 256, 339,
     345, 346, 350
immigration · 206, 209
incarnation · 133, 141
Incarnation · 253, 254
incentive · 52, 53, 54, 145, 166, 173,
     174, 188, 194, 198, 221, 231, 238,
     271, 309, 312, 313, 314, 337, 364,
     365, 369
     disincentive · 17
income · 10, 35, 51, 52, 53, 54, 65, 89,
     224, 226, 230, 233, 237, 265, 266,
     273, 294, 305, 314, 315, 317, 359,
     360, 365
     distribution · 182, 185, 206
     high · xxvii, 206, 210, 211, 213, 219,
          232
     (in)equality · 36, 51, 101, 102, 103,
          104, 185, 202, 203, 204, 206,
          208, 209, 211, 212, 214, 215,
          216, 217, 220, 221, 222, 224,
          225, 227, 230, 231, 232, 233,
          359, 360, 367
     inequality · 217
     low · 50, 184, 206, 211, 213, 219,
          231, 309
     mobility · 36, 206, 211, 212, 213,
          214, 233
     redistribution · 5, 204, 214, 278,
          345, 367, 370, 371
     Supplemental Security Income · 312
individual · 12, 32, 61, 64, 82, 87, 133,
     138, 173, 199, 223, 247, 270, 288,
     294, 299, 301, 302, 303, 350
     individualism · 247, 248, 250, 251,
          252
     rights · 269
industrial · xxi, 10, 82, 125, 127, 135,
     245, 330, 332, 334
     Industrial Revolution · 10

inequality · 124, 185, 314, 359. *See*
     income (in)equality
inflation · 188, 323, 367
informal economy · 189, 190, 191
infrastructure · 195, 196, 326
injustice · 6, 16, 47, 161, 233, 339, 360
innovation · 119, 143, 145, 197, 220,
     221, 232, 242, 271, 367, 371
institution · xxi, 9, 12, 13, 14, 16, 25,
     28, 31, 32, 87, 150, 152, 154, 155,
     170, 171, 172, 173, 175, 177, 178,
     179, 194, 196, 248, 249, 252, 265,
     284, 286, 304, 327, 347, 357, 361,
     367
     New Institutional Economics · 171,
          365
interest · 7, 103, 176, 183, 191, 227,
     338
International Monetary Fund (IMF) ·
     xxiii, 187, 208, 360
investment · 21, 30, 101, 157, 177, 187,
     193, 196, 198, 200, 210, 211, 216,
     229, 241, 271, 327, 329, 332, 333,
     339, 345, 359
     angel · 191, 194
     cherry-picking investment · 197
     foreign direct · 361, 371
     foreign direct investment · 186, 189
     impact · 198
     impact investment · 195
     shared value · 198, 361
invisible hand · 124, 144, 362
Isaac · 6, 21, 40
Isaiah 1:17 · 46
Isaiah 3:14 · 39
Isaiah 3:15 · 45
Isaiah 5:8 · 101
Isaiah 5:8-10 · 45
Isaiah 10:1-2 · 45
Isaiah 10:2 · 47
Isaiah 14:32 · 39
Isaiah 58:1-12 · 47
Isaiah 61:1 · 105, 398
Isaiah 61:1-2 · 62

M

Endnotes

Chapter 1: Who Are the Poor?

1 Luke 6:20, 24; 18:22, 25 (ESV).

2 This will be developed more fully in chapter three.

3 In the ancient world, loans were given to people who needed them to survive; investment loans had not yet been developed.

4 Chapter two will expand on this in greater detail.

5 Glenn Sunshine, "The Image of God and Work," *Christian Worldview Journal*, (2010), http://www.breakpoint.org/the-center/columns/call-response/15715-the-image-of-god-and-work.

6 These were the Mosaic Law's provisions; it is unclear whether they were ever followed in practice. We know that the land's Sabbaths were not observed, so it seems likely that the law of freeing slaves may not have been observed either.

7 Similarly, one use of the Old Testament tithe was to provide for the needy. Although the tithe is sometimes described as a tax, it was administered by the priests and Levites, not the civil government.

8 For more on the historical and contemporary aspects of this idea, see T. M. Moore's, "Kudzu Government series," *Viewpoint*, The Colson Center, May 10-16, 2010, http://www.colsoncenter.org/images/content/wilberforce/ViewPoint_Studies/VPKudzu.pdf.

9 Such as the Italian city states that worked to insure their supply of bread to prevent food riots by the poor.

10 This began to change with the Reformation in the Swiss Cantons and the city states in the Holy Roman Empire, whose governments frequently took on the task of caring for the poor with roots in their cities. Foreign poor and refugees continued to be supported through private charitable institutions.

11 This will be covered in great detail in chapter ten.

12 Psalm 96 is instructive here: after warning us not to put our trust in princes, because even the best of them eventually die (vv. 3-4), it tells us only the Lord can be relied on to provide social justice (vv. 6-9).

13 Loren Collins, "The Truth about Tytler," January 25, 2009. http://www.lorencollins.net/tytler.html.

14 John Locke, *The Second Treatise on Civil Government* (1690), chapter 2, paragraph 6.

15 See Kinnaman and Lyons, *UnChristian*, for a sobering examination of how the church is viewed today. While I have questions about some of the conclusions and methodology of the book, it is nonetheless an eye-opening look at how our failure to live out the gospel in the here and now has discredited the church in the eyes of the world.

16 Ched Myers, *The Biblical Vision of Sabbath Economics* (n.p.: Tell the World, Church of the Savior, 2001), 5.

17 This interpretation of early human history has its roots in Rousseau's *Social Contract*, which claimed that human inequality comes from private; property I have only found the particular form of this argument that appears in *Sabbath Economics* in Soviet-influenced historiography, where it is used to demonize private property and land ownership.

18 Myers, *The Biblical Vision of Sabbath Economics* (Washington, DC: Tell the World Press, 2001), 31.

19 Ibid., 24.

20 E.g. the Eucharist is really about redistribution of goods and remembering the poor rather than remembering Jesus (chapter six).

21 Sunshine, "The Image of God and Work."

22 See chapter four, which will address the Acts text in detail.

23 These widows may have been deaconesses such as Phoebe (Romans 16:1) or the deaconesses arrested in the early second century by Pliny the Younger.

24 For a discussion of this, see Sunshine, "The Image of God and Work."

25 Immigrant groups in Geneva had their own organizations, known as *Bourses*, to take care of the poor in their communities.

Chapter 2: Poverty and the Poor in the Old Testament

26 As reported by Timothy C. Morgan, "Purpose Driven in Rwanda," *Christianity Today*, October 2005.

27 See E. Bammel, "The Poor in the Old Testament," *The Dictionary of the New Testament* 6 (1968): 888-94; C. U. Wolf, "Poor," IDB 3 (1962):843-44;

F.C. Fensham, "Widow, Orphan and the Poor in Ancient Near Eastern Legal and Wisdom Literature," JNES 21 (1962): 129-39; Donald E. Gowan, "Wealth and Poverty in the Old Testament: The Case of the Widow, the Orphan and the Sojourner," *Interpretation* 41/4 (1987): 341-53; D. Baker. *Tight Fists or Open Hands? Wealth and Poverty in the Old Testament Law* (Grand Rapids: Eerdmans, 2009); Richard D. Patterson, "The Widow, the Orphan, and the Poor in the Old Testament and Extra-Biblical Literature," BibSac 130 (1973): 223-34.

28   This suggestion comes from Edward C. Banfield. *The Unheavenly City Revisited* (Boston: Little, Brown and Co., 1974), 56-61 as pointed out by Ronald H. Nash, *Poverty and Wealth: The Christian Debate over Capitalism* (Westchester: Crossway Books, 1986), 173.

29   Jim Wallis, "Of Rich and Poor," *Post American* (February/March 1974): 1 as cited by John Jefferson Davis, *Your Wealth in God's World: Does the Bible Support the Free Market?* (Phillipsburg, NJ: Presbyterian and Reformed Publishing Co., 1984), 39.

30   Ron Sider is the author of *Rich Christians in an Age of Hunger.*

31   John Jefferson Davis, *Your Wealth in God's World*, 54.

32   For the material in this section I am beholden to John D. Mason, "Biblical Principles Applied to Welfare Policy," in *Biblical Principles & Public Policy: The Practice*, Richard C. Chewning, ed. (Colorado Springs: NavPress, 1991), 81-99.

33   See Walter C. Kaiser, Jr., "The Old Testament Case for Material Blessings and the Contemporary Believer," *Trinity Journal* 9 (Fall 1988): 151-170.

Chapter 3: Remember the Poor—A New Testament Perspective on the Problems of Poverty, Riches, and Redistribution

34   Bruce W. Longenecker, *Remember the Poor: Paul, Poverty, and the Greco-Roman World* (Grand Rapids: Wm. B. Eerdmans Publishing Company, 2010), 53.

Chapter 4: Does God Require the State to Redistribute Wealth? An Examination of Jubilee and Acts 2-5

35   Jubilee was the basis for "Jubilee 2000," which called for cancelling Third World debt by the year 2000, claiming that at Jubilee "all debts are cancelled." It is also used to justify periodic redistribution of land and property by the government.

[36] For historical evidence of the observance of sabbatical years, scholars point to the extra-biblical works of 1 Maccabees (6:49), the Talmud ("Moza'e Shebi'it"), and the writings of Josephus (*Antiquities*, bk. 11, ch. 8, sect. 4-5). Historical evidence for the celebration of Jubilee years is less prevalent and more disputed. Some scholars point to mentions of Jubilee in the Babylonian Talmud (Arakin 12a and Megillah 14b) and the Samaritan "Book of Joshua" (Chapter XV) as possible evidence of its celebration.

[37] In the year of Jubilee there is no distributive injustice (no loss of capital).

[38] Michael Harbin estimates that a crop was worth about "one and half to two years' wages," depending on "the quality of the soil," "how well watered it was," and other market forces of supply and demand. Because of the inherent variance in harvests, Harbin conjectures that the future crop yields might have been priced at "an understood depreciated flat-rate value for a year of crops" ("Jubilee and Social Justice," *Journal of the Evangelical Theological Society* 54, no. 4 (2011): 692). Jacob Milgrom asserts that the buyer would still bear significant risk, however: "for in the case of a crop failure, the loss was the buyer's" (*Leviticus 23-27* (AB 3B; New York: Doubleday, 2001), 2178).

[39] Matthew Henry, *Commentary on the Holy Bible (Genesis to Esther)* (Nashville: Royal Publishers, Inc., 1979), 279.

[40] *The Interpreter's Bible, Volume II* (Nashville: Abingdon Press, 1953), 122.

[41] R. K. Harrison, *Leviticus* (Downers Grove, IL: InterVarsity Press, 1980), 225.

[42] Gordon Wenham, *The Book of Leviticus (NICOT)* (Grand Rapids: Eerdmans, 1979), 317.

[43] Derek Tidball, *The Message of Leviticus* (Downers Grove, IL: InterVarsity Press, 2005), 296.

[44] Ron Sider, *Rich Christians in an Age of Hunger, 5th Edition* (Nashville: Thomas Nelson, 2005), 68.

[45] Walter C. Kaiser, Jr., "Ownership and Property in the Old Testament Economy," *Journal of Markets & Morality* 15, no. 4 (2012): 234.

[46] Cal Beisner points out that Leviticus 25 has indeed radical implications for laissez-faire capitalism but not for the reasons many give: "It would seem radical because it put a strict requirement on borrowers by requiring collateral to secure all loans, and because it put a maximum limit on the number of years for which a loan could be extended" (*Prosperity and Poverty* (Eugene, OR: Wipf and Stock Publishers, 2001), 64).

47   Leviticus 25:39-41: [39]If a countryman of yours becomes so poor with regard to you that he sells himself to you, you shall not subject him to a slave's service. [40]He shall be with you as a hired man, as if he were a sojourner; he shall serve with you until the year of jubilee. [41]He shall then go out from you, he and his sons with him, and shall go back to his family, that he may return to the property of his forefathers.

48   Leviticus 25:47-52: [47]Now if the means of a stranger or of a sojourner with you becomes sufficient, and a countryman of yours becomes so poor with regard to him as to sell himself to a stranger who is sojourning with you, or to the descendants of a stranger's family, [48]then he shall have redemption right after he has been sold. One of his brothers may redeem him, [49]or his uncle, or his uncle's son, may redeem him, or one of his blood relatives from his family may redeem him; or if he prospers, he may redeem himself. [50]He then with his purchaser shall calculate from the year when he sold himself to him up to the year of jubilee; and the price of his sale shall correspond to the number of years. It is like the days of a hired man that he shall be with him. [51]If there are still many years, he shall refund part of his purchase price in proportion to them for his own redemption; [52]and if few years remain until the year of jubilee, he shall so calculate with him. In proportion to his years he is to refund the amount for his redemption.

49   Lampe, Peter, "Early Christians in the City of Rome" in *Christians as a Religious Minority in a Multicultural City*, vol. 243 of *The Library of New Testament Studies* (London: T&T Clark International, 2004), 24.

50   Michael Harbin, "Jubilee and Social Justice," *Journal of the Evangelical Theological Society* 54, no. 4 (2011): 696.

51   Ibid., 685.

52   John Schneider, *The Good of Affluence* (Grand Rapids: Eerdmans, 2002), 82-84.

53   Derek Tidball, *The Message of Leviticus* (Downers Grove, IL: InterVarsity Press, 2005), 301.

54   John Schneider, *The Good of Affluence*, 70.

55   Ibid., 84.

56   E. Calvin Beisner, *Prosperity and Poverty* (Eugene, OR: Wipf and Stock Publishers, 2001), 65.

57   John Schneider, *The Good of Affluence*, 83.

58   John Calvin, *Calvin's Commentaries, Volume III* (Grand Rapids: Baker Books, 1984), 169.

Michael Harbin echoes Calvin's comments on a universal application of the Jubilee law:

While it may be true that private property would be good for everyone, this is never expressed as an objective and certainly does not seem to be part of the Jubilee principle. The fact that the Jubilee principle only applied to one group of people out of the entire world on a one time basis seems to undermine the argument of those who would universalize this Jubilee principle. ("Jubilee and Social Justice," *Journal of the Evangelical Theological Society* 54, no. 4 (2011): 696.)

[59] There is in Jesus's inaugural sermon, sometimes called the "Nazareth Manifesto" (Luke 4:18-19), a possible allusion to Jubilee. Jesus's text was Isaiah 61:1f.:

The Spirit of the Lord God is upon me, because the Lord has anointed me to bring good news to the afflicted; He has sent me to bind up the brokenhearted, to proclaim liberty to captives, and freedom to prisoners.

Robert North observes that the word "release" from Isaiah 61:1 was the same as the word in Leviticus 25:10 (*Sociology of the Biblical Jubilee* (Rome: Pontifical Biblical Institute, 1954), 213-231). So perhaps the acceptable or favorable year of the Lord is inspired by the Jubilee year. For instance, in his commentary on Isaiah, Alex Motyer draws out of Isaiah 61:1 that Jesus had both a "salvific purpose" and a "judgmental component" – themes of liberty and judgment that are certainly present in the Jubilee text as well (*The Prophecy of Isaiah* (Downers Grove, IL: InterVarsity, 1993), 499). The physical application of Jubilee to the land thus becomes a spiritual application to be applied as a result of the gospel. So although the Jubilee (Lev. 25) was not applied universally (to all people), perhaps it serves as a type, shadow, or hint of a larger spiritual application of the gospel.

[60] Craig L. Blomberg, *Neither Poverty nor Riches* (Downers Grove, IL: InterVarsity Press, 1999), 162, 165.

[61] Ron Sider also looks to the Greek tenses and draws a similar conclusion on the early church:

The earliest church did not insist on absolute economic equality. Nor did they abolish private property...The tense of the Greek words confirms this interpretation. In both 2:45 and 4:34, the verbs denote continued, repeated action over an extended period of time. Thus the meaning is "they often sold possessions," or "they were in the habit of regularly bringing the proceeds of what was being sold." The text does not suggest that the community abolished all private property or that everyone immediately sold everything. It suggests instead that over a period of time, whenever there was need, believers sold lands and houses to aid the needy. (*Rich Christians in an Age of Hunger* (Nashville: Thomas Nelson, 2005), 78-79.)

62 John Stott, *The Message of Acts* (Downers Grove: InterVarsity Press Academic, 1994), 83-84.

63 N.T. Wright, *Acts: 24 Studies for Individuals and Groups* (Downers Grove: InterVarsity Press, 2010), 23.

64 Rachel Cohon, "Hume's Moral Philosophy," *The Stanford Encyclopedia of Philosophy (Fall 2010 Edition)*, ed. Edward N. Zalta, http://plato.stanford.edu/archives/fall2010/entries/hume-moral/.

65 C.S. Lewis, *The Abolition of Man; or, Reflections on Education with Special Reference to the Teaching of English in the Upper Forms of School* (Oxford: Collier, 1947), 42.

66 R.C. Sproul, *Discovering the God Who Is: His Character and Being, His Power and Personality* (Ventura: Gospel Light Publications, 2008), 116.

67 For good biblical guidance on helping the poor, see Glenn Sunshine's blog series "Poverty and the Church" (Institute for Faith, Work & Economics, http://blog.tifwe.org/part-1-2/).

Chapter 5: Evangelicals and Poverty—the Voluntary Principle in Action

68 Richard Turnbull, *Shaftesbury, The Great Reformer* (Oxford: Lion Hudson, 2010), 24.

69 The title Lord Ashley will be used for reference to the period prior to 1851, Shaftesbury for the post 1851 years. Shaftesbury will also be used for generic description and assessment.

70 Turnbull, *Shaftesbury*, 83, 226.

71 The issue of what constitutes an evangelical Christian is beyond the scope of this particular chapter. For a succinct review see Richard Turnbull, *Anglican and Evangelical?* (London: Continuum International Publishing Group, 2007, reprinted 2010), especially chapter 2.

72 Adam Smith (1723-1790) was a Scottish moral philosopher and economist who developed the early theoretical foundations of modern economic thought. His religious views are contested, although he most easily fits into the model of many Enlightenment thinkers as a deist—that is, a believer in some overarching divine force rather than a

personal deity. John Calvin (1509-1564) was the leading thinker of the second generation of Protestant Reformers. He was based in Geneva for most of his life, and his great work, which went through several editions, was *The Institutes of the Christian Religion.*

73 B.A. Corry, *Money, Saving and Investment in English Economics 1800-1850* (London: St. Martin's Press, 1962), 1.

74 E.L. Paul, *Moral Revolution and Economic Science* (Westport: Praeger, 1979), 5.

75 Adam Smith, *An Inquiry into the Nature and Causes of the Wealth of Nations*, 3rd edition (London: Cadell and Davies, 1812), 19.

76 Paul, *Moral Revolution*, 11.

77 Paul, *Moral Revolution*, 20.

78 See, for example, the exchange between Emil Brunner and Karl Barth in E. Brunner, *Nature and Grace* and K. Barth, *No!* contained in P. Fraenkel, trans., *Natural Theology* (London: Geoffrey Bles, 1946).

79 Calvin, *Institutes*, 1.5.1.

80 David Bebbington, *Evangelicalism in Modern Britain* (London: Routledge, 1989), 50ff.; A.M.C. Waterman, "The Ideological Alliance of Political Economy and Christian Theology, 1798-1833," *Journal of Ecclesiastical History*, volume 34, number 2 (1983): 232.

81 Thomas Malthus (1766-1834) was a prominent early economist who viewed poverty as inevitable due to the exponential growth of population. Attempts to interfere with this natural (divine) order through enforced redistribution would not succeed. The scenario and mechanism for self-correction were severe. but Malthus supported all moves to increase production and remove unnecessary drains on resources in order to increase productive capacity as much as possible.

82 Chalmers, *Natural Theology*, volume 2.4.4.6, in *Works*, volume 2, 136-137.

83 Ibid., 137.

84 Chalmers, *Natural Theology*, volume 2.4.4.6, in *Works*, 128.

85 Ibid., 130.

86 A.M.C. Waterman, "The Ideological Alliance of Political Economy and Christian Theology, 1798-1833," *Journal of Ecclesiastical History* 34 (April, 1983), 2.

87 R.J. Morris, "Voluntary Societies and British Urban Elites, 1780-1850," *Historical Journal*, 26.1 (1983): 95.

88 K. J. Heasman, *Evangelicals in Action* (London: Geoffrey Bles, 1962), 8.

89 The Tories were generally the party of land and property, constitutional rights, duty, localism, and a small state. The Whigs were the party

of reform, rights, manufacturing, and free trade. There was some crossover in the area of economics, especially as the nineteenth century progressed.

90 Turnbull, *Shaftesbury*, 16.

91 Lord Ashley, Diaries, Oct 13, 1825, Turnbull, *Shaftesbury*, 21.

92 Lord Ashley, Diaries, April 22, 1827, Turnbull, *Shaftesbury*, 24.

93 Lord Ashley, Diaries, Feb 22, 1827, Turnbull, *Shaftesbury*, 24.

94 Turnbull, *Shaftesbury*, 213.

95 Turnbull, *Shaftesbury*, 214.

96 Turnbull, *Shaftesbury*, 216.

97 Ibid.

98 Turnbull, *Shaftesbury*, 217.

99 See Turnbull, *Shaftesbury*, for full analysis.

100 Turnbull, *Shaftesbury*, 222-223.

101 "Shaftesbury at the Mansion House," *LCM Magazine*, vol. 46 (April 1881): 65.

102 "Lord Shaftesbury—Responsibility and the Welfare of Humanity," Introduction to *Our Veterans* by J.M. Weylland (London: S. W. Partridge & Co., 1881).

103 Lord Ashley, Ragged Schools Union, Second Annual Report, 1846, 35.

104 RSU Second Annual Report, 1846, 6f.

105 RSU, Eighth Annual Report, 1852.

106 Shaftesbury, Diaries, March 16, 1870, Turnbull, *Shaftesbury*, 151.

107 R.H. Tawny, *Religion and the Rise of Capitalism* (London: G. Bell & Sons, 1926), 282.

108 Ibid., 284.

109 Max Weber, *The Protestant Ethic and the Spirit of Capitalism* (London: Allen and Unwin, 1930).

110 J.H. Yoder, *The Politics of Jesus* (Grand Rapids: Eerdmans, 1974, second edition, 1994), 2.

111 Ibid., 39.

112 R.J. Sider, *Rich Christians in an Age of Hunger* (London: Hodder and Stoughton, 1977), 154.

113 R. Heinberg, *The End of Growth* (U.K.: Clairview, 2011), 101

114 Sider, *Rich Christians*, 178.

115 Donald Kraybill, *The Upside-Down Kingdom*, (Harrisonburg: Herald Press, 1978), 113.

116 Ibid., 155.

117 David Sheppard, *Bias to the Poor* (London: Hodder and Stoughton, 1983).

118 Ibid., 133-134.

119 Roger Scruton, "Charity," *Conservative Home Thinkers' Corner*, February 11, 2012.

Chapter 6: Markets and Justice

120 John Calvin, *Institutes of the Christian Religion*, trans. Henry Beveridge (Grand Rapids: Eerdmans, 1989).

121 Craig Bartholomew, "The Relevance of Neo-Calvinism for Today," *The Kuyperian*, 2004, http://kuyperian.blogspot.com/2004/09/relevance-of-neocalvinism-for-today.html.

122 Ibid.

123 Ibid.

124 Economists reading this paragraph should see that my approach could be seen in the spirit of Ronald Coase, although I do not want to assert that he would agree with all that I have written.

125 Gordon Tullock, *The Rent Seeking Society: Fifth Volume of the Selected Works of Gordon Tullock*, ed. Charles K. Rowley (Indianapolis: Liberty Fund 2005).

126 Sid Gally, "Black-Gold Rush Came to Early Los Angeles Downtown," Pasadena *Star-News*, September 2, 2012, http://www.pasadenastarnews.com/ci_21455898/black-gold-rush-came-early-los-angeles-downtown.

127 Division of Labour, "Common Property Bicycles—Won't They Ever Learn?" 2005, http://divisionoflabour.com/archives/001768.php.

128 In Chapter 4, Lindsley also addresses at length the debate as to whether the Jubilee was ever actually celebrated, and whether that matters for Christians.

129 It should be emphasized that even though I view the Jubilee as a kind of a safety net akin to bankruptcy in modern society, I agree with Lindsley in Chapter 4 that the Jubilee was not a "forgiveness" of debt but rather a reclamation of land after the expiration of a long-term land lease. My argument is that if it was practiced as described, the Jubilee would have had a functionality similar to bankruptcy in modern society.

130 R.C. Sproul, *The Reformation Study Bible: English Standard Version* (Orlando: Ligonier Ministries, 2006).

131 Robert H. Nelson, *The New Holy Wars: Economic Religion vs. Environmental Religion* (University Park: Pennsylvania State University Press, 2010); Elia Kazan's 1960 movie *Wild River* is only one example of the revisionist view of FDR's dam-building policies through the TVA.

[132] Deirdre McCloskey, *The Bourgeois Virtues: Ethics for an Age of Commerce* (Chicago: University of Chicago Press, 2006).

[133] In the associated references for these authors, I have attempted to choose writings that are easily accessible to non-economists. For example, the reader will see several references to the public lectures given by Nobel laureates at the prize ceremony. These are good places to start to understand the authors' thinking in relatively non-technical presentations: Vernon L. Smith, "Constructivist and Ecological Rationality in Economics," Nobel Prize in Economic Science Lecture, December 8, 2002, http://www.nobelprize.org/nobel_prizes/ economics/laureates/2002/smith-lecture.pdf; Elinor Ostrom, "Beyond Markets and States: Polycentric Governance of Complex Economic Systems," Nobel Prize in Economic Science Lecture, December 8, 2009, http://www.nobelprize.org/nobel_prizes/economics/laureates/2009/ ostrom_lecture.pdf.

[134] James M. Buchanan, "An Economic Theory of Clubs," *Economica* 32 (1965): 1-14.

[135] See classics such as Coase and Williamson for significant elaboration.

[136] David Boaz, "Private Property Saved Jamestown, And With It, America," Cato Institute, May 14, 2007.

[137] Mancur Olson, *The Logic of Collective Action* (Cambridge: Harvard University Press, 1971).

[138] Mark R. Isaac and James M. Walker, "Group Size Hypotheses of Public Goods Provisions: An Experimental Examination," *Quarterly Journal of Economics* 103 (1988): 179-199.

[139] R. C. Sproul, *The Reformation Study Bible: English Standard Version* (Orlando: Ligonier Ministries, 2006).

[140] Rodney Stark, *The Rise of Christianity* (Princeton: Princeton University Press, 1996).

[141] Lactantius, *On the Manner in Which the Persecutors Died*, trans. J. Vanderspoel, 1998), http://people.ucalgary.ca/~vandersp/Courses/ texts/lactant/lactperf.html

Chapter 7: Fighting Poverty through Enterprise

[142] John Paul II, "Centesimus Annus," *Encyclical Letter* (1991): 31.

[143] "Income Inequality," UN Atlas, September, 23, 2013, http://ucatlas. ucsc.edu/income.php.

[144] Dato Kim Tan, *The Jubilee Gospel* (Authentic Media, 2008); Brian Griffiths, "The Challenge of Globalisation: A Christian Perspective," *Making Globalisation Work,* ed. J. H. Dunning (Oxford: Oxford University Press, 2004).

[145] Deuteronomy 14:28-29.

[146] Ibid.

[147] "12,000 fewer children perish daily in 2010 than in 1990," United Nations Children's Fund & World Health Organization, September 23, 2013, http://www.who.int/mediacentre/news/releases/2011/child_mortality_estimates_20110915/en/

[148] United Nations, *The Millennium Development Goals Report* (2012), http://www.un.org/millenniumgoals/pdf/MDG%20Report%202012.pdf.

[149] "The Forgotten 1 Billion," Worldwatch Institute, June 20, 2013, http://www.worldwatch.org/forgotten-1-billion.

[150] Department of Economic and Social Affairs, "Goal 2: Achieve universal education," *Progress towards the Millennium Development Goals, 1990-2005* (United Nations, 2005), http://unstats.un.org/unsd/mdg/Resources/Attach/Products/Progress2005/goal_2.pdf.

[151] The World Bank, "Poverty at a Glance," April 2013, http://web.worldbank.org/WBSITE/EXTERNAL/NEWS/0,,contentMDK:20040961~menuPK:34480~pagePK:64257043~piPK:437376~theSitePK:4607,00.html.

[152] Ibid.

[153] Ibid.

[154] The United Nations, "Millennium Development Goals Report 2012," http://www.un.org/millenniumgoals/pdf/MDG%20Report%202012.pdf.

[155] William Easterly, *The White Man's Burden* (Oxford: Oxford University Press, 2006), 4.

[156] The United Nations, "Millennium Development Goals Report 2012," http://www.un.org/millenniumgoals/pdf/MDG%20Report%202012.pdf.

[157] "Poverty: Not always with us," *The Economist,* 1 June 2013, http://www.economist.com/news/briefing/21578643-world-has-astonishing-chance-take-billion-people-out-extreme-poverty-2030-not.

[158] "GINI Index," *Data,* World Bank, 2013, http://data.worldbank.org/indicator/SI.POV.GINI.

[159] Ibid.

[160] Ibid.

[161] Ibid.

[162] Ibid.

[163] Sonalde B. Desal, et. al, *Human Development in India: Challenges for a Society in Transition*, (New Delhi: Oxford University Press, 2010), 11, http://ihds.umd.edu/IHDS_files/02HDinIndia.pdf.

[164] "Key Messages," *The State of Food Insecurity in the World*, Food and Agriculture Organization of the United Nations, 2013.

[165] United Nations, *The Millennium Development Goals Report*.

[166] "Aspiring Africa," *The Economist*, 2 March 2013, <http://www.economist.com/news/leaders/21572773-pride-africas-achievements-should-be-coupled-determination-make-even-faster>.

[167] "Economy Rankings," *Doing Business*, International Finance Corporation, June 2012, http://www.doingbusiness.org/rankings.

[168] "Africa. "'Patronizing' West Risks Losing Trade, Influence to Emerging Powers, Warns Think Tank," *All Africa*, 1 June 2010, http://allafrica.com/stories/201006021222.html.

[169] "The hopeful continent: Africa rising," *The Economist*, 3 December 2011, http://www.economist.com/node/21541015.

[170] "The sun shines bright," *The Economist*, 3 Dec 2011, http://www.economist.com/node/21541008.

[171] P. Bauer & C. Onslow, "Fifty Years of Failure" (Centre for Policy Studies, 1999); W. Easterly, R. Levine & D. Roodman, "New Data, New Doubts: A Comment on Burnside and Dollar's 'Aid, Policies, and Growth'" (Center for Global Development, 2003); Simon Jenkins, *The Guardian*, 2013, http://www.theguardian.com/profile/simonjenkins; Dembisa Moyo, *Dead Aid: Why Aid Is Not Working and How There Is a Better Way for Africa* (London: Penguin Books, 2010).

[172] Ibid.

[173] "Compare HIV/AIDS Statistics Worldwide: Swaziland," *United Nations Knowledge Centre Global Report on AIDS*, Real Clear World, http://hiv-stats.realclearworld.com/.

[174] John Schneider, *The Good of Affluence: Seeking God in a Culture of Wealth* (Grand Rapids: Wm. B. Eerdmans Publishing Co., 2002), 19.

[175] "Report on Support to SMEs in Developing Countries Through Financial Intermediaries," Dalberg, November 2011, http://www.eib.org/attachments/dalberg_sme-briefing-paper.pdf.

176 Dato Kim Tan, "Enterprise, Not Aid, for Social Change," Lien Centre for Social Innovation (2012): 65, http://www.lcsi.smu.edu.sg/downloads/SocialSpace2012-KimTan.pdf .

177 Hernando De Soto, *Mystery of Capital* (New York: Basic Books, 2000).

178 Dato Kim Tan, "Enterprise, Not Aid, for Social Change."

179 "Lending Interest Rate," *Data*, The World Bank, http://data.worldbank.org/indicator/FR.INR.LEND/countries.

180 Ibid.

181 "Lending Rates Still at 30%," *Modern Ghana*, February 12, 2011, http://www.modernghana.com/news/316122/1/lending-rates-still-at-30.html.

182 Magali Rheault & Bob Tortora, "At Least 1 in 5 African Youth Plan to Start a Business," *Gallup World*, June 30, 2011, http://www.gallup.com/poll/148271/Least-African-Youth-Plan-Start-Business.aspx.

183 "Commodity Markets and Commodity Mutual Funds," *ICI Research Perspective*, 18.3 (2012): 7.

184 J.P. Morgan, "Impact Investments: An Emerging Asset Class," *Global Research,* November 29, 2010, http://www.jpmorgan.com/cm/BlobServer/impact_investments_nov2010.pdf?blobkey=id&blobwhere=1158611333228&blobheader=application%2Fpdf&blobcol=urldata&blobtable=MungoBlobs.

185 Amira Farid and Sherif Kamel, "Socioeconomic Implications of Mobile Technology in Emerging Markets: the Case of Egypt," http://www-marshall.usc.edu/assets/006/5578.pdf

186 "Mobile Phone Access Reaches Three Quarters of Planet's Population," The World Bank, July 17, 2012, http://www.worldbank.org/en/news/press-release/2012/07/17/mobile-phone-access-reaches-three-quarters-planets-population.

187 Dembisa Moyo, *Dead Aid: Why Aid Is Not Working and How There Is a Better Way for Africa* (London: Penguin Books, 2010); Brian Griffiths and Kim Tan, *Fighting Poverty through Enterprise* (Transformational Business Network, 2005).

188 Michael Porter and Mark Kramer, "Creating Shared Values," *Harvard Business Review* (January-February 2011); Deborah Cadbury, *Chocolate Wars From Cadbury to Kraft: 200 Years of Sweet Success and Bitter Rivalry* (HarperPress, 2010).

189 Dato Kim Tan, "Enterprise, Not Aid, for Social Change."

Chapter 8: Why Does Income Inequality Exist? An Economic and Biblical Explanation

190 World Bank, "Gini Index," http://data.worldbank.org/indicator/ SI.POV.GINI.

191 Central Intelligence Agency, World Factbook 2009, https://www.cia.gov/library/publications/download/download-2009.

192 Frank Levy, "Distribution of Income," *The Concise Encyclopedia of Economics*, http://www.econlib.org/library/Enc/DistributionofIncome. html.

193 United States Department of Labor, Bureau of Labor and Statistics, "Labor Force Statistics from the Current Population Survey," http:// data.bls.gov/timeseries/LNS11300002?years_option=specific_ years&include_graphs=true&to_year=2006&from_month=3.

194 Florence Jaumotte, Subir Lall and Chris Papageorgiou, "Rising Income Inequality: Technology, or Trade and Financial Globalization?" IMF Working Paper, 2008.

195 R.W. Fogel, "The Escape from Hunger and Premature Death, 1700-2100," (Cambridge: Cambridge University Press, 2004), 40-45.

196 Jaumotte et al., "Rising Income Inequality."

197 Ibid.

198 Congressional Budget Office, "The Role of Immigrants in the U.S. Labor Market: An Update," July 2010, http://cbo.gov/ftpdocs/116xx/ doc11691/07-23-Immigrants_in_Labor_Force.pdf.

199 George J. Borjas, Richard B. Freeman, and Lawrence F. Katz, "How Much Do Immigration and Trade Affect Labor Market Outcomes?" Brookings Papers on Economic Activity, 1997 (1), 1-90; Council of Economic Advisors, *Economic Report of the President* (Washington, DC: U.S. Government Printing Office, 1997), 11-16; Robert Lerman, "U.S. Income Inequality Trends and Recent Immigration," *American Economic Review*, vol. 89, no. 2 (1999), 23-28.

200 Congressional Budget Office, "Role of Immigrants."

201 Walter C. Kaiser, Jr., "Ownership and Property in the Old Testament Economy," unpublished paper presented at Evangelical Theological Society, San Francisco, November 16, 2011.

202 Simon Kuznets, "Economic Growth and Income Inequality," *The American Economic Review*, vol. 45, no. 1 (March 1955), 1-28.

203 Thomas A. Garrett, "U.S. Income Inequality: It's Not So Bad," Federal Reserve Bank of St. Louis, *Inside the Vault*, Spring 2010, http://www. stlouisfed.org/publications/itv/articles/?id=1920

204 U.S. Department of the Treasury, "Income Mobility in the U.S. from 1995 to 2005," November 13, 2007, http://www.treasury.gov/resource-center/tax-policy/Documents/incomemobilitystudy03-08revise.pdf.

205 Alan Reynolds, "Has U.S. Income Inequality Really Increased?" *Policy Analysis*, no. 586 (January 8, 2007), http://www.cato.org/pub_display.php?pub_id=6880.

206 Ibid.

207 Ibid.

208 Thomas Piketty and Emmanuel Saez, "Income Inequality in the United States, 1913-1998," *The Quarterly Journal of Economics*, Vol. CXVIII, February 2003, Issue 1: 3-71.

209 Robert Rector, "Means Tested Welfare Spending: Past and Future Growth," *Policy Research and Analysis*, Heritage Foundation, March 7, 2001, http://www.heritage.org/research/testimony/means-tested-welfare-spending-past-and-future-growth.

210 Congressional Budget Office, "Trends in the Distribution of Household Income Between 1979 and 2007," October 2011, http://cbo.gov/publication/42729.

211 Ibid.

212 Simon Kuznets was aware of this when in 1955 he wrote a paper exploring income inequality and economic growth: "Without such a long period of reference and the resulting separation between 'resident' and 'migrant' units at different relative income levels, the very distinction between 'low' and 'high' income classes loses its meaning, particularly in a study of long-term changes in share and in inequalities in the distribution." Simon Kuznets, "Economic Growth and Income Inequality," *The American Economic Review*, vol. 45, no. 1 (March 1955), 1-28.

213 U.S. Department of Health and Human Services, Office of the Secretary, "Annual Update on the HHS Poverty Guidelines," *Federal Register*, vol. 76, no. 13 (January 20, 2011), http://aspe.hhs.gov/poverty/11fedreg.shtml.

214 U.S. Energy Information Administration, "Residential Energy Consumption Survey." (2009).

215 World Bank, "World Bank Updates Poverty Estimates for the Developing World," August 26, 2008, http://go.worldbank.org/C9GR27WRJ0.

216 Kaiser, "Ownership and Property."

[217] CelebrityNetWorth, "Billy Graham Net Worth," http://www.celebritynetworth.com/richest-celebrities/billy-graham-net-worth/.

Chapter 9: The Moral Potential of the Free Economy

[218] Ludwig von Mises, "Profit and Loss," *Planning for Freedom* (Grove City: Libertarian Press, 1952), 120.

[219] See, for example, Todd Zywicki, "The Auto Bailout and the Rule of Law," *National Affairs* 7 (Spring 2011): 66–80, http://www.nationalaffairs.com/publications/detail/the-auto-bailout-and-the-rule-of-law.

[220] Mark J. Perry, "Q1: Exxon Paid Almost $1M per Hour in Income Taxes and Its Effective Tax Rate was 42.3%," *Carpe Diem*, April 28, 2011, http://mjperry.blogspot.com/2011/04/exxonmobil-paid-almost-1m-per-hr-in.html, citing figures from *Yahoo! Finance* (http://biz.yahoo.com/p/sum_qpmd.html). Eleven months later, as of March 16, 2012, the profit margin for the sector was 7.90%, higher but still well below that of dozens of other industries.

[221] Francis de Sales, *Introduction to the Devout Life* (New York: Doubleday, 1950), 164.

[222] Ayn Rand and Nathaniel Branden, *The Virtue of Selfishness* (New York: New American Library, 1964), 44.

[223] Ibid., vii.

[224] Merriam-Webster's Collegiate Dictionary, 11th ed., s.v. "Selfishness."

[225] John Larrivee summarizes well the moral damage done by Communism in "It's Not the Markets, It's the Morals," *Back on the Road to Serfdom: The Resurgence of Statism*, ed. Thomas E. Woods Jr. (Wilmington: ISI Books, 2010).

[226] Mother Teresa, *No Greater Love*, ed. Becky Benenate and Joseph Durepos (Novato, Calif.: New World Library, 1989), 97-98.

[227] Pope Paul VI, "Pastoral Constitution on the Church in the Modern World: *Gaudium et Spes*," (December 7, 1965), no. 39. http://www.vatican.va/archive/hist_councils/ii_vatican_council/documents/vat-ii_cons_19651207_gaudium-et-spes_en.html.

[228] Dietrich Bonhoeffer, *Barcelona, Berlin, New York 1928-1931*, ed. Clifford J. Green, trans. Douglas W. Stott, volume 10, *Dietrich Bonhoeffer Works* (Minneapolis: Fortress Press, 2008), 521.

[229] James Madison, "The Federalist No. 51," *Independent Journal*, February 6, 1788, http://www.constitution.org/fed/federa51.htm.

Chapter 10: A Poverty Program that Worked

[230] Franklin D. Roosevelt, "Annual Message to Congress" (Washington, DC, January 4, 1935), http://www.presidency.ucsb.edu/ws/index.php?pid=14890.

[231] Ibid.

[232] Ronald W. Reagan, "State of the Union Address" (Washington, DC, January 25, 1988), http://www.presidency.ucsb.edu/ws/index.php?pid=36035.

[233] Dr. Barry Asmus, "American Economic Progress," *The Freeman* (August 1985), http://www.fee.org/the_freeman/detail/american-economic-progress/#axzz2T0vgCISQ.

[234] Thomas Jefferson, "First Inaugural Address" (Washington, DC, March 4, 1801), http://www.bartleby.com/124/pres16.html.

[235] James Madison, "On the Memorial of the Relief Committee of Baltimore, for the Relief of St. Domingo Refugees" (U.S. House of Representatives, Washington, DC, January 10, 1794).

[236] Andrew Jackson, "Fourth Annual Message" (Washington, DC, December 4, 1832), http://www.presidency.ucsb.edu/ws/index.php?pid=29474.

[237] Andrew Jackson, "Second Inaugural Address" (Washington, DC, March 4, 1833), http://www.bartleby.com/124/pres24.html.

[238] Ibid.

[239] Franklin Pierce, "Veto Message" (Washington, DC, May 3, 1854), http://www.presidency.ucsb.edu/ws/index.php?pid=67850.

[240] Ibid.

[241] Philanthropy Roundtable, "A Passion for Performance: An Interview with Peter Drucker" (March/April 1999) http://www.philanthropyroundtable.org/topic/excellence_in_philanthropy/a_passion_for_performance.

[242] Burton W. Folsom, "The Difference Between a Fire and a Flood" (Midland: Mackinac Center for Public Policy, June 9, 1997), http://www.mackinac.org/27.

[243] Ibid.

[244] Ibid.

[245] Marvin Olasky, *The American Leadership Tradition: Moral Vision from Washington to Clinton* (New York: Simon & Schuster, 1999), 153.

246 "American Presidents Life Portraits" (Cable News Network (CNN), August 13, 1999). See accompanying Teacher Guide: http://www.americanpresidents.org/classroom/22guide.asp).

247 Grover Cleveland, "Veto of the Texas Seed Bill" (U.S. House of Representatives, Washington, DC, February 16, 1887), http://mises.org/daily/3627.

248 Ibid.

249 Olasky, 160.

250 Robert Rector and William Lauber, "America's Failed $5.4 Trillion War on Poverty" (Washington, DC: Heritage Foundation, 1995), 7.

251 Auberon Herbert, "The Right and Wrong of Compulsion By the State" (1885), http://oll.libertyfund.org/index.php?option=com_staticxt&staticfile=show.php%3Ftitle=591&layout=html.

252 Frederic Bastiat, "The Law" (New York: Foundation for Economic Education, 1990), 76, http://www.fee.org/files/doclib/20121116 TheLaw.pdf.

Chapter 11: Alleviating Poverty Through Provision of Welfare

253 David Naugle, *Philosophy* (Wheaton: Crossway, 2012), 29.

254 Ibid., 30.

255 Marvin Olasky, *The Tragedy of American Compassion* (Washington: Regnery, 1992), 193.

256 S.I. Hayakawa, *Language in Action* (New York: Harcourt, Brace, 1964).

257 Ibid., 16.

258 *The Mary Thomas Story*, NBC, December 3, 1989.

259 Marvin Olasky, "What Children Live By," *World* (Nov. 3, 2012), 89.

260 Ibid., 90.

261 Ibid.

262 Ibid.

263 Ibid.

264 Ibid., 91.

265 Ibid.

266 Ralph and Muriel Pumphrey, eds., *The Heritage of American Social Work* (New York: Columbia University Press, 1961), 22.

267 Pumphrey and Pumphrey, 29.

268 Franklin, quoted in Philip Klein, *From Philanthropy to Social Welfare* (San Francisco: Jossey-Bass, 1968), 282.

269 Ibid.

[270] *Southern Evangelical Intelligencer,* vol. 2 (1820-1821), 244-247.

[271] Ibid., vol. 1 (1819-1820), 215.

[272] *Report of the Secretary of State on the Relief and Settlement of the Poor,* reprinted in State Board of Charities of the State of New York, 34th Annual Report (1900), vol. I, 939-963.

[273] *Report of the Committee,* 29.

[274] Ibid. The three exclamation marks were in the original.

[275] *American Quarterly Review,* 14 (1835), 78.

[276] Ibid.

[277] Michael B. Katz, *In the Shadow of the Poorhouse: A Social History of Welfare in America* (New York: Basic Books, 1986), 17-18.

[278] William and Alexander McGuffey, *McGuffey's Newly Revised Eclectic Reader,* 1844.

[279] Nathaniel Ware, *An Exposition of the Weakness and Inefficiency of the Government of the United States of North America* (New York: Leavitt, Trow, 1845), 191.

[280] William Ruffner, *Charity and the Clergy* (Philadelphia: Lippincott, 1853), 138.

[281] Ibid., 141.

[282] *Providence Journal,* December 16, 1857; an editor responded that this idea was "full of danger, and full of discouragement to industry."

[283] Boston, *City Document.*

[284] *Waltham Sentinel,* March 12, 1858.

[285] *Congressional Globe* XXVIII, 2 (1854), 1062.

[286] Ibid.

[287] Mary Richmond, *Friendly Visiting Among the Poor* (1899; reprint, Montclair, N.J.: Patterson Smith, 1969), 151.

[288] Ibid., 28.

[289] Ibid., 28.

[290] Ibid., 4.

[291] Ibid., 13.

[292] Jacob Riis, *How the Other Half Lives* (1890; reprint, New York: Dover, 1971), 148.

[293] Ibid., 199.

[294] Ibid., 151.

[295] Ibid., 68.

[296] Associated Charities of Boston, *Ninth Annual Report* (Boston: George Ellis, 1888), 10.

[297] Associated Charities of Boston, *Fourth Annual Report* (1883), 43-44.

[298] Ibid.

[299] Amos G. Warner, *American Charities: A Study in Philanthropy and Economics* (1894; reprint, New Brunswick: Transaction, 1989), 367-368.

[300] Charles Loring Brace, *The Dangerous Classes of New York and Twenty Years' Work Among Them*, 3rd ed. (1872; reprint, New York: Wynkoop & Hallenbeck, 1880), 93-94.

[301] Walter Johnson in *Lend a Hand*, quoted in *The American Hebrew* LI (May 27, 1892), 123.

[302] Warner, *American Charities*, 367-368.

[303] William Graham Sumner, *The Forgotten Man, and Other Essays* (Whitefish, Montana: Kessinger Publishing reprint, 2010), 472.

[304] E. Wright Bakke, *Citizens Without Work: A Study of the Effects of Unemployment Upon the Workers' Social Relations and Practices* (New Haven: Yale University Press, 1940), 362-366.

[305] Amity Shlaes, *The Forgotten Man* (New York: Harper, 2008).

[306] Frank Bruno, *Trends in Social Work, 1874-1856* (New York: Columbia University Press, 1948), 300.

[307] Marvin Olasky, *The Tragedy of American Compassion*, 154.

[308] Grace Adams, *Workers on Relief* (New Haven: Yale University Press, 1939), 11.

[309] *New York Times*, January 5, 1935.

[310] Ibid., November 30, 1935.

[311] *New York Times*, Nov. 8, 2008; *Wall Street Journal*, Nov. 21, 2008. The following March, Emanuel elaborated on his axiom: "Never waste a crisis. It can be turned to joyful transformation" (*New York Times*, March 17, 2009).

[312] Milford conference 1932-1933 report, quoted in Jacob Fisher, *The Response to Social Work to the Depression* (Boston: G.K. Hall, 1980), 71.

[313] Dorothy C. Kahn, "Some Professional Questions About Relief," in *Four Papers on Professional Function* (New York: American Association of Social Workers, 1937), 38-39.

[314] Ibid.

[315] Quoted in Bruno, 314.

[316] Mary Van Kleeck, "Our Illusions Concerning Government," *Proceedings of the National Conference of Social Work*, 1934 (Chicago, 1934), 284-303.

[317] Ibid.

[318] Gertrude Springer, "Rising to a New Challenge," *The Survey*, 70 (June 1934), 179.

[319] Van Kleeck, "Our Illusions Concerning Government," 504-516.

[320] Eduard C. Lindeman, "Basic Unities in Social Work," *Proceedings of the National Conference of Social Work*, 1934, 504-516.

[321] Bruno, 320.

[322] Ibid., 653.

[323] Hearings on J.J. Res. 83 [work relief], U.S. House Committee on Appropriations, 76th Congress, 1st Session, 1939, 184.

[324] Ibid., 829-830.

[325] Ibid., 832.

[326] Ibid., 835.

[327] See Daniel P. Moynihan, *Maximum Feasible Misunderstanding* (New York: Free Press, 1969), 35, 40-41. Ylvisaker headed the Ford Foundation's Public Affairs Program.

[328] James N. Morgan, Martin H. David, Wilbur J. Cohen and Harvey J. Brazer, *Income and Welfare in the United States* (New York: McGraw-Hill Book Company, Inc., 1962), 3.

[329] *Time*, February 8, 1971, 17.

[330] Nathaniel Dunford, "N.Y.C., True to Form," *New York Times*, April 10, 1990, A21.

[331] Ibid.

[332] Robert L Rose, "For Welfare Parents, Scrimping Is Legal, But Saving Is Out," *The Wall Street Journal*, February 7, 1990, A1, A11.

[333] Ibid., A11.

[334] Marvin Olasky, "Food Stamps Surge," *World*, Nov. 19, 2011, 38; http://www.worldmag.com/issue/2011/11/19/ezine.php.

[335] Alan Berube and Matt Fellowes, "Leaving Money (and Food) on the Table" (Washington, DC: Brookings, 2005), http://www.brookings.edu/research/reports/2005/05/childrenfamilies-fellowes.

[336] Olasky, op. cit.

[337] Ibid.

[338] Ibid.

[339] Ibid.

[340] Ibid.

[341] Ibid.

[342] Ibid.

[343] Ibid.

[344] Sprint Newsroom, "Sprint 4G Helps Chicago Food Bank Feed More," accessed October 30, 2013, last modified May 17, 2010, http://newsroom.sprint.com/article_display.cfm?article_id=1510.

[345] Ibid.

[346] Ibid.

[347] Marvin Olasky, "Disabling Security," *World*, Dec. 17, 2011, 47, http://www.worldmag.com/issue/2011/12/17/ezine.php.

[348] Ibid.

[349] Ibid.

[350] Ibid.

[351] Ibid.

[352] Marvin Olasky, "Poverty Politics," *World*, April 19, 2011, 51, http://www.worldmag.com/issue/2011/04/9/ezine.php.

[353] Ibid.

[354] Marvin Olasky, "Myth Makers," *World*, Oct. 6, 2012, http://www.worldmag.com/2012/09/myth_makers.

[355] Interview by author, Dec., 2011.

[356] Ibid.

[357] Ibid.

[358] Ibid.

Chapter 12: "Stop Helping Us" – A Call to Compassionately Move Beyond Charity

[359] 1 John 3:17.

[360] James 2:16.

[361] Brian Fikkert and Steve Corbett, *When Helping Hurts: Alleviating Poverty Without Hurting the Poor . . . and Yourself* (Chicago: Moody Publishers, 2009), 53.

[362] Chris Ordway, "Poverty is an Empty Heart," *Inside Microfinance: HOPE International Blog*, October 10, 2011, http://blog.hopeinternational.org/2011/10/10/poverty-is-an-empty-heart/.

[363] Robert Lupton, *Toxic Charity: How Churches and Charities Hurt Those They Help (And How to Reverse It)* (New York: HarperCollins Publishers, 2011), 129-130.

[364] "Can Ukraine Avert a Financial Meltdown?" World Bank, 2008, http://web.worldbank.org/WBSITE/EXTERNAL/NEWSLETTERS/EXTTRANSITION/EXTDECBEYTRANEWLET/0,,contentMDK:20692620~isCURL:Y~menuPK:1544646~pagePK:64168445~piPK:64168309~theSitePK:1542353~isCURL:Y,00.html, accessed Oct. 13, 2011.

[365] Matthew 25:31-36.

[366] Matthew 25:40.

367 Matthew 25:35.

368 Matthew 25:36.

369 Matthew 25:36.

370 "Haiti Earthquake 2010," http://www.oxfam.org/en/haitiquake.

371 Giles Bolton, *Africa Doesn't Matter* (New York: Arcade, 2008), 76.

372 "Microfinance in Ukraine: Country Profile," 2010, http://www.
mixmarket.org/mfi/country/Ukraine/.

373 Genesis 2:15.

374 Leviticus 19:9.

375 2 Thessalonians 3:10.

376 Ephesians 4:28.

377 Laurence Chandy and Geoffrey Gertz, "A Stunning Reduction in
Global Poverty Goes Unnoticed," *Real Clear World*, July 8, 2011, http://
www.realclearworld.com/articles/2011/07/08/unnoticed_a_stunning_
reduction_in_global_poverty_99583-full.html, accessed Dec. 10, 2012.

378 Shaohua Chen and Martin Ravallion, "The Developing World Is
Poorer Than We Thought, But No Less Successful in the Fight Against
Poverty," paper presented for the Development Research Group, World
Bank, Washington, DC, August 26, 2008.

379 Martin Ravallion, "A Comparative Perspective on Poverty Reduction"
(Policy Research Working Paper, Development Research Group,
World Bank, October 1, 2009), https://openknowledge.worldbank.org/
bitstream/handle/10986/4333/WPS5080.pdf?sequence=1.

380 "Paul Collier — Improving Aid with Smarter Compassion," http://
www.povertycure.org/voices/paul-collier/.

381 Dambisa Moyo, *Dead Aid: Why Aid Is Not Working and How There Is a
Better Way for Africa* (New York; Penguin Books, 2009).

382 "From Aid to Enterprise," PovertyCure, http://www.povertycure.org/.

383 William Easterly, *The White Man's Burden: Why the West's Efforts to Aid
the Rest Have Done So Much Ill and So Little Good* (New York: Oxford
University Press, 2006), 4.

384 Teju Cole, "The White Savior Industrial Complex," *The Atlantic*, March
21, 2012, http://www.theatlantic.com/international/archive/2012/03/
the-white-savior-industrial-complex/254843/, accessed December 9,
2012.

385 Quoted in Easterly, *White Man's Burden*, 4.

386 "Africa Rising," *Time Magazine*, December 3, 2012, 52.

[387] "Africa's Future and the World Bank's Role in It," http://siteresources.worldbank.org/INTAFRICA/Resources/Africa_s_Future_and_the_World_Bank_s_Role_in_it.pdf.

[388] "The sun shines bright: The continent's impressive growth looks likely to continue," *The Economist,* December 3, 2011.

[389] *Sub-Saharan Africa: Maintaining Growth in an Uncertain World* (Washington, DC: International Monetary Fund, 2012), 2.

[390] *The New Africa: Emerging Opportunities for Business and Africa* (Business Action for Africa, 2011), 24.

[391] "JfL Stories and Impact," http://www.jobsforlife.com/media/index.html.

[392] Brian Fikkert, interview by Peter Greer, HOPE International, December 10, 2012.

[393] Kris Frieswick, "Ex-Cons Relaunching Lives as Entrepreneurs," *Inc.,* May 29, 2012, http://www.inc.com/magazine/201206/kris-frieswick/catherine-rohr-defy-ventures-story-of-redemption.html, accessed December 6, 2012.

[394] Catherine Rohr: Redeeming Justice," last uploaded January 3, 2008, http://www.youtube.com/watch?v=tgqn31cx05g.

[395] Adam Liptak, "U.S. prison population dwarfs that of other nations," *New York Times,* April 23, 2008, http://www.mytimes.com/2008/04/23/world/americas/23iht-23prison.12253738.html?_r=0, accessed December 7, 2012.

[396] Ibid.

[397] "What We Do: The Problem," http://www.prisonentrepreneurship.org/what/problem.aspx.

[398] Uriah King and Leslie Parrish, *Payday Loans, Inc.: Short on Credit, Long on Debt* (Center for Responsible Lending, 2011), 7.

[399] *Payday Loans, Inc.: Short on Credit, Long on Debt,* http://www.responsiblelending.org/payday-lending/research-analysis/payday-loans-inc.html.

[400] King and Parrish, *Payday Loans, Inc.,* 19-20.

[401] Jesse James DeConto, "Lending With Grace: Breaking the Cycle of Payday Loans," *The Christian Century,* June 19, 2012.

[402] "The sun shines bright: The continent's impressive growth looks likely to continue," *The Economist,* December 3, 2011.

Conclusion

[403] David Roberts, "1953: First Steps—Sir Edmund Hillary and Tenzing Norgay," *National Geographic Adventure*, April 2003, http://adventure.nationalgeographic.com/adventure/everest/sir-edmund-hillary-tenzing-norgay-1953/.

[404] Gregg Morgan, "How Early Technology Helped Sir Edmund Hillary Conquer Everest," *The Telegraph*, May 28, 2013, http://www.telegraph.co.uk/news/worldnews/asia/nepal/10084710/How-early-technology-helped-Sir-Edmund-Hillary-conquer-Everest.html.

[405] Nina Porzucki, "Remembering Sir Edmund Hillary and Sherpa Tenzing Norgay's Climb Up to the Top Everest," *PRI's The World*, May 29, 2013, http://www.theworld.org/2013/05/remembering-sir-edmund-hillary-and-sherpa-tenzing-norgays-climb-up-to-the-top-everest/.

[406] From "Mythopoeia," II. 70, *Tree and Leaf*, 99, quoted in Brian Rosebury, *Tolkien: A Critical Assessment* (New York: St. Martin's Press, 1992), 110.